8-20-21

John W.

2612 Violett Rd.

Goshen, Ind. –

John knew Mrs. Clark
from meeting while in military in
South

CAPTAIN'S BRIDE, GENERAL'S LADY

The Memoirs of
Mrs. Mark W. Clark

CAPTAIN'S BRIDE,

McGRAW-HILL BOOK COMPANY, INC.

GENERAL'S LADY

BY *Maurine Clark*

NEW YORK   TORONTO   LONDON

CAPTAIN'S BRIDE, GENERAL'S LADY

SECOND PRINTING

Library of Congress Catalog Card Number: 56-8860

Published by the McGraw-Hill Book Company, Inc.
Printed in the United States of America

To Wayne, Ann, and Bill

For his valuable help in the writing of this book, I want to express to Howard Handleman my warmest thanks and appreciation.

Illustrations will be found following page 118.

CHAPTER ONE

THERE COMES A TIME IN THE LIFE OF EVERY woman when something happens that makes everything seem wonderful and worthwhile, when all the little irritations and complaints are washed away in one moment. For me that moment came by candlelight, at a time of great sadness and joy, when my only daughter, Ann, was married. The cause was not really the marriage itself but the truly classic thoughtfulness of my only son, Bill.

It was June 12, 1952, at Fort Monroe, Virginia. My husband, Gen. Mark Wayne Clark, was half a world away, in Tokyo and Korea, running a three-front war. War was the only thing that could have kept him away from Ann's wedding, and he had plenty of it. He had to command the United Nations forces fighting the Chinese and North Korean Communists at the front. He had to direct the United Nations military men trying to arrange a cease-fire with the Communists in the diplomatic front at Panmunjom. And he had the terrible problem of fighting the Communist prisoners of war on Koje Island and weeding out the leaders who had been ordered by their Red masters to surrender so they could organize revolt in the prison camps. He had had this job little more than a month, so it was impossible for him to attend Ann's wedding.

That is the kind of irritation every Army wife learns to live with.

Army orders, duty, take the husbands away so much of the time that they always seem to be somewhere else when the really important family events occur. And it was the kind of irritation and complaint that was washed away for me the day Ann was married.

The irritation had reached a peak, too. Not only was Wayne to miss the wedding, but we had 150 out-of-town guests, in addition to all the regular work that goes with weddings. To top it all, Ann and I were living in an empty house. All our furniture and furnishings were packed for storage. I was scheduled to board an airplane at seven o'clock the morning after the wedding to fly to Tokyo and join Wayne. Take-off was just eleven hours after the ceremony.

The mere mechanics of the week were closing in on me. It was one job to get Ann ready for the wedding and the honeymoon ; it was another to get all the furnishings of the house packed for storage. And to live through that final few days, we had to have beds and linen and chairs from the Quartermaster and pots and pans and dishes from the commissary.

Then the reception had to be planned. It was to be in the rose garden, a formal garden with fine walks, that lies behind the home of the commandant of Fort Monroe. A spotlight was rigged to play on the huge wedding cake that was set outdoors at the far end of the garden.

Arrangements in the chapel, too, took detailed planning. A spotlight outside sent soft light spreading through the stained-glass window above the altar. Inside, the only light came from candles, hundreds and hundreds of them in clusters of eight in the small windows, on tree-shaped candelabra along the walls, in the balcony, and around the altar.

Planning all this and a trip to Tokyo too almost got me down, and I must confess I was a little sorry for myself that day Ann was married. Bill had come down from Walter Reed Hospital in Washington, where he was under treatment for the lung and leg wounds he had suffered in Korea as an infantry company commander, and he was still limping noticeably when he walked down the aisle of the post chapel at Fort Monroe with Ann on his arm.

The organ played softly, and I was proud of my two children, and happy. But at the same time I was sad and miserable. Later I learned that in classical Japanese literature there is a word that is translated as "joy and sadness," and the day Ann married I learned the meaning of the word before I ever heard it.

But Bill gave me joy that evening. He was substituting for Wayne in the ceremony. He was giving away the bride—his sister—and the moment came when he was asked, "Who gives this woman in marriage?"

Bill said simply, "Her mother, her father, and I."

I was overwhelmed. In six words Bill had summed up, for me at least, the fact that the Clarks had succeeded as a family. Despite the fact that we never really had a home town or even a home state, we were four people bound by the strongest of family ties. Wayne and I had been successful in creating the most precious of all things, a loving family.

After the ceremony was concluded, Ann and her wonderful new husband turned from the altar and began walking back down the aisle. I was in an aisle seat up front and when Ann saw me she stopped and gave me a quick hug and kiss. My cup ran over.

We all knew, of course, that Wayne was with us in spirit that night, but it wasn't until after I joined him in Tokyo that I learned just how deeply his thoughts were with us. Wayne had accepted the Tokyo command with the full understanding of Gen. Omar Bradley that he would get time off to fly home for Ann's wedding, then only a month and a half away. The understanding was clear, and General Bradley, bidding farewell to Wayne at Washington National Airport in the first week of May, 1952, repeated that barring unforeseen developments he would expect to see Wayne again in a few weeks.

The unforeseen happened, of course, as it so often does. Stalemate in Korea was the keystone in Wayne's plan to come home. So long as the war and the armistice talks continued in stalemate he could get away. Under those conditions six weeks were more than enough for him to take over from his long-time friend, Gen. Matt Ridgway, who was going to Paris and NATO, and get squared away in the new command.

But stalemate ended the day Wayne landed in Tokyo. It was

3

broken in the most unlikely of all places—the main camp for Communist soldiers captured as prisoners of war. When Wayne left Washington for Tokyo he had never heard the name of Koje Island. The day after he arrived the whole world knew all about Koje-do. That was where a hard-core gang of Communists, some of whom had permitted themselves to be captured at the front so they could stir up trouble in the rear, kidnaped the American general commanding the prison island and held him for political ransom.

Stalemate was over and Wayne was stuck. He sent a message to General Bradley, a difficult message. He said there was nothing he ever wanted to do more than fly back for Ann's wedding, but that he realized that under the circumstances he just couldn't get away. General Bradley sent back word that he was sorry but that he agreed the time was not right for Wayne to come home. Wayne didn't come.

As a matter of fact, at the moment Ann was being married Wayne was in an airplane over the Sea of Japan, en route to Korea with his old comrade-in-arms from Italy, Lord Alexander, who, as Defense Minister of Great Britain, was in the Far East to visit Wayne and inspect British Commonwealth units fighting in Korea.

Wayne had asked us to write him the precise time of the wedding ceremony so he would know the moment his Annie was being married. It was 10 A.M., Tokyo time—8 P.M., our time—when the ceremony began. At ten o'clock Wayne, in the airplane, closed his eyes and tried to visualize the ceremony. He knew the chapel well. He had attended services there each Sunday he was home while Chief of Army Field Forces with headquarters at Fort Monroe. Just after Wayne closed his eyes, Lord Alexander thought of something and said, "Say, Wayne, when we . . ."

That was as far as he got. Wayne opened his eyes, glared at his old and close friend, and said, "Nothing doing, Alec, my little girl is being married right this minute and I want to be alone with my thoughts."

Wayne never did tell me whether he ever found out what Lord Alexander had on his mind.

4

When I remember our beginnings together, Wayne's and mine, they seem in comparison like nothing so much as wild slapstick.

It was the late summer of 1923 in Washington, D.C. It was another age, another life. There still was elbow room in the capital. Wars had been ended for all time, we were told, by the "war to end wars" that had ended only five years before. Life was easy, beautiful, and secure, and I was young.

I went to Washington after finishing my studies at Northwestern University. It was to have been a short visit with my adopted aunt and uncle, who was Gen. William Hart, then Quartermaster-General of the United States Army. He and his sister Mary lived together in Washington. Neither was married. "Uncle Will" was a childhood friend of my mother's and the two families always were very close.

The visit was to have been short but Uncle Will secretly had other ideas. He had a problem. Everybody else in the Army had a welfare department, but his Quartermaster Corps did not. He wanted a welfare department just like the Infantry, the Air Corps, the Engineers, and all the rest. Uncle Will told me of his problem at great length. He spent a whole evening at it, telling me how sad he was that he still was unable to offer his people the same advantages that men and women got working for other parts of the Army.

Uncle Will went into detail. The Army took care of its uniformed personnel all right, but special provision had to be made to help the civilian employees. And there were a large number of civilians working for the Quartermaster. Uncle Will wanted a number of things. He wanted somebody to visit his civilians when they were sick, make certain they were getting proper medical care, and try to cheer them up—all this to show the Army was interested in them. He wanted someone who would lend a sympathetic ear to the civilian men and women when they were in trouble and give them advice when possible. And he wanted a room in his headquarters where both military and civilian personnel could relax with a magazine, a cup of coffee, or a sandwich.

Uncle Will was a fine salesman. I didn't even know he was trying to sell anything until, at the tag end of the evening, he said, "Renie, would you be willing to stay on in Washington and run a welfare department for me?"

By that time he had built up quite an excitement in me about his plans. I was so excited, in fact, that I couldn't possibly have said no to him. I dashed off a letter to my parents in Muncie and they gave me permission to stay on in Washington. I found an apartment, furnished it, and for the first time in my life was a working girl, on my own.

I was running the welfare department for Uncle Will when I first met Wayne.

In the morning of that very big day in my life President Harding was laid to rest. In the Presidential funeral guard of honor was a young captain, Mark Wayne Clark, tall and straight and handsome. He was—though I didn't know it then—an officer who had made a brilliant record in France, where at the age of twenty-two he had been put in command of an infantry battalion.

I paid no attention at all that morning to the funeral service for the President. My mind was taken up with other things. I had a blind date for a picnic that afternoon, and it kept me busy all morning, dressing carefully and fixing my half of a box luncheon for four. My blind date, built up as a romantic type by the mutual friends who arranged the thing and were going with us, was none other than Captain Clark. I never really could decide whether they arranged the date to introduce us or whether they got Captain Clark a date so they could use his automobile for the picnic. Automobiles were hard to come by for young people back in 1923.

We met and took off. The captain was poised and had exceptional qualities in his voice. He was, in fact, quite an exceptional young man. But he was hopeless as a picnic date. The glamour was frozen on him that afternoon. Maybe the funeral had affected him. Maybe something was on his mind. Maybe he just was reserved and cautious meeting a new girl. But whatever the reason, the afternoon began on a dull note.

Captain Clark drove down to Chesapeake Bay, his eyes glued to the road. He sat at ramrod attention while he drove. He would not talk and would not smile. In the back seat our two friends were giddy with excitement and fun. They laughed and chattered and had a marvelous time. And I was bored completely and made a mental note that this would be my last blind date.

It was, but not in the way I thought then. In fact, nothing worked out the way I planned. For one thing, the rains came, in cloudburst proportions. Our beach picnic was washed out and we were carbound, parked at the side of the road. We decided to have lunch in the car, and the picnic boxes were brought out. The car top was canvas and it dripped. The world around us dripped. Everything inside the car, including the sandwiches and little cakes, was damp and sticky. So were we.

The party continued in the back seat, however, with gay talk and laughter by two young things who appeared very much in love. I felt like a fifth wheel and if anybody had asked me at that moment to describe my date, I would have called him the sixth wheel.

He sat there munching my egg-cucumber sandwiches, one after another, glum and silent. He ate so many that my gloom was partially dispelled by wonderment at his appetite. I later learned this was a most unusual display, for though Wayne is a big man, he is an extremely light eater.

Some bees attracted by the food buzzed around inside the car, and I thought they seemed more vocally appreciative of the lunch I had prepared than did my munching Captain Clark.

I decided at least to make the back-seat gaiety three-sided and leaned back to join in the fun. Then the captain spoke. He was poking around in the box lunch between us and he muttered, "Got more of these what-you-call-'em sandwiches in here?"

I moved to help him search the box, and in moving sat back on the seat. In less than a second I shot to my feet and leaped from the car into the rain, yelling and slapping as I went. I had sat on a bee and he had stung back—plenty.

Outside, I sloshed around, stamping and slapping and shaking my skirts. I yelped some more, turning and jiggling and doing the weird kind of dance people do only after they have been stung by a bee.

7

After a bit the sting stopped hurting and I quieted down enough to hear an unfamiliar sound. Pushing my rain-soaked hair back out of my eyes, I looked up and saw my captain leaning out the car door, fascinated and in convulsions of laughter. It was the first time I ever saw Wayne Clark laugh, or even smile. And he helped me stagger back into the car.

Maybe I should have slapped his face and walked out of his life right then. He had earned it. But I didn't and I'm glad.

Once in the car, he grinned and said, "I'll bet you're a good dancer."

The ice was broken; a thaw that has now lasted thirty-three years set in. It was a gradual thaw, no immediate romance. We just became friends. We danced together; we walked through the Indian-summer glow in Washington's Rock Creek Park; we went to movies to see people like Douglas Fairbanks and Mary Pickford and Wallace Reid. We laughed a great deal and talked and were terribly impersonal. But I did begin to learn about Mark Wayne Clark.

The bee sting was the first bit of humor in our life, but fortunately not the last. Silly little troubles and mishaps that can be laughed about in later years have their place in building up the private memories which bind two people, and I think it is an important place.

As an example, Wayne took me to the theater one night after a big snowfall. By the time we left, the snow was still deep, but melting, leaving a horrible kind of dirt and slush. I was all decked out that night, long skirt and all. Wayne was gallant, and when the cab stopped in front of my house, he took me in his arms to carry me through the slush and protect my party-going best. The inevitable happened. He slipped a bit, struggled to keep his balance, but struggled in vain. Down he went, with me in his arms. I hit the slush first and he came tumbling down on top of me, all six feet two of him.

The beautiful new Spanish comb I wore in my hair that night, a comb I treasured with all my heart, went flying into the deep snow. I never will forget the sight of my dressed-up captain scuffing and kicking through the slush which soaked him almost to the knees. But he scuffed and kicked until he found my little treasure.

Trite as it may be, one of my favorite sayings is that great oaks from little acorns grow. Maybe I like it because I can see how it worked in my life. The big things in life so often are tied to or started by the little things, and that's the way it was with me.

Wayne and I were no more than friends for a long time. He went out with other girls and I went out with other boys. But our friendship was moving along quite nicely and we built up a large store of common interests. Long before there was any thought of romance, I found that I liked him, admired him, and enjoyed being with him.

It was a whole host of little things that spun the web of our romance. One night, for instance, he brought me some chrysanthemums and when I admired them he surprised me by talking as though he knew and loved flowers. For a moment or so I felt as though he had intruded into my private world. Flowers had always been an important part of my life at home in Indiana and now that I was walled up in an apartment in Washington, I missed the joy of seeing my garden grow and the pleasure of the work and talk of gardening.

But then, as Wayne talked more about flowers, I got the warm kind of feeling one gets suddenly hearing English spoken in a foreign land. Wayne told me he had learned about flowers from his mother, who, he said, was "crazy about gardening." Then he looked at me with that grin. "Just like you."

That caught me unprepared. I had no idea he knew anything of my love of flowers, but he did. And that, I have always believed, was the little thing that led to the biggest thing in my life—marriage to Mark Wayne Clark. It was because of the flowers that Wayne took me home to meet his parents. At least that is the reason he gave. And the way things developed, so slowly, I believe him.

Mother and Dad Clark lived in a charming old Colonial home in North Arlington on Glebe Road near the intersection with Lee Highway. It was about eight miles from Washington, on the Virginia side of the Potomac. Dad Clark bought the house and a large acreage around it when he retired from the Army. And Mother

9

and Dad Clark together converted the sprawling grounds into a delightful garden of vegetables and flowers. Dad did the heavy work, the carpentry and the trellis building, while Mother Clark tended the flowers with loving hands.

The garden was the first thing I saw that first day Wayne drove me out to meet his parents. After all those months in the city, those fallow months of apartment living and hard, cold pavements, I was ecstatic. I talked so much and so fast about the garden as we drove through it to the house that Wayne looked at me, amused, and said, "Would you prefer to meet the garden first, or Mother?"

That brought me down to earth, and to the always uneasy moment when a girl meets a boy's parents for the first time. But the uneasiness was dispelled the moment I saw Mother Clark. She awaited us in her living room smiling, and held out her hand to me. "I'm so glad you've come," she said.

Her words were simple and so was her manner, the kind of simplicity that creates a warm welcome and a feeling of friendliness and ease right away. She was a striking woman. Few women hold themselves as well, and in her face was wit and intelligence and a quick, light spirit. And something else. I found myself staring at her, and when I realized what I was doing I became flustered and embarrassed and blurted out the explanation: "Wayne looks so very much like you."

Mother and son exchanged glances and smiled. There always was a strong tie between them; there still is to this day.

Mother Clark said, "Wayne has told me of your love for gardening, Renie," and then added, "It's too early in the year, but I shall show you my garden after luncheon, if you like."

That invitation to Mother Clark's garden actually turned out to be an invitation to marriage, or, at the very least, a long step toward marriage. After lunch we walked together over the frozen ground. It was the first of many, many walks Mother Clark and I were to take there, among her cherished plants. Nothing was alive that day. There were only bare branches and empty beds. But it seemed to come alive through a combination of my yearning to be among growing things and the loving way Mother Clark talked about the splash of color that would come out of this bed and the delicate green that would cover that branch. It all seemed to blossom as she talked.

On an impulse I said, "May I come and help you garden as soon as spring begins?"

"Of course you may," she said, and I was happy, both at the prospect of getting to know her and at that of a refuge from the manmade walls of apartment living.

And so I took another step into the future. In the months that followed, Wayne and I saw each other more often and more easily than we would have otherwise, without our mutual interest in the garden and, as time went on, our mutual love for Mother Clark.

That spring I spent as much time as I could in the garden. And often, as I would kneel there trimming, digging, lifting young plants out of flats, a pair of large male feet would stop beside me. And I would look up, and up and up, to see Wayne grinning down at me. He would say, "Hi, Renie," and I would smile back. And that was all, friendly and detached.

He was only a visitor at the Clark home, too. He lived in the city, at the Army-Navy Club, to be close to his work in the War Department. We saw each other when we met at Mother Clark's house. In the city he had his friends and I had mine.

During this phase Wayne was part of my pleasant Clark surroundings, but only a part. That pleasant, uncomplicated relationship continued until one afternoon when I left the Clark home earlier than usual. The next day Wayne telephoned and with almost an accusing tone in his voice said, "You weren't with Mother when I got to Arlington yesterday and I was going to ask you to go to dinner with me."

"I'm sorry, Wayne, but I had a date."

There was a moment of silence. Then he said, "Well, that's too bad, but how about dinner with me tomorrow night instead?"

That was the turning point and Maurine Doran, family friend, became Renie Doran, girl friend.

After that, everything was glorious in a way that only a girl in love can know.

I suppose it is true that the way to a man's heart is through his stomach. I loved to cook then, as I do now, and I liked to think I was a fairly good cook. Wayne made me think so, at least. He always liked to come to dinner at my apartment. It had a cute kitchen and there were lots of modern gadgets—modern for 1923, that is—which made cooking easy. It was fun working in that kitchen while Wayne watched or stretched out in a comfortable living-room chair to read the evening paper.

It wasn't long before I learned that although Wayne ate sparingly, he loved good food. He would eat almost anything if it was simple, well cooked, well seasoned, and not too rich.

Two things Wayne liked to do, however, were beyond me. He loved tennis and hiking. He was six feet two and I was five feet one. I never tried to play tennis with him, but I always loved to watch him. He was a fine player. His long arms and legs gave him an advantage over most men and few were able to beat him. I always marveled that such a tall, lanky man could move about the courts with the ease and grace and skill that Wayne showed.

Hiking was another thing. To Wayne a good hike has to be at least ten miles long. He still likes to tramp through the woods for hours, his long legs covering the ground rapidly. If there are no woods available he will spend a whole afternoon or evening walking through city streets "just to stretch my legs."

In Washington there were plenty of places for hiking. Rock Creek Park was a favorite. So were the rural areas of Virginia just across the Potomac. But I was no good at this. For one thing, I couldn't walk ten miles at my own pace. For another, I couldn't walk ten yards at his pace. The few times I tried to go with Wayne on a hike I found myself trotting after him in desperate little spurts.

Other things we shared, however. We spent many hours enjoying music together. I played the piano and Wayne sang. He had a good voice then, and still has. It really was more than a good voice. It was full and rich with melody. Sometimes he would whistle, and that was magnificent because Wayne could whistle as well as many of the professionals who were a part of every vaudeville bill in those days.

And we danced. Maybe we didn't look as though we should be

dancing together. He towered over me by thirteen inches. But he was as graceful and easy on the dance floor as on the tennis court, and I still say he's the best dancer I know or ever knew.

I'm prejudiced, of course. Somebody once said that every woman thinks the man she loves is the handsomest and most irresistible man in the world. Certainly I did and do.

He was my hero and there was no doubt about it. He was quite tall and he carried himself straight and with a wonderful military bearing. He had jet-black hair, dark brown eyes, and an olive complexion. To me he was the kind of man girls dream about.

But most of all, the thing that attracted me first was his voice, the musical, deep modulation of his speaking voice that I first noticed after that bee sting broke down his reserve or boredom or whatever it was on that almost disastrous picnic. It was all exciting and glorious and he saw less and less of other girls and I dated fewer and fewer other boys. It just worked that way. Nothing was ever put into words. He never even said he loved me. We were just having fun together and each of us seemed willing to let it go at that—for a while, anyway.

Sometimes, particularly toward the end of the month when Wayne's spending money was running out, we would just sit at home, in my apartment, and talk. I always knew when those evenings were coming because when we made the date to have dinner at my house he would say nothing about going to the movies or a dance afterward.

On one of these nights at home Wayne was thoughtful and quiet. He had something on his mind, some worry about the office or something, I thought. I wanted to get him out of that mood so I suggested a game of cards. I went into the other room and was carrying the cards back when he said, ever so softly, "You wouldn't think of marrying me, would you?"

I thought I had misunderstood. I tried hard to keep my voice in control despite the pounding of my heart, and said, "Will you say that again?"

No, there was no mistake. I had understood correctly.

Long before, I had tried to think what I would do when a man

asked me that question. I had tried to steel myself for it. I had so
wanted to act as though a proposal of marriage was an everyday
occurrence in my life.

But my plans and hopes all went smash. So did I, just about. I
was all aflutter. The cards fell from my hands and scattered over
the floor. I had to back into a chair to keep from falling down.

Wayne sat there with his face as red as could be. I knew mine
was the same color. We must have looked like a couple of boiled
lobsters.

Then I got very formal. "Is that to be taken in the form of a
proposal?" I asked.

"It was intended for such," he said, as formal as I.

We sat there looking at each other. Then I muttered something
about never wanting to marry a man who didn't say he loved me,
and the spell was broken and everything was spilled out in a torrent
of words. He did love me, he had loved me for ever so long, would
I marry him and if so when, how soon?

We thought we would keep it all as our secret for a little while,
a secret to be cherished and held against the whole world. But who
can keep such things a secret? It showed in our eyes and our faces
and the way we talked.

Mother Clark saw the change. One day in the garden she surprised me by saying, "Do you know, some of these flowers would
make a lovely bride's bouquet."

They did, too. Mother Clark cut the blooms herself while the
morning dew was still on and sent them to a florist, who arranged
them into as lovely a bouquet as any bride ever carried. To me it was
the loveliest.

In many ways, years later, my daughter Ann had the same kind
of romance I had. Her man was a captain in the Army, too, Gordon
Oosting, West Point, class of 1946. He was Wayne's aide at Fort
Monroe and saw Ann almost every day. They liked each other,
just as Wayne and I had liked each other, but no more. Gordon
was a family friend. Secretly I always hoped it would develop
because I had the greatest admiration for Gordon and loved him
deeply, but it seemed a vain hope, particularly when Gordon took

a one-month leave in 1951 to spend the Christmas holidays with his family from Michigan on a Florida vacation. Gordon wrote Ann once but Ann never got around to answering him. Something clicked after he returned, however, and the first thing we knew they announced their engagement.

Wayne and I were married at the Washington Cathedral in May of 1924 in a simple church wedding. After the ceremony and reception we drove away in a shiny new Buick my parents had given us. It was a handsome machine—we called them machines in those days. It had silken blinds and a graceful cut-glass flower holder bracketed against a door frame.

In that wonderful car, which seemed like a royal carriage to me that day, we drove off into a future we could not have imagined, toward long, good years, and years of slow inch-by-inch progress, to happiness and gaiety, heights and drama that no one could have forecast.

As we drove along, our hands clasped on the car seat between us, I looked out at the new sunshine. I looked proudly at my new husband. I listened to the steady hum of the new Buick and took pleasure in the sight of its rich upholstery. Sprigs of our wedding flowers had been cut and put in the glass flower holders inside the car by some thoughtful friend. I was charmed. "We'll always keep fresh flowers in the cut-glass holder," I said, "won't we, Wayne?"

"We'll always keep fresh flowers in all our cars, always," he promised stoutly.

They don't put flower holders in automobiles any more so Wayne was not able to keep his promise literally.

I never minded, though, because Wayne did not let the change in styles force him to go back on the spirit of his promise. To this day he keeps flowers in my bedroom, flowers that he picks himself and puts in little vases. Maybe it's only a sprig of buds from a tree, or a single flower, but every three or four days he puts a new one on my bedstand.

CHAPTER TWO

ONE OF THE NICEST THINGS ABOUT BEING MAR-
ried to Mark Wayne Clark has been that no matter how busy or
harassed he was with his work of soldiering, he always found some
unexpected little way to let me know that he was thinking of me,
some little thoughtfulness that went beyond a duty letter when he
was away.

Wayne demonstrated that quality before we were married, when
he was courting me, but he proved himself a rare husband by continuing these wonderful little attentions all through our married
life. Some of my nicest memories are of the times he did things
to make me feel I was more important to him than his work or a war
or anything else.

For one thing, I believe I am one of the few women, or at least
wives, who got a bouquet of violets from an army reconnaissance
patrol. We were at Fort Benning where Wayne was in infantry
training. Bill was only two days old. Wayne was assigned a reconnaissance problem in which he had to lead eight men over a prescribed route of five miles and report back anything he saw of military value.

I never heard whether there was anything at all of military significance on that five-mile route, but I know there were plenty of violets. Wayne began picking them for me as soon as he was out of sight of his commanding officer, and the eight men with him thought that was more fun than scouting so they picked violets too. All the violets picked on that five-mile patrol were delivered to me at the hospital in a magnificent bouquet.

Wayne had to pay for that bouquet the hard way, though. Not more than once a year did a colonel come out to meet a patrol returning from a mission. Wayne drew that one time. The colonel was outside waiting for him and his patrol when they came in with their posies. He was stern and became sterner when his questioning showed that Wayne and his patrol had failed to see all kinds of militarily significant things they should have spotted and reported. Wayne tried to win the colonel's sympathy with a burst of parental pride. He told the colonel proudly that his first son was just two days old, and said, "It's a wonderful feeling, Colonel. Do you have children?"

Now one of the first things a young officer should do at any post is learn something about his commanding officer. Wayne certainly should have learned that long before as he was raised in Army posts, son of an Army officer. Maybe he had learned it, but if so he forgot all about it in the great excitement and happiness of becoming a father. Whatever the reason, Wayne didn't know or had forgotten that the colonel was a bachelor, and his colonel did not take kindly to the question at all.

The colonel was absolutely furious. He allowed that Wayne lacked what it took ever to become an effective combat leader. Later Wayne confided to me that he thought maybe the colonel was not only a bachelor himself but maybe came from a long line of bachelors!

On rare occasions I felt that Wayne had something in common with that colonel. Just after we were married and still living in Washington, Wayne took me to a very large party. It seemed to me the party was made up of nothing but old Army friends. At least he was with a group of them all the time, talking man-talk. I couldn't have cared less about stories of West Point classmates

17

or the one who spilled soup in his lap when he was a plebe. But Wayne and his pals seemed to think these things uproarious.

Wayne more or less got lost at this party. He talked with his old friends so long that momentarily he forgot that he was even married. He said good night to his friends and left—without me.

He didn't stay gone long. Almost before I realized he had deserted me, he was back at my side, breathless and, I always thought, a little frightened. I wasn't sizzling, I was boiling mad. But Wayne was so apologetic and so humble that my anger melted. I didn't know it then, but that was to be the pattern of my life with Wayne. No matter what problems or irritations arose, I never was able to stay angry with him for more than a few minutes at a time—and those times were few and far between.

Benning was our first Army post as newlyweds. For me it was the introduction to Army life. My previous life had been about as far removed from the military as it could be. I was born in Wisconsin and raised in Muncie, Indiana, where my father was an official in the Ball Brothers Glass Company which makes Mason Fruit Jars. He had been raised in Pennsylvania on the farm next to the Ball farm, and his boyhood friends were the five sons of the Ball family.

One of the brothers, Ed, and my father decided one summer in Pennsylvania that they would try to make some extra money to help pay for their schooling. Both families were having a difficult time getting enough money to educate the children. The two boys succeeded by tramping the countryside on foot as peddlers. They sold a one-package item—twelve sheets of letter paper, twelve envelopes, a bottle of ink, a pen and penholder—all for twenty-five cents.

Some years later four of the Ball brothers started a small glass factory in Pennsylvania. The oldest of the five brothers became a doctor. It was most natural for the Ball Brothers Glass Company to move from the Dutch to the Hoosier State after natural gas was found in Indiana, for that would save them much money on fuel. It was also natural for them to ask my father to join them because he was such a close friend and he had had business experience by then with the Ivory Soap Company.

My memories of childhood in Muncie are happy ones of a long-ago world of horses and buggies, the forbidden nickelodeon, the piano in the parlor, matinee dances, taffy pulls, fudge, sleigh rides, a grammar-school principal whose name was Longfellow and who wore bushy white whiskers just like the poet's.

My allowance was ten cents a week as a girl, but that was not bad when I could buy three huge jumbo pickles for three cents and a sackful of crackers for two cents. I used to walk along the river with girl friends, eating pickles and crackers and dreaming the wonderful imaginative dreams of girlhood.

The corner drugstore became important to us as we grew older. We passed it as we went to and from school. Behind the plate-glass window were the fountain and the twisted-wire chairs that were so much the mark of early American soda fountains. Whenever I had a nickel to spare I would go in for a cherry crush with lots of chipped ice and I would sip it sparingly to make it last as long as possible so I could watch all the kids on their way home from school, especially the boys.

As we grew older there were group dates, never individual dates. We would picnic in the country with hamburgers, potato salad, and other delicacies. And there were girlish crushes, secret crushes, on both boys and men, the kind of crushes which led us to walk in pairs or small groups by a boy's house to try to make him notice us. My main crush on an older man involved a matinee idol in Minneapolis, where I spent some summers with my cousin Mildred. We never met him, of course, but we were mad about him and saved our money until we not only had the price of two matinee tickets but thirty-five cents left over for a bunch of forget-me-nots. We sent them backstage to him with a note signed, "Two Girls in the Third Row." Then came tragedy. In the third act the leading lady came out on the stage wearing our forget-me-nots as a corsage. We were crushed.

My childhood summers were spent on my grandparents' farm in

Minnesota, where Mildred and I got into all the trouble two city youngsters can get into on a farm. We pulled tail feathers from the roosters to make hats for our dolls. We mixed Grandmother's eggs in our mud pies. We ate the greenest apples and devoured pieplant (rhubarb) raw. In later summers, when money became important to us, we sold Grandmother's eggs until she caught us. Then we sold her flowers.

Each year we spent Christmas with my grandparents. It always was an old-fashioned Christmas, like the ones in American legend and folklore. A bobsleigh piled high with heavy blankets met us at the railroad station, or depot, as we used to call it. There were plenty of big fur gloves for everyone, and we would pile in and bundle up and away we'd go, just as in "Jingle Bells." At the farm Grandfather cut down the Christmas tree, trimmed it, and set it up in the parlor. Decorations consisted of strings of cranberries and popcorn that we made ourselves. Christmas was more for the family and less for the department stores in those days.

Suddenly childhood was gone and I was entering young womanhood, with all its special problems and fluttering and embarrassment. It was the era of the diary, and I kept one. All my hopes and dreams and fears went into that precious, secret little book, and I took it with me when I visited my cousins in Minneapolis, Mildred and her two older brothers. There, without a room of my own, I hid it under the seat of the Morris chair in the living room.

But I knew my secret was out and my soul bared when my cousin Earl teased, "Have you got on your corset?" I was mortified. The only place anyone could have learned about my corset was from my diary, in which I had noted with such pride that I had purchased and worn my first Royal Wooster corset, a real landmark on the way to womanhood. The discovery of the diary subjected Mildred and me to almost interminable teasing from the two boys. It was all part of the price of growing up.

There was more to pay for the process, of course. There was the inevitable heartbreak at the fraternity dance when I caught another girl kissing the boy whose fraternity pin I wore and who, to me, was the only man in the world I could think of marrying. That was

20

when I was attending Northwestern University at Evanston, Illinois, majoring in music, and the sight of that kiss crushed me. Later, the boy rejoined me in the ballroom, unaware that I had seen him kissing another girl. He took me home and I said good night without once hinting that I knew his secret.

Upstairs in my dormitory room I confided to my roommate, Louise Reynolds, dragged out a suitcase, and packed a few clothes. I called a taxi and went to the railroad station, after swearing Louise to secrecy.

My refuge was in Gary, Indiana, with my good friend Jean Highlands and her family. The Highlandses had moved to Gary from Muncie and were old family friends. I knew Jean's parents would take me in.

Once at the Highlandses', I sobbed out my story. Everything was out of focus for me. I knew all the consequences. I knew the school would notify my parents I was missing and that they would be frantic. I knew I would probably be expelled. But right then all I could feel was a broken heart, and none of these other things seemed at all important.

I suppose Mr. and Mrs. Highlands suffered most of all, harboring a fugitive and wondering what to do with me. But it didn't last long. Back at Northwestern the pressure was put on Louise. Finally she broke down and told the school authorities where I had gone. Two days later I was taken back to school, chagrined, ashamed, unhappy. But I knew by then I had to face the music. The sentence was a rough one, too. For three months I was permitted to leave the dormitory only for classes.

It was a dreary three months. But during it my ardor for the boy disappeared, and with it went the broken heart. When I was freed I immediately returned his fraternity pin, and he almost as immediately pinned it on another girl. I was glad to see that she was not the girl he had kissed at the dance.

I finished school that year and returned to Muncie, but was bored almost from the first. Mother was busy with her club and charitable work, so busy that the telephone kept ringing for her when she was home and I hardly got a chance to use it at all. My job was to keep house mostly, and I was far from enthusiastic about it. When the invitation came to visit the Harts in Washington, therefore, I jumped at it, never knowing how it would change my life.

That, in general terms, was my background before I married into the Army, a background as civilian as a blue serge suit. After I married Wayne I not only had to go through all the normal troubles of a new bride but had to learn to live the Army way.

And it was different! My first feeling was that I was living in a goldfish bowl. Everybody knew everything about me. I didn't have a chance to hide a thing or pretend a thing.

My husband wore his salary on his shoulders. Everybody knew just how much a man earned when he wore the two bars of a captain. The lieutenants and their wives were bucking for that salary, and the majors and lieutenant colonels knew all about it because they had lived through it. Besides, it was listed in public records which every Army man had to know by heart if he wanted to dream and plan for the future.

In civilian life a man can keep his salary secret and, if he is so inclined, can put up a bold front with an empty pocket. Not in the Army! If you try to live beyond your means everybody knows it, and resents it because it puts some pressure on them.

Then in civilian life, many times people hardly know their next-door neighbors. In the Army that's impossible. The men work together on the same general kind of problems. Everybody goes to the same club, the same commissary, the same post movie, the same post exchange, which is more like a super drugstore than anything else. Then, too, the neighbor you snub might turn out to be your commanding officer ten or twenty years later. Snubbing was kept at a minimum in the Army.

Since we all had the same money problems and each of us knew what everyone else was making, we discussed budget problems without restraint and were always delighted to receive suggestions from other Army wives about how to cut corners and save pennies.

Gradually, as I got to know Army life, I found I had to think about my personal behavior constantly, just as every other Army wife must. This was particularly true when we had quarters on a post and after the children came along. If I offended someone in a back-fence argument, for instance, or if the children annoyed a neighbor by leaving their toys on his lawn, Wayne got a black mark. It wasn't a formal thing, but word spread from post to post and other officers and their families would have a bad impression of people before they even met.

We heard it in the Officers' Club and when the women got together to talk and gossip. Someone would say, "I hear Captain Jones and his family are moving into the post next month," and someone else would confide, "Oh, if that's the Captain Jones from the Presidio it will be awful. He has three terrible little boys. Real brats all of them."

Those were some of the things I found I didn't like about Army life, but there were many, many compensations. The interest our neighbors showed in us was not mere idle curiosity but more of a feeling of kinship that grows among people who are in the Army a long time. Any post is like a big family, and the people living on it often know each other better than they know their own families. I found, after the strangeness wore off, that these other women who asked questions and made suggestions really were being friendly and simply wanted to help me adjust to this new way of life.

And there were so many problems. We didn't get married and move into a dream cottage to live happily ever after. Sometimes I felt we got married so I could learn interior decorating the hard way. Certainly I got enough practice settling into new homes.

I don't know how it happened, but it seemed that every new house had longer windows than the old. If they gave degrees for lengthening short curtains to fit long windows, I would have my Ph.D. hands down.

Then there was the cost. The Army pays the basic transportation and moving costs, but the basics do not include all the little things a woman must have to pretty up her home or fix the garden or add shelves and coat hooks and all the other small but vital incidentals.

School was always a problem, too. I can't count the number of times Ann and Bill were yanked out of school in mid-term, to lose a few weeks during a move and then have to work like Trojans to catch up in a new school where the teachers and students were strange to them.

All this moving about did have a good side for the children. It forced them to learn to make friends and to adjust to new situations. They acquired poise, learned how to meet people, and got to know many parts of our great country.

We didn't really have to "put on the dog" in the Army, but we did have to keep up, at least. An officer in the United States Army is expected to make a good appearance, and so are his wife and children. Money is the easiest way to do it, but on a captain's pay we didn't have enough money to do the whole job, so we had to improvise. Sewing circles were most popular among Army wives, and we made clothes for ourselves and our children.

Another big difference for me between civilian and Army life was that in the Army I could not escape from my husband's work. Army wives cannot retire into the kitchen even if they want to. A wife plays too big a part in her husband's career in the Army and in extreme cases can make or break him.

I found that in addition to the necessity of keeping such a close watch on my own deportment and that of my children, I had to do many positive things. There were social obligations. I had to pay my respects to the wives of senior officers whenever we moved to a new post, and I had to pay them early no matter how much work I had to do to get settled in my new house. There were all the post activities, and a wife had to do her share. These included church, clubs, nurseries, Boy Scouts, Girl Scouts, the thrift shop where Army people sold everything from an old pair of golf shoes to an outgrown baby carriage, PTA, Army Relief, and ever so many other things.

All these made up the life of our Army community, and it was the wives who had to keep it going. Actually I enjoyed this work, as do so many of the Army wives. It gave me a feeling of belonging and of helping my husband and of having a real purpose in life. And there was nothing like it to cement friendships securely.

The most difficult part of Army life is the separation. In peacetime there are summer maneuvers, field trips, inspections, conferences and all those other things that take an officer away from his family. But in wartime there is just separation, of the worst possible kind. In wartime the wives simply wait and hope.

It is sad to say that I saw many previously happy marriages, some that had lasted twenty years or more, go on the rocks because of the wartime separation. The husband or wife just could not keep it going alone. One or the other would find somebody new.

Each time one of us wives saw that happen to a marriage we felt a twinge of fear. The marriages that broke up during the war had seemed as firm as our own. Could it happen to us? None of us was ever really free of that fear.

During World War II, I was living in Washington and Wayne was away for such a long time I was heartsick to see how many women I loved dearly were losing their husbands through divorce. In most cases it was the man who found someone new. We women back home were so helpless and there seemed nothing we could do in a positive way to hold our men when they were overseas.

I prayed that it wouldn't happen to me. There was nothing I knew that could possibly mar our marriage, but other people I knew, people who had seemed so happy with each other, were breaking up and I could not wipe out the gnawing concern in my heart.

That, over-all, was the Army to me. Some of it was strange and even annoying. Most of it, as I got used to the new way of living, was wonderful.

For a short time after we were married we lived in an apartment in Washington, just like civilians.

But then came the Army, and with it adventure, humorous and otherwise, in large doses. It was built on everything from bedbugs to sweet potatoes.

Our first home was Fort Benning and our first gas bill was for eighteen dollars. Nobody had ever told Wayne married life would cost that much and he paled a bit. So did I. Wayne decided to find out why the bill was so high because, after the initial shock, he figured eighteen dollars was way out of line for a gas bill.

So he turned detective in his own home and found the answer in the only place it could be, in the gas range in the kitchen. We had a six-dollar-a-week cook, Mattie, who was a real find, not only because she worked so well herself but because every night her five children came to the house to help her clean our kitchen until it shined. But Mattie and her five children were the answer to our eighteen-dollar gas bill. She had a passion for sweet potatoes, and so did her five children. Every day she kept the oven burning to bake her sweet potatoes, which she ate almost constantly, and then, before leaving for home, she and her five children filled up on some more sweet potatoes.

Wayne was a thorough detective on that job. He not only learned why the gas bill was so high, but he learned to appreciate the work that Mattie and her five little helpers did in our first home. So he said, "Our cook gets six bucks a week? Make it eight."

It sounded like a snap decision but later Wayne explained his thinking to me. He said, "Those are wonderful kids, all five of them, and they do help Mattie a lot in the kitchen, and, well, I just don't think they ever get enough to eat. I think they can use the money better than we can."

So actually we didn't save at all but we solved the mystery of the gas bill.

That first home we rented, furnished, was charming, and I was so proud the first time my parents came from Muncie to stay with us at Christmastime, and so crushed when they left after the first night with an excuse that I thought pretty flimsy. Cleaning the room, I learned the real reason, which I had to admit was pretty good. Overnight visitors had to share our only guest room with bedbugs!

Our closest friends at Benning were the Matt Ridgways, who lived across the street from us. Matt was a classmate of Wayne's at West Point and later, of course, became Army Chief of Staff. At Benning they were two serious young captains. Frequently we put our dinners together and shared a table at one house or the other. After these dinners Matt and Wayne would spend hours talking over military problems, sometimes agreeing, sometimes not. Mrs. Ridgway and I would sit quietly doing the family mending or darning and listening to the shoptalk of our husbands.

Each captain had a keen mind and an avid interest in military science. Their discussions were lively and, as I look back, their thinking was advanced. Each had a strong, commanding personality and each had definite ideas on the tactics and strategic concept of war, that is, how and under what circumstances America should fight. Wayne has always had a warm place in his heart for Matt Ridgway, not only as a friend but as an outstanding combat officer. They retained a mutual admiration for each other throughout their long years of service together.

Matt had been Cadet Adjutant, one of the highest-ranking cadets in the Corps, during his final year at West Point. He had a splendid physical and soldierly appearance and was a real athlete. Wayne and Matt played tennis together often at Benning, and also played handball and went on long hikes together.

There was a world of animal energy wrapped up in those two young officers. Near the end of the Benning course they were tent-mates while studying field problems away from the fort. Sundays they would return home together to relax. One Sunday night after returning to their tent they started a friendly wrestling match for want of anything else to do. They grabbed and clawed, tumbled together to the tent floor, rolled under bunks. Then they rose and wrestled on top of the bunks. By the time they were through the tent was a wreck and so were they. But they were happy.

The Ridgways were still our across-the-street neighbors and close friends when Bill, our first child, was born at Benning. Another important date was coming up for Wayne right at that time. Each student at the infantry school had to present what they called a "monograph" on a particular military problem. The monograph, much like a thesis for a graduate degree, had to be presented before the entire infantry-school student body and faculty and was at least as important to a young Army officer as a thesis is to the aspirant for an added degree. The monographs were judged on succinctness, grasp of the problem, and ingenuity of presentation. Actually, the student had to brief the infantry school on a military problem or exercise, preferably a personal experience in combat.

The young officers went to the greatest lengths to impress their instructors with these monographs. One ingenious fellow, in a monograph on a World War I problem, used little cutout bulldogs wearing German helmets to mark the location of German units on his map.

Wayne planned his monograph carefully, right down to the timing. He got the best reading the doctor could give him on when our baby would be born and set the date for his monograph well after the estimated date.

But some things even the Army cannot plan. Bill malingered. He did not arrive until 1 A.M. of the morning that Wayne was to give his monograph. The time set for the monograph was 8 A.M.

Wayne was much more of a father than a soldier that day and he forgot all about his monograph. He picked me some wild flowers. He celebrated with Matt Ridgway, who stayed up through the night with him. Wayne had become a father and he was doing it right.

But Matt Ridgway wasn't becoming a father that day and he could think of other things. About dawn Matt brought Wayne down to earth by asking him if he were really set for that eight-o'clock monograph. Wayne was startled. Hastily he groped his way back to realities. Matt lent a guiding hand with some questions. Yes, Wayne said, he could focus all right on the problem and give his briefing. After all, he was talking about a reconnaissance patrol in his own sector of France in World War I. Yes, he had his notes and he had his map.

Map markers? That question by Matt threw the whole thing out of kilter. Wayne had forgotten his map markers. There was a moment of panic as the two friends remembered the good impression the bulldogs with the German helmets had made on the instructors.

It was much too late to go shopping for clever map markers and even too late to dream up some originals and make them. Wayne looked around the house in desperation. All he could see was baby stuff—bottles, clothing, blankets. And packages of diapers. That was it! He and Matt looked at each other questioningly for a moment and then leaped for a package and tore it open. Somewhere

Wayne found a bold crayon, and quickly the diapers were converted into great big map markers with unit numbers and designations drawn on them in crayon.

He pocketed a handful of the out-sized safety pins that went with the diapers and marched off to give his monograph with some map markers that probably were as unique, if not quite as ingenious, as any ever used at Benning. And despite the excitement of the baby, the loss of a whole night's sleep, and the emotional turmoil of the forgotten map markers, Wayne carried off his monograph with great success.

Our second post was the Presidio of San Francisco, and on arrival I got another lesson in Army life. Our quarters were not ready. They had to be vacated by an Army family moving somewhere else. We would stay in the Bachelor Officers' Quarters until the family went to their new post. I had been prepared at Benning for such things in the Army. But then orders came through for Wayne to go immediately to Monterey, about 125 miles down the coast, for summer maneuvers. This time I rebelled. I wasn't going to stay in Bachelor Quarters with my infant baby and my dog while Wayne spent the summer tramping around in the hills behind Monterey. I determined to follow him, thus beginning my life-long, and largely unsuccessful, battle to stay with my husband.

The very first morning after we arrived in San Francisco, Wayne had to take off for Monterey. It was just impossible for me to go with him so early after our trip across the country with baby and dog. Wayne gave me the keys to the car and casually told me it was parked in the Bachelor Quarters garage. He said the garage was "up there" and pointed to a rickety-looking row of stalls on the peak of a typical San Francisco hill. Then he took off.

I had absolutely nothing to do, except take care of my baby and dog, until our house was vacated and I could go to work on that. So I decided that first morning that I would go sight-seeing in San Francisco. Bill was packed in a basket, and Barney, my German shepherd, was whistled along. We trudged up the steep hill to the garage. I put Bill's basket on the front seat beside me and Barney in back. We were ready for adventure in San Francisco—and got it a whole lot faster than I had planned. Nobody, least of all Wayne, had ever told me that in hilly San Francisco people leave parked cars in gear for safety so they won't roll away. Wayne automatically had left the car in forward gear.

I stepped on the starter. The car crashed through the back of the garage carrying my baby, dog, and me out into space, into the air, falling along an almost sheer cliff face.

About halfway down we hit a tree that stopped our fall. Baby Bill was upside down and all mixed up in the gear shift. Barney was up front with us. None of us was hurt, why I shall never know.

After checking the baby and then the dog, I crawled out of the car, surveyed the deplorable wreck, and almost fearfully peeked back up the hill down which we had just flown.

The landscape had changed. There were no more garages. Our car had brought them all tumbling down like a house of cards. Where they had stood was a man on horseback looking down on me. He was Capt. John Ferguson of the post police. I literally wailed, "I suppose you'll arrest me and put me in the guardhouse now?" But he appeared to be only too glad that I hadn't killed myself and could still speak. Much to my relief, he shook his head and said, "They were condemned anyway. You saved us the trouble of tearing them down."

The whole script might have been written for Mack Sennett. Just like one of his two-reel comediennes, I had a one-track mind and a single purpose—to get to Monterey. And just like one of his comediennes I went from one trouble to another.

The car was repaired and a few days later I started out for Monterey, again with baby and dog. Through friends I had rented a house down there, sight unseen, for the few weeks of the maneuvers. We arrived late on a Saturday afternoon so I stopped by the camp to pick up Wayne on the way to the house. He had the weekend off.

We were pleasantly surprised. The owners had left everything in most livable condition. They had even left their personal things. While I was putting Bill to bed and beginning to unpack, Wayne

30

even found a bottle of gin upstairs and we decided to celebrate. The drinks were just about ready when we heard someone come in downstairs. Wayne was indignant and shouted in his booming voice, "Who are you?"

An equally angry answer came back: "Who are *you?*"

"I've rented this house," Wayne shouted down the stairs.

"You have not," came the answer. "I own it and I happen to live here."

The only fortunate thing about the incident was that Wayne was bigger than our involuntary host, who was mad enough to have started something if he hadn't been so outmanned. He was particularly furious when he realized we were drinking his gin. It was Prohibition time and decent gin was not easy to get.

The man finally cooled down enough to recall that he had heard that the house next door, identical to his, had been rented to some Army officer, and he let us move from his house to ours without calling the police. Wayne later replaced his gin.

I, of course, felt like the most befuddled of all brides. I had remembered the street name but not the house number and, by coincidence, the key fit the locks to both houses.

My score with Wayne was not very high right then. I had wrecked the car. I had moved into the wrong house. I was messing things up to a fair-you-well. With the tolerance of the new husband, Wayne was not angry but he was plenty annoyed. I felt I had to do something to get back into his good graces, and womanlike I decided the quickest way would be to get prettied up. So Monday morning I went in search of a hairdresser. That would fix up everything, and almost did.

I found a small beauty shop and told the operator something had to be done with my hair. "A rinse?" she suggested. "Henna, perhaps?" I had never heard of henna, but it sounded new and glamorous, just the thing to right all the wrongs of which I had been guilty. I asked the price and the girl said five dollars. That was a lot of money, but I felt it would be worth it, so I told her to put it on. I was shampooed and then came the henna. The girl covered my head with a towel turban and went to work manicuring my nails. Suddenly she looked up and said, "How long do you think we should keep the henna on you?"

I was lost. "Don't you know?" I asked.

She shook her head. "Never gave one of them before," she confessed.

I remembered the five dollars and wanted my money's worth so I said, "Well, keep it on until you finish the manicure."

In time the turban was removed and my hair was rinsed and I went to the mirror to take a look. What a horror! My hair was the color of the red stripe in the American flag. The hairdresser had a pinched look around her nose. "Let's rinse it again," she said in a try-anything mood. She rinsed it not once but several times, and each time my hair got even redder. We finally had to give up. The only saving element for the moment was that my cloche hat, then the height of fashion, covered my whole head.

Back home I kept that hat on for dear life. Wayne found me in the kitchen fixing dinner and wearing an apron and the hat. He looked surprised but, thinking this was just another odd female quirk, said nothing. He couldn't remain silent, though, when I sat down to dinner with the hat still on. He had to ask me about it. I smiled brightly and said, "I like the hat, don't you?"

What could a young husband do? He backed away from something he didn't understand, of course, and made a game effort to wipe the look of mystification from his face.

The evening wore on—with the hat. Finally it was bedtime, the time I had dreaded all evening. I just couldn't sleep in that hat. It was difficult enough to keep Wayne from exploding into anger when I wore it into the dressing room to change to my nightgown. It was there that I finally was forced to take off that protective hat and reveal my hair in all its horrifying new color.

Cautiously I slipped back into the bedroom. Wayne stared at me, openmouthed. Just as I reached for the switch that would plunge the room into blessed darkness, I saw the color slowly creeping up into his neck.

The pain of that experience was with me for a full year. It took that long for the red hair to grow long enough to be cut off.

The mishaps of Monterey behind us, we returned to the Presidio and got settled into our own quarters in the beautiful old post that overlooks the Golden Gate. The Presidio of San Francisco, one of the oldest Army posts, is on a hilly peninsula on the San Francisco side of the Golden Gate. It was at the Presidio that I gradually came to understand the responsibilities of an Army wife. There were the social responsibilities, of course, which take up a good deal of the time and energy of any Army wife. I had to learn about protocol and the established social procedure of the service. The wife of every young Army officer must learn, with her husband, how to conform to social obligations. She should also give part of her time to post activities. I started to do my bit, at first from a sense of duty. As time passed, however, I found that these activities gave me that "good" feeling of contributing to things worthwhile, even if only in a small way.

Life on an Army post in peacetime gives the Army wife far more opportunity, and probably more obligation, to help her husband in his career than most wives find in civilian life. The reasons are fairly obvious. An Army post is something like a company town. Everybody is working for the same outfit. Everybody goes to the same post clubs and chapels and movies and buys their food at the same commissary and miscellaneous articles at the same post exchange. Living on the post, the husband is never far from either his home or work. The people the wife sees at night, at parties or in her home, are the people her husband works with or for. Army protocol requires that the wife get to know the commanding officer and his wife socially. And it is quite common in Army life for the wife to call a ranking officer by his first name while her husband must address him by rank, as "colonel" or "general."

These were the kind of things I had to learn at the Presidio, where Wayne was an officer on duty, not an officer-student as he was at Benning. And there was a break in my training period, too, because of domestic reasons. Another baby was on the way.

33

This time Wayne, serving in San Francisco's own Thirtieth Infantry Regiment, had a colonel who could understand how it was with fatherhood. The colonel had five children of his own. So on a pretext, he excused Wayne from part of the summer maneuvers at Monterey and gave him special duty at the Presidio, just so he could be with me when the baby came.

The second baby, like the first, came late. Wayne got more and more nervous about the duty he was missing at Monterey. Finally one night he asked me for perhaps the millionth time how I felt. I smiled back, "Just wonderful." Then he explained that his own unit was going into a most important phase of the exercises and he felt he just couldn't wait any longer. He said he would go down to Monterey in the morning and that I could call just as soon as I felt the baby was near. He got up at 5 A.M. the next day, and once again asked how I felt. I said I was tops and told him to run along and not worry.

Wayne got into his little Ford with Joe Sullivan, his classmate at West Point and, down through the years, one of our very dearest and closest friends, and started out.

Half the outfit lined the roadway screaming as they pulled into camp. The call had just come from the hospital. The baby was being born. Wayne and Sully jumped back into the Ford and took off for San Francisco as though their lives depended on it. Sully, a San Franciscan born and bred, said he knew a short cut through the mountains and the redwood groves north of Santa Cruz. Wayne took that. The hills were high and the roads were bad and Wayne burned out just about everything needed to make that Ford run. But he got back to the Presidio, breathless and a little late. Ann was born some time before he arrived.

Ann was sixteen months younger than Bill, and two babies in the house kept my hands full. But I did have to pick up my educational training as the wife of an Army officer.

My first lesson, a painful one, was that as long as Wayne was in the Army I had better do what I could to learn the likes and dislikes, the quirks and whims, of the wives of his superior officers.

Ann was still a tiny infant when we gave our first formal dinner party. We were determined to make it perfect. An officer doesn't have to be an accomplished host to make his way up in the Army, but it helps.

At the time we had a part-time maid but this was such an important party to us and there was so much to do that I worked all day in the kitchen, in the house, and especially in the dining room which was to be my showpiece for the evening. I brought out all of our wedding silver for the first time, and saw that every bit of it was polished till it gleamed. I handled the pieces almost lovingly as I set them out on the table and beamed with what I thought was justifiable pride. When Wayne came home he and I walked around and around that table, hand and hand, admiring it. It sparkled with sterling and was ablaze with the color of banked flowers.

Wayne was proud too. "Nobody," he said, "ever has set a more beautiful dinner table, Renie."

Like so many other young couples, we were way behind in our social obligations, and our guest list included only people who had entertained us in their homes. I can remember still the wonderful sense of anticipation I felt as guests began to arrive. We were about to return hospitality we had been given, and we could be proud of the beautiful way in which we were returning it. Everything was ready and perfect; nothing could go wrong.

But of course it did.

After gay talk at cocktails we moved into the dining room and if the roof had caved in I couldn't have felt worse. The voice of a colonel's lady speaking to another woman floated through the room loud and clear with the terrible words—"What a vulgar display of silver for a junior officer."

My big effort was ruined. I was miserable. Later I learned that this colonel's wife was a crusader who held that it would be easier for the ranks if the officers set more simple standards of social life. Apparently she limited her sympathies to the enlisted men for she rode roughshod over my feelings that night she ate at my table. But a colonel's lady has the power to sear the soul of a captain's wife, and that lady did. For years afterward, every time I remembered her shocking words, I winced.

Perhaps it was coincidence, or a sum of such small things, but shortly after that dinner Wayne made his first and only serious move to take us out of the Army. He even traveled off to Florida, spending more money on the trip than we could afford, to study a tempting business offer. On his return he decided that he had too much love for service life and we went on in our Army way, poorer for the travel money he spent but happy in the decision.

The most exciting news we had from the Army during that first three-year tour of duty at the Presidio was the assignment Wayne got to take the Pacific Coast Army Basketball championship team to Honolulu.

Neither of us had ever been there and we were thrilled with the prospect. The big day came and we boarded the tiny Army transport, the *St. Mihiel,* and away we went toward the open sea, beautiful Hawaii and adventure. It was a rough start, though, with the waters of San Francisco Bay kicking up such a fuss that almost everybody was seasick soon after we went through the Golden Gate. We were learning why the *St. Mihiel* had the reputation of being the smallest and worst of the transports the Army had. She was still in service more than ten years later and carried assault troops to the beach of Massacre Bay on the island of Attu in the Aleutians in 1943. The troops aboard the *St. Mihiel* in northern waters got an even rougher ride than we did, but ours was rough enough.

Wayne and I had decided to take Ann and Bill along but to leave our nurse behind and depend on the stewardess to give me what help was needed in caring for them en route. Unfortunately the stewardess broke her arm the first day out.

It was no pleasure cruise to Honolulu and we arrived pale and wan. The heat was stifling on the dock, and Ann, Bill, and I had to stand there and wait for Wayne to make arrangements for the basketball players to get transportation to their hotel. An open car came for the officers and it was suggested that, instead of going directly to the hotel, we take a cooling ride amid the beauty of Oahu. The ride was cooling, all right. Both children, overheated by the wait on the dock, were chilled by the ride in the open car and came down with the croup. I was torn between two duties—

attending the games with my husband or staying in the hotel caring for my croupy babies. The problem was solved by hiring a dependable trained nurse.

Our voyage back to the States was smooth and delightful, but we had learned a lesson. Next time we would leave the babies at home!

CHAPTER THREE

MARK WAYNE CLARK BEGAN HIS MILITARY career just about as auspiciously as anyone could. A President of the United States helped get him his appointment to West Point. Woodrow Wilson gave Wayne a hand because he was a friend of Wayne's aunt, Mrs. Marshall, of Highland Park, Illinois.

Wayne learned early, though, that such attention from high places was not all good. Shortly after he arrived at West Point as a plebe, an Assistant Secretary of State, Dudley Field Malone, visited the Academy and there was a review of cadets. The Secretary knew of the President's interest in Wayne, so he asked that this plebe cadet be called from the ranks so he could meet him. Introductions were made all around, to the Superintendent, the Commandant, and the First Captain, and the eyes of every cadet were on Wayne.

The eyes were not particularly friendly, either. It was a very hot day and the sun beat down on the cadets standing in ranks, at attention. Wayne knew that he would suffer at the hands of the upperclassmen for this, and he did. The heat of the sun on the cadets' heads that day was nothing compared to the heat they later put on Wayne. Upperclassmen got even by making Plebe Clark stand at attention in his room for hours.

The President's interest in young Wayne in 1913 didn't help him, either, to win promotion in the Army during the seventeen-year period after World War I when few, if any, of the younger officers were moved up in rank. Wayne was luckier than some because he was a captain during this Army stalemate. Many of the men who were generals in World War II spent those seventeen years as junior officers, and they had real difficulties with money during the years when they were doing their best to raise their children properly. The long stalemate was caused by the many young men commissioned by the Army during World War I who decided to make the Army a career. It took seventeen years to break the jam and retire enough people to begin to move men up in rank again.

Although we considered ourselves lucky, we still had to cut a few corners. The pay scale for a captain with a dependent in 1930 was $372 a month, including his rental and subsistence allowance. Wayne was such a proud young husband he rejected the help my family offered. And he also insisted that we always have help in the house because, as he put it, "I don't want you to do so much work, Renie, that you get old before your time." So we always had a girl to help in the house and with the children.

Captains just didn't get enough money to pay for these things without scrimping on others, so we scrimped some. Fortunately, my mother had made a seamstress out of me when I was a little girl by teaching me how to use patterns and do all the sewing for my dolls. She also taught me to make coats and hats for the dolls. This training stood me in good stead all those years Wayne was drawing a captain's pay. I had a little electric sewing machine, and I made all the clothes for Ann and myself and most of the clothes for Bill.

The second source of saving was on the food budget. We were always particular to set a good table, but there were ways to save and I found them. We would splurge on steak and roast beef occasionally and then level off the food bill with such things as tuna fish and chipped beef.

The Buick wedding gift from my parents in 1924 saved us from having to go into debt to become automobile owners, debt that was so heavy for many of our young friends at that time. We were so grateful for this gift and the financial boost it gave us in our first years together that when Ann and then Bill were married, our wedding gifts to them were automobiles.

Social obligations were the biggest budget busters. At every Army post, the higher the rank, the more an officer's wife is obliged to entertain. And in that strange seventeen years of no advance, seniority in service began to take on the aspects of rank. Wayne, who in 1917 was one of the youngest battalion commanders in the American Army, gradually was becoming one of the senior captains.

The development was quite natural. The more years Wayne served and the more friends we made in the service, the more parties we went to and the more parties we had to give to return the favors. Nobody has to keep up with the Joneses like an Army family.

As a result, we not only had to plan parties and pay for them, but we had to be ready at all times for the social blitz when high-ranking officers or civilian friends would drop in for a weekend. In the close-knit, family atmosphere of the Regular Army, people are expected to be ready for these unexpected social invasions.

During those years we often used to say, only half jokingly, that we were but one jump ahead of the sheriff. And sometimes Wayne, with his unfailing sense of humor, would grin after we talked like that and say something like, "Yes, Renie, but think of the poor lieutenants."

The tour of duty at the Presidio was a wonderful period in our lives. The two children were still infants and weren't too much of a chore, and we had besides the beauty of California and the sea all around us. But Army orders ended that idyllic era, as Army orders were to end all other eras for us in the next thirty years. I was heartbroken to leave the Presidio and all the friends we had made there, just as I was heartbroken every time I had to leave every other post at which Wayne served. It seemed that I hated to move to each new past, and hated to leave it after we had settled into it.

We drove to our new post, across the desert to Fort D. A. Russell in Cheyenne, Wyoming. The Buick was really loaded. There were the four Clarks with luggage, the nurse, the German shepherd, and a canary. Capt. Harold Gilbert (later General) drove ahead of us with his wife, Sarah, and their two children in the car. Happily Harold was leading the way, for when we hit a sandstorm, his car practically blazed a trail through it for us.

When we got to Fort Russell we were given an apartment over the Gilberts' and were most comfortable. It, too, was a happy post and soon we were building up a backlog of people to whom we owed dinners. At last we were sufficiently straightened around and I invited five couples. That was all I could ask because we had just twelve of everything—silverware, china, chairs. Our dining room was built for a maximum of twelve people. One more couple would have crowded us out of it.

Again I was happy in anticipation of giving a party and almost danced to the door when the bell was rung by the first guests. I reached out my arms in greeting and then stopped dead in my tracks. They were utter strangers!

For an instant I could say nothing. And in that instant they greeted me by name and I knew a terrible mistake had been made. They were not at the wrong party. They had been invited, somehow by someone.

It was a nightmare. These two strangers made it fourteen for dinner and I didn't even have fourteen plates or chairs. Frantically I whispered to Wayne. It didn't bother him. He just said, "You handle it." For an instant I thought he was even enjoying my predicament. In any event, he went right on being the perfect host, laughing, talking, enjoying himself.

Finally the ninth and tenth guests arrived and I was beside myself. I set my smile hard, trying to hide the panic within me. The doorbell would herald disaster any minute. My moment of agony was extended, as the doorbell just didn't ring. Our last two guests were overdue. It happened that they were good, close friends.

I excused myself and went to the telephone, for now I was caught between two social blunders. The first was having more guests than I could feed. The second, and growing one, was failing to feed my guests on time. I called the overdue guests. No, they had not planned to visit us that evening. No, they had not been invited. Yes, they understood they were left out because we had limited facilities and certainly they understood we had so many obligations we couldn't fulfill them all with one dinner party and had to space out our invitations. No, of course they didn't mind.

The whole thing was beyond my understanding right then, but I was so relieved that I fear I became a rather giddy hostess. It did turn out well and we had a fine party. Later I figured out what had happened. The name of the strangers was quite similar to that of our friends and the telephone operator had given me the wrong couple when I asked for my friends by name. The strangers saw nothing unusual in the invitation since people on Army posts like to get acquainted with one another and frequently invite people to dinner without knowing them too well.

The commanding general at Fort Russell was Brig. Gen. Frank Bolles, known throughout the service as "Bowser" Bolles because he barked so much. Bolles had received reports that the Chinese operator of the concessions restaurants was holding back some of the take that should properly have been given to the post, and asked Wayne to conduct an investigation. The Chinese, worried about losing the source of his livelihood, had tried to spread good will by taking little presents to the ladies on the post, and Wayne therefore advised me to accept *no* presents but did not tell me why. Then he went off for a week-long inspection trip.

While he was gone a Chinaman brought me a bolt of gorgeous white liberty silk. I really had forgotten that I was not to accept a gift from him, but I don't really know if I would have been able to resist that silk even if I had remembered. It was so beautiful. I grabbed it happily and made a dress for Ann and a dress for myself and curtains for our apartment and was delighted with the surprise I had waiting for Wayne.

When Wayne came home he was surprised all right. But surprise quickly turned to suspicion when I appeared in a new dress. He asked if "by any chance" that was silk from the Chinese. I admitted it was and he was furious. The offender was ordered off the post.

It wasn't very nice of me, but since the silk was all cut up and made into dresses for Ann and me, as well as curtains for some windows, I kept it.

My mother spent some time at Fort Russell helping take care of the children while Wayne was in the hospital in Denver having his gall bladder removed and while I was having some trouble with my teeth. Sarah Gilbert, living downstairs, had to help her out of one crisis, when Bill and Ann smeared my cold cream all through their hair, on the walls, and on the curtains and rug in my bedroom, and Bowser Bolles himself had to get her out of another.

I was at the dentist's office that day and Mother took the two children out to see a post review. She didn't know that after each review there was a wild field-artillery charge with the horses dragging the caissons across the parade grounds at breakneck speed. Nobody had told Mother about that charge, so as soon as the foot soldiers completed their marching, she took a child by each hand and started crossing the parade ground. General Bolles spotted her and ordered his automobile driver to beat that charge and make the rescue. The driver made it, General Bolles grabbed Mother and the two children and hustled them into the car, and the driver got them all out safely before the horses and the caissons came crashing through.

Some time later, still in the dentist's office, I heard an officer complaining, "Some fool woman with a couple of kids almost got trampled during the artillery charge. They all would have been killed for sure if someone hadn't pulled them out. Can't women do the craziest things?"

I agreed and wondered who could have been so foolish as to have done that. Only later did I find out it was *my* family who had such a narrow escape.

After eight months at Fort Russell, later renamed Fort Francis E. Warren after Wyoming's famous senator, we were ordered to Indianapolis, where Wayne was to serve as an instructor with the Indiana National Guard. It was wonderful to be moving so close to home in Muncie, and to add to our bounty Wayne had two months' leave coming to him before he had to report for duty. We decided to go to Muncie, where we had spent vacations with my parents. We were overjoyed when word came that one of the Ball brothers, with whom my father worked, had offered to let us stay in his home for the whole two months, since he and his wife were to be out of the

43

city on vacation during that time. By this time, 1930, the Ball Brothers Glass Company was very big business. The brothers had bought up a whole boulevard on the river in Muncie and built for themselves five magnificent houses, one of which we were to have rent free, no work, no responsibilities, no office hours. We looked forward to a wonderful two months of rest and play.

We settled into the house as soon as we arrived in Muncie. The next morning at seven the doorbell rang. Wayne struggled into a robe and slippers and answered the bell, a disheveled, sleepy man.

At the door was Mr. G. A. Ball, stern and straight. He was a great driving spirit in Ball Brothers, and years later, after his ninetieth birthday, was still the active head of the company as chairman of the board.

When Wayne opened the door, Mr. Ball said, "Captain Clark?" He yawned out a "Yes, sir."

"I understand," said Mr. Ball, "that you have two months' leave. That is too long for any young man to loaf. We are shorthanded right now. I want you to report to me at my office at nine o'clock— this morning." He looked Wayne up and down and added, "You can work those two months."

Taking orders from a civilian was something new for Wayne. But Mr. Ball was the kind of civilian who knew how to give orders with full confidence that they would be obeyed.

They were, too. Wayne reluctantly gave up his dream of a two months' rest with me and the children. He got dressed and was in Mr. Ball's office at nine o'clock sharp. Mr. Ball put him right to work at fifty dollars a week, which was not bad in that first year of the Depression. The company was expanding into the field of glass jars for prepared food companies and Wayne went to work in that department.

It was Wayne's first civilian job and he learned to like it.

At the end of two months Mr. Ball called Wayne back into his office and said quite bluntly, "I want you to resign from the Army." He added, "There is no future in it for you and you can do much better with us."

44

It was a temptation, and we considered it seriously, but once again Wayne decided in favor of the Army.

I learned a lot about just how devoted Wayne was to the service when this job was offered him. The situation in Muncie must have put tremendous pressure on him. We were living in a mansion, a magnificent home, the kind of home he could hardly hope to get in the Army, and living so close to the Balls, we could see all around us the rich rewards of success in private enterprise.

It had to be Wayne's decision. I tried to make it clear to him that either way I would be happy, so long as he was certain in his own mind that he was doing what he thought best for him and our happiness. It was easy for me to take this attitude because I myself was pulled both ways. Money could buy a lot of happiness and security, and I had not the slightest doubt about Wayne's ability to forge ahead in the business. But by that time I was used to the Army and there was much in it that I loved. We had made a legion of friends and, with all the trouble of moving, I still enjoyed traveling about the country as we did.

We talked many hours before we came to a decision. Wayne thought long and hard of what a change would mean to the family, and what the Army would mean to it. Finally, he made his choice. He said, as he has said so often since, "If I had started out with the idea of becoming rich I wouldn't have gone into the Army in the first place."

There was security in the Army, too, not the security that a fortune would bring but the security of a pension and the other privileges an Army officer received in those days, to say nothing of the honor of service to country. Since World War II ended, those privileges have been whittled down considerably, and that has worried Wayne. He is constantly concerned that the caliber of the men attracted to the Army as a career will decline as the benefits of Army life are reduced. So long as the pay cannot be commensurate with what men get for jobs of similar responsibility in civilian life, Wayne feels there must be such other inducements as good medical care for the families, good pensions for retired officers, and adequate pensions for their widows.

I was so excited about going home to Indiana that when we got to Indianapolis and Wayne reported for duty I began to dream of owning our own home. I urged Wayne to buy but he resisted. The tradition in the Army is that it's just not smart to buy a house because of the number of moves you have to make. But fate was on my side this time. We looked and looked but had no luck finding a place to rent so we almost had to buy. It was not much of a house, but it was ours, we thought it beautiful, and it did have a garden. After we bought the house I dug a big hole in the garden and sunk the children's bathtub in the ground. We fixed it up with a dirt bottom and filled it with water hyacinths and water lilies.

Dr. and Mrs. Charles O. McCormick were our close friends in Indianapolis. Many evenings they came to our house to play bridge, the McCormicks against the Clarks. Often they suggested we visit their house but we always pointed out that our children were young and had to be tended so it was better all around to meet at ours. Finally, however, they prevailed on us, pointing out that the two houses were back to back and that our children were getting bigger now. We went to the McCormicks' to play our bridge one night.

The radio was playing softly in the living room as we matched wits, family against family, at the card table. Suddenly the music was halted and a voice broke in to say: "Squad Car No. 10, Squad Car No. 10, go to 4026 North New Jersey. Burglars. That's 4026 North New Jersey."

That was not only 4026 North New Jersey, that was our home!

Wayne took off like a scared rabbit. He knocked over the bridge table, hurdled the back hedge, and raced into our house and up the stairs to the children's room. Wayne was in a terrible state because he found stockings and underwear on the steps, but at least the children were all right.

Then he grabbed a gun and went searching from room to room, hunting burglars until the sound of laughter stopped him. Dr. McCormick was doubled up, roaring. Through tears of laughter he explained that his seventeen-year-old son was a radio bug and had plugged a gadget into the radio so he could cut off the regular program and read the "police bulletin." Wayne didn't see the joke, and told the doctor, "Both Renie and I put on ten years in ten minutes." The hose on the stairs had been carried there by our playful chow puppie Chan, who had replaced our faithful old police dog Barney.

Practical joking seemed to run in the McCormick family. I used to drive the youngest son, Gene, to school each day along with Ann and Bill. One morning he had a matchbox in his hand when he got into the car and told me proudly, "I've got sumpin'." "What?" I asked. "Sumpin' for teacher," he said; "some false teeth." "Whose?" "Daddy's."

I had to talk Gene out of that gift for the teacher. After I got home I ran over to the McCormick's to return them. Dr. McCormick had delivered a baby in the middle of the night and was asleep, so I gave the teeth to the maid, Daisy, who hid them so well they weren't found for a month.

Another Indianapolis friend was Col. Joseph Marmon, Wayne's commanding officer in the Indiana National Guard. His family made the old Marmon automobiles. He was urbane and charming, finely educated and brilliant. Later, after we knew him in Indianapolis, he married the actress, Pauline Frederick. Colonel Marmon dined with us often in those Indianapolis days. Once, while Wayne was on inspection, he invited me to dine with him at his club. It was during the summer and I waited for him out in the garden, in a swing. He came walking across that garden looking like a matinee idol, his white shoes and white trousers spotless, his clothes beautifully tailored.

Then he inadvertently stepped into that bathtub-pool I was so proud of.

He was mud to the knees.

But I said he was urbane. He excused himself for a little while, went home, changed his clothes, returned, avoided the mud pool, and we went to dinner.

Wayne got his promotion to major in 1933 shortly before we ended our more than three-year stay in Indianapolis. The pay jump from captain to major was one of the big ones in those days and our financial problems were eased a great deal. The promotion also was the one that more or less separated the men from the boys. In the

Army the lieutenants and captains are classified as company officers. The majors, lieutenant colonels, and colonels are field-grade officers.

Wayne's pay and allowances jumped almost $100 a month, from the $372 he got as a captain to $468 monthly as a major. When that first pay check came through at the major's rate, we felt we really could begin living.

We were kidding ourselves, a little. The raise came just before a transfer, with all the expense of moving the family once again. And besides that, we had known for years what we were going to do with at least part of the raise when it came. Wayne's insurance premium had always been extremely high because of his World War I wounds, and he had never been able to afford the extra insurance he thought he should have for our protection. Now, as a major, with a major's pay, he bought the extra amount.

But new problems were on their way. Wayne was assigned to the Command and General Staff School at Fort Leavenworth, Kansas, an assignment every Regular Army officer covets even though he knows it means two years of sheer slavery. The course is so tough that officers' families are given quarters only on condition that one room in the house will be devoted exclusively to the officer's study and that nobody else in the family can use that room for anything whatsoever. It was an Army order that created an ivory tower for every man on the post.

Army orders went even more deeply into the private lives of the officer-students, however. From Sunday night until Friday night the wives had to be on their own. That was by order, too. Except for weekends, the student-officers were permitted no relaxation, no amusement, no time at the club or the movies. They had to concentrate on studying.

Further than that, all post residents were expected to be quiet. From Sunday night until Friday night we wives talked in whispers. We hardly laughed aloud. We shushed our children. The whole post was as quiet as a church.

For the wives it was a sort of martyrdom, but a proud one because we felt our husbands had been singled out for particular honor when they were assigned to Fort Leavenworth for that tough

48

course. That is where men are trained to be generals and that's what we all wanted our husbands to be.

Leavenworth was a terrific ordeal. The course was tough and the competition tougher. The officers battled for grades as though their careers depended on it—as indeed they did. Each student knew full well what he was working and struggling to get. The young officers who came through Leavenworth with high marks were the young officers tabbed for bigger things in the Army. In one sense Leavenworth was the prep school for the Army War College. In another very real sense, high marks at Leavenworth won an officer consideration for future high-command duty.

The big hurdles were what the men called the "pay" problems. They were something like a final examination in importance to the students, but they were handled differently. The pay problems were time-limit affairs. Wayne would be handed a problem and told he had twelve, twenty-four, or forty-eight hours to complete it. Those were the trying days at Leavenworth. Wayne would rush home with his problem and lock himself in his study. Sometimes he remained locked in for as long as twenty-four hours working on a pay problem. The only disturbance allowed during these periods was the food break. I would carry a tray of food in to him and he would wolf it down quickly so that he could get back to his work. Outside in the rest of the house, I would be busy quieting the children so that nothing would disturb Wayne's concentration.

In fact, every weekday at Leavenworth was devoted to arranging things so that Wayne could study. That was the orbit of our life there.

I missed Wayne's companionship during those long, dreary months. There were some compensations, though. The Army recognized how difficult the Leavenworth course was for families and did all it could to provide things for us to do. Actually it was a wonderful place for the children because of the planned recreational program. They were given instruction in horseback riding, swimming, baseball, basketball, archery, and other sports. There was scouting for both the boys and girls. And for the teen-agers there were matinee "coke" parties and dances.

School was out for Wayne on Saturday and Sunday, so he and the other officers relaxed at the regular Friday night dance at the club. "Relaxed" is putting it mildly—they were like a bunch of schoolboys suddenly turned loose for the long weekend. Saturdays Wayne usually played golf or tennis, and Saturday nights, like Fridays, were party nights. Sunday morning we went to church together, and that ended our weekend. For immediately after church Wayne went back into that study, and for all intents and purposes we wouldn't see him again until Friday.

During those long weeks we fashioned a woman's world, and the women on the post were wonderful people who became wonderful friends.

We had afternoon teas for every imaginable reason. I remember one I gave at my house for the PTA. My maid, Laura, made dozens of delicious little tidbit sandwiches. There were all kinds of these, but one was a puzzler. I couldn't quite figure out what Laura had put in it, and afterward, after the guests were gone, I happened to look for the little dish of cat food we had in the refrigerator. It was gone, too!

We ladies took horseback-riding lessons, and we had a handsome young polo-playing officer as our instructor. He was the beau of the post and we all were a little silly about him. Our lives revolved around those riding classes and I suppose it was natural for us to center our attention on the glamorous male who conducted them. I was in the advanced class, and proud of it, too proud. I tried a jump I couldn't make and landed on my head, far away from my horse. Fortunately, we always dressed properly for those classes, including derbies, and my derby helped save me from being hurt more than I was. That was enough, though, because my jaw swelled and I lived on soup for several days.

I didn't give up, either in the riding classes or in that foolish girlish race for a sign of favor from the handsome teacher. The competition for that sign of favor was always toughest at the regular Saturday night dances. That is where I really came cropper.

Wayne looked particularly fine that evening. As we left the car to enter the clubhouse, however, I noticed something on his trouser cuff. It was chewing gum. "Those kids, I'll bet," Wayne moaned. He pulled at it but to no avail. The stuff wouldn't come off.

I dashed inside the ladies' room and came out with a bottle of cleaning fluid. Off in a corner, among the parked cars, I rubbed the gum from his trouser. The trouser looked as good as new and Wayne looked spic and span and wonderful again. I felt I looked my best, too, all dressed up and perfumed. We were gay as we started in toward the sound of music and laughter.

And suddenly it was better than ever. That dashing, gallant riding instructor was walking across the floor right toward me, smiling and cordial. None of the girls had ever enjoyed such a display of attention and friendliness from our hero. Maybe he would even ask me to dance.

He took my hand and then was a trifle too gallant. Nobody ever kissed anybody's hand at Leavenworth, but he did. At least he started to. Halfway to my hand he stopped suddenly and seemed to recoil without moving. As he straightened his back, I saw a peculiar look in his eyes. He was polite, but there was no invitation to dance. Neither did he say anything, nothing at all. He simply smiled stiffly, and as soon as he could leave politely, he left. Full realization of what was happening did not come to me until, in bewilderment, I put my hand to my face. I almost choked on the benzine fumes.

Sometimes the Saturday night hops were costume parties, and those were the most fun of all. They would announce a theme for the party and people were supposed to dress accordingly—like the time they had a Shipwreck Party and I went as a Fiji Islander in long underwear, dyed black, a wig made of Quartermaster mops, black gloves, curtain rings in my nose and ears, and round steak bones around my neck. Wayne didn't look much better in pajama bottoms, a shirt, and whiskers, with our cocker spaniel on a leash and our canary in a cage. Our cocker spaniel Pal had replaced the chow. I spent the evening with an officer made up as a cannibal. We both looked pretty horrible.

But my evening was tainted because Wayne, bad as he looked, spent what seemed to me to be the whole evening with a fellow officer's wife, a charming girl who had had the foresight to be ship-wrecked in as nice a negligee as anyone ever wore. There she was all glamorous and beautiful and there I was with a ring in my nose. I kept thinking it was downright immoral and unfair competition.

At Fort Leavenworth the children reached the age where they really were personalities, real people with minds of their own rather than little dolls. Bill was an energetic, restless, and imaginative ten. Ann was just nine, trying so hard to act like ten and keep up with her brother.

Wayne lived in a world of books and problems, as far removed from us as he could be, but now and then he was pulled back to reality, usually by the children. There was the day when he was ordered out of class, a thing that only happened for the most serious kind of emergencies. The adjutant was ominous when he said, "The Commandant wants to see you, Clark." The Commandant was a new general who already had the reputation of being rough.

"I've got a complaint about your children, Clark," the general snapped after Wayne presented himself. "They're annoying people on the post with anonymous telephone calls. You've been in the Army long enough to know that unless you control your children, I'll have to have them moved off the post."

There was real danger in that warning. A general could break a man for such a thing, even if it seemed small. Everything Wayne had worked for during all his years in the Army was in jeopardy. Wayne knew the Army book and his rights, however, and said as evenly as he could, "I would like to know, sir, who made the charge."

"You'll get the details from the Adjutant," the general snapped. The details were about as bad as they could be. The complainant was a colonel's wife, a woman whose sharp tongue and cantankerous attitude were the fear of every officer's wife on the post.

At lunch that day Wayne was tight-lipped and worried. Success at Leavenworth was important to him, and to us, and he did not like to think it would be denied him because of his children's pranks.

He questioned the children and cross-questioned them. Wide-eyed, they denied everything. They seemed so innocent and truthful that Wayne and I looked significantly at each other. We remembered many things. Our last post-exchange bill had been enormous because Ann and Bill had charged candy and ice cream and Popsicles for themselves and all their friends. And they had not denied it at all, not for an instant. They had said simply that this was the way things were bought and paid for—on the charge account we had at the PX.

We remembered, too, that the preceding summer at Fair Hills in Minnesota, Bill had thrown his first good signet ring into the lake because a boy had said, "I'll bet if you throw it way out in the lake, you can't find it again." Bill was a good swimmer for his age, but not good enough to fish that ring out of the muddy lake bottom. But he had never tried to cover up or lie about how he lost the ring.

Ann had the same quality of truthfulness. Once she had splurged her whole weekly allowance—a nickel—in a slot machine. She hit the jackpot, and the nickels came tumbling down all around her. It was real beginner's luck for she never had been allowed to play a slot machine. We confiscated her winnings as quickly as we could to head off any get-rich-quick ideas that jackpot might have given her. And solemnly we told her she must never, never put any money in a slot machine again. But she did. Three times. Her luck had run out by then, however, and she lost the three nickels. She had been naughty and she knew it. But she did not lie to escape the punishment she expected—and got.

The memories went on and on. We just couldn't remember a time that our children had lied to us to escape responsibility and punishment. And this time they persisted in their denials that they had telephoned anybody to annoy them.

Wayne believed them. Risky as it was, he said he would tell the general that he believed in his children and did not believe the charges the colonel's wife had made.

He left the house looking like a man on the way to battle. I simmered with anger. I was boiling because my children had been maligned. The longer I sat, the madder I got, until I no longer could sit helpless and motionless. Anger rid me of the fear of the colonel's wife and her barbed tongue. I raced from the house, leaped in the car, and drove to her house, feeling something like a dragon killer. My assault carried the day to at least a minor victory. She admitted she was not really certain that Ann and Bill had made the telephone calls and agreed to withhold her charges until more evidence was in.

The calls continued, and that made us feel better because we were sure that if the children had made the calls before our family meeting, they most certainly did not make any afterward. Finally the two real culprits were found, and Ann and Bill were completely exonerated.

Ann was a Brownie at Fort Leavenworth and I helped somewhat with her troop. One Saturday afternoon I parked the car outside the Girl Scout House and went inside. After the meeting, when I went back outside, the car was gone. I knew I had locked it so I called the Military Police and reported a stolen car. What I didn't think of was that Wayne had duplicate keys.

It was still Prohibition time and we had to go across the Missouri River from Kansas into Missouri to get beer. Wayne, returning from his regular Saturday-morning round of golf, spotted our car in front of the Girls Scout House and took it to go over the river to get some beer. He was still in his golf clothes and more than a little unkempt after his eighteen holes.

He got the beer all right but the MPs stopped him as he returned to the post. The beer was hidden carefully under a blanket in the back seat, but Wayne was alarmed and thought somebody had spotted him buying the forbidden beer and reported him to the police.

But the MPs were not interested in beer, at least not in anybody else's beer. They were after a stolen car, and stolen cars were big things at Leavenworth. Some months before, a couple of prisoners had escaped from the Federal penitentiary at Leavenworth and made off in an officer's unlocked car. From that time, all cars on the post had to be locked at all times they were not occupied.

54

The MPs were understandably tough about such things, and here was a messy, slightly dirty man in old clothes driving the stolen car of Maj. Mark Wayne Clark.

They explained the situation to Wayne. He said with authority and conviction, "I'm Major Clark." The MPs were polite but firm. "May we see your identification, Major, sir?" The authority and conviction went out of Wayne's voice. He didn't carry identification out to the post golf course. That cut it. The MPs dropped the "sir" and told Wayne he was being held. Wayne was fighting, not to beat an MP rap, but to protect that forbidden beer in the back seat. He suggested the MPs telephone our house for identification.

Our maid Laura answered the phone. They asked if the major was at home, and she said brightly, "Yes, sir, he's in the study but I can't disturb him." Those were standing orders in the house for weekdays. Laura told the MPs they should call back later.

Wayne could see that things were developing rapidly to the point where the MPs would begin searching the car for stolen gems or something. In desperation he asked that they drive home with him. Somehow they agreed, although all the evidence by then was against Wayne. Laura answered the doorbell and beamed. "Why, Major, sir, I thought you were inside, studyin' as usual. . . ."

Men are so unreasonable sometimes. When I got home Wayne was furious with me just because I had reported our car stolen, as I should have. I was confused and asked him why he was upset with me. He gave up, stalked off to the safety of his study muttering, "Women, too darn many women in this world. . . ."

Money was a constant problem to us during the days at Leavenworth, so our private Twenty-dollar Bill Mystery was a real tragedy to us. It all started innocently enough. I bought some material to make up into curtains and asked that it be sent to me C.O.D. Wayne left me a twenty-dollar bill to make the payment. Twenty dollars was a lot for us to spend in one place in those days and I took particular care in hiding it.

The package arrived and my mind went blank. Where did I

put the money? I looked in all the usual places. It wasn't in the tea-pot. It wasn't in the sugar bowl. There was no twenty-dollar bill in my handkerchief drawer. Nothing was under the flower pot. The longer I looked, the worse I felt. What would Wayne think?

I dreaded having to tell him when he came home, but the moment he walked in the door I blurted out the story. He questioned me in great detail but he was really very kind about the whole mess. However, I still felt uncomfortably guilty and upset.

My search went on for days, weeks, and then for months. Our private mystery wouldn't let me rest. I just had to find that bill. I searched every drawer, every shelf, every cupboard time and time again. But no luck.

At last I just gave up the hunt, convinced that our Twenty-dollar Bill Mystery never would be solved. All I could do was try to forget it, but I never really did. It was one of those things that continued to haunt me.

The ordeal of Leavenworth finally ended. Wayne finished his course and we were able to look forward to living together as a normal family again—as normal as a family can be in the Regular Army. The movers came and the carpenters who had to crate and box all our things. One carpenter took a picture from the wall. As he moved the frame, a dusty, wilted piece of green paper fluttered to the floor.

It was my long-lost twenty-dollar bill!

I had never before in my life hidden money behind a picture frame. And I haven't since, either.

I was overjoyed. The mystery was solved and we had the twenty dollars. And with the expenses of moving to a new post, breaking up one home and setting up another, we needed the twenty dollars much more when we found it than we had when I lost it.

CHAPTER FOUR

DESPITE ALL THE TRIALS AND TRIBULATIONS, Wayne did all right at Fort Leavenworth. He did very well, in fact, and the coveted notation, "Recommended for High Command," was appended to his official Army service record.

That was not absolute insurance of a bright and happy and successful future, but it was about as good insurance as a young Army officer could get. Only about one-third of each class won the recommendation. Those who got it were tabbed for big things in the Army, command of divisions and corps and armies. It didn't always work that way, of course, but it was easier to get high command with that recommendation than without it.

The almost monastic life of Leavenworth finally ended in 1935 and I was happy that Mark Wayne Clark could become a husband and father again after those two years in his ivory tower. It was just the right time for him to begin at it, too, for Ann and Bill were at the age where they needed a father and the strong hand of a man in the house. Pranks had almost become the order of the day in our house, harmless, childish pranks, but pranks nonetheless.

By 1935 I had been an Army wife for more than ten years and felt I knew the ropes. I was to learn that my education had just begun. Our first assignment after Leavenworth was Fort Sam Houston in San Antonio, and I was thrilled to have the chance to live in the Texas I had heard of so much but did not know.

As soon as I arrived, I applied the first lesson that every Army wife learns. That was that when you were transferred you dug in and fixed up your house as fast as you could. With tours of duty running two years or even less, you had to fix your house fast or you wouldn't have any time at all to enjoy living in it.

When we got to San Antonio, therefore, I went to work feverishly. Wayne was not there to help me. Gen. Frank "Bowser" Bolles, our old commander at the Presidio and Fort Russell, the man with the terrible bark who had saved my mother and children from the charge of the field artillery, was in command at San Antonio. He had requested that Wayne be assigned to him for duty, and as soon as we arrived the general whisked Wayne away on maneuvers with him.

I was left alone to arrange the home in which we planned to spend the next two years of our life. It was a pleasant house and new, but the grounds around it had not been developed. This disappointed me, for there in Texas so many things would grow and I felt there was no reason why this home should not be surrounded by all kinds of flowers and color. But nobody had even bothered to plant a tree or seed in the grounds. My green thumb not only itched, it fairly ached.

Before the furniture was arranged inside the house I was working outside, planning and dreaming of the wonders that could be done with a few plants and some care. The first need was obvious. The earth itself was so bare and neglected that it needed a covering of topsoil. That was first on the agenda. Next I ordered hundreds of poinsettias, and after the old, parched soil was dug up and carted away and the topsoil dumped in to replace it, the poinsettias were put out to give a great splash of brilliant red in contrast to the lawn I set out.

It was all so expensive that I had to prepare my explanation to Wayne very carefully, but it was all going to be so beautiful I knew he would be as happy as I.

Altogether the whole job, inside and out, took six weeks. Inside, the furniture was arranged as I liked it, and on the last day of the sixth week I hung the last picture and the last drape and stood back and surveyed my handiwork. I was pleased as Punch.

Then the mail came. The bill for the topsoil was there, and it was a mighty big one. I would have a lot of explaining to do to Wayne and would have to count heavily on his love for flowers to see me through. I concentrated on thinking how much he liked gardens and well-kept lawns. I had to in order to build up confidence to face him.

Then the telephone rang. I still had the bill in my hand when I answered. New orders. We were going to Fort Omaha at Omaha, Nebraska. That bill suddenly began to look like the most extravagant thing in my whole life. And I was going to have one sweet time convincing Wayne that I had done the right thing even though someone eventually was going to have a mighty beautiful lawn.

Before we left San Antonio, though, Ann turned the place upside down. She was fascinated with the bugle calls the soldiers played at all Army posts, and persuaded us to buy her the instruments and get a sergeant to teach her to play both the bugle and the trumpet. Her ambition was to join an all-girl band.

Ann turned our Fort Sam Houston home into a bedlam with her tentative blasts. She played every sour note possible, but finally was able to put out an acceptable bugle call. Apparently feeling it was no use knowing something unless you could use it, she slipped from the house one dark night and went out to the middle of the parade ground, all alone.

There she stood and sounded fire call on her bugle.

The entire post turned out to find and fight the fire, including her dad. Everyone finally realized it was a false alarm, and every bugle-blowing soldier on the post came under suspicion.

Wayne knew better, however. After starting all the commotion, Ann had slipped back into the house. She overlooked one thing, though, and left her bugle on a chair in the hall, where Wayne spotted it when he got home. After Ann had confessed everything, Wayne simply gave up and never told her secret.

Ann's tenth birthday was celebrated during the six weeks we

59

were at San Antonio, and she was especially pleased because she thought the sunset review was staged just in her honor. She stood stiffly at attention, so cute nobody had the heart to tell her the review wasn't really for her.

Our stay at San Antonio was cut short because of the unexpected death of the commanding general at Fort Omaha, Maj. Gen. Stewart Heintzelman. General Bolles was named to succeed to the Omaha post and he requested that Wayne be ordered to go along.

Fort Omaha was in a lovely setting on the outskirts of the city, and the comfort and charm of our new home helped take the sting out of my loss of the newly landscaped grounds in San Antonio. Our new home had a huge screened porch, and in the summertime I could sit out there and watch my children play and swim in the big post swimming pool close by our house.

The children were becoming ever more interesting and part of our lives as they grew older. Bill was eleven and Ann ten at that time, growing up faster than we liked to admit. Most of the time they were buddies, but now and then they got into fights as all children do and one or the other would come running home with a bloody nose or a black eye and a long story about how awful the other one was. Fortunately, the knock-downs and drag-outs were far between.

There were the anxious moments that every parent knows so well, such as the time of the polio scare in Omaha. Our children seemed so healthy and full of life that we had given little thought to this scare. They swam in the post pool as always and had a marvelous time, right under my eyes where I knew they could come to no harm.

But one night at dinner both Bill and Ann looked peaked. They were listless and toyed with their food. Long before dinner was over they excused themselves and went upstairs to bed. Alone and frightened at the table, Wayne and I stared at each other, neither daring to utter the awful word "polio" that crowded all other thoughts from our minds. Guests came that evening, but on a succession of flimsy excuses I left the living room time and again and went upstairs to feel first one feverish forehead and then the other. When I returned to our guests, I noticed that Wayne would make an elaborately casual exit and hurry upstairs. I followed him once and saw him just as he was leaving Bill's bedroom. It was a long, bad evening.

But in the morning the two children bounced downstairs, noisy and full of life and energy. Wayne and I were so relieved and happy that we asked no questions. And it was months before we learned that on the way home from the swimming pool that afternoon, Ann and Bill had sneaked beneath a neighbor's porch and tried their first cigarettes.

The post swimming pool was just one of the advantages our children had from Army life. In later life both Ann and Bill often told us how grateful they were that they were raised in the Army, as Army "brats." Almost every post had a swimming pool. Many had stables of riding horses and instructors for the children. Generally Army posts are on big reservations which include wooded areas. Ann and Bill therefore almost always had woods in which to play, something that would have been denied them if we had been city dwellers. Bill and his friends built lean-to shelters in the woods, and treehouses. Ann helped as much as she could and participated fully in the games of make-believe. And such games! With all those trees and all that freedom, the children were given complete opportunity to let their imaginations run riot. They could be Daniel Boone or Davy Crockett one day, Mad Anthony Wayne or Lighthorse Harry Lee the next.

Never did the children seem to think they were missing anything by being cut off from civilian life. Rather, they seemed to pity the children who had to live in town and who had to live in one house all their lives. There was so much excitement for the Army "brats." They rode their bicycles behind parades. The post movie was a party place for the children on Saturday afternoons. The children took pride in learning the bugle calls so well that they could tell time by them. They also were proud to stand at attention with the big people during retreat.

There always was added excitement on Christmas Eve because men from the Army band would travel the post in open trucks to serenade everyone with Christmas carols.

But most of all the children liked the feeling of belonging to something, something they knew was big. That was the Army. They got this feeling chiefly from their ever-growing circle of friends. As they grew older they came to know that in each new post they would meet old friends, children they had gone to school with or played with at some other post. And the Army gave the children a common bond missing in civilian communities. Their fathers all worked for the same boss, all had the same career interest, all worked for a common goal. In civilian life a child hardly realizes it when his father gets a promotion or raise. Not so in the Army. When father gets an Army promotion it shows on his shoulder, where he puts his new insignia. All the other children know about it, too, and the Army child can bask in a reflected glory.

As children, of course, Ann and Bill could not have put these feelings into words. For one thing the civilian world was a mystery to them. As they grew up, though, they often talked with me about the advantages they had.

There were disadvantages, too. Neither Ann nor Bill enjoyed the physical process of moving from one post to another. So often we traveled between posts by automobile, and the children became uncomfortable and restless during the long drives in the crowded car. They did not like the job of getting settled in a new house, either. They had their chores to do in getting settled and had to work when they were most anxious to get outside and play with their new neighbors. There also was a pang of remorse in leaving old friends to go to a new post, but that usually was short-lived. For one thing Ann and Bill always were confident that at the new post they would find old friends. For another they came to realize that, being in the Army, they were leaving their old friends only temporarily and that they would be together again sometime, somewhere. But most important of all, I believe, was the fact that by moving about from post to post in the Army, Ann and Bill, like most other children of Army officers, learned to make new friends quickly.

The Army posts were so big, and there was so much for the children to do inside the reservation, that they rarely felt any need or desire to go outside. The post always provided more than enough room and facilities for their amusement and development.

Bill was developing, all right. General Bolles and Wayne were on an inspection of the post at Omaha. One day the general stopped and pointed to the top of a very high radio tower, around which were innumerable "No Trespassing" signs.

"Clark, do you see that?" asked the general.

Wayne took a long, hard look, squinting his eyes against the sun, and said slowly, "I think it's my son, general."

The two angry men—one, at least, with a great lump of fear in his stomach—watched breathlessly as the figure of that precious small boy crawled down the tower ladder inch by inch to safety.

From Omaha, Wayne went to the War College for his last tour of formal Army study. His course ended in 1937. He did return to the War College as a staff officer in 1940, and, of course, the Army is a constant tour of study for any regular officer, since to know the tools of his trade he must be constantly familiar with the new weapons being developed, and to prepare himself for whatever duty call he might get, he must keep abreast of the great political forces shaping our world.

Bill was at the age where trouble came naturally, and more often than not, little Ann got into the act. Their pranks continued after we left the War College and went to Fort Lewis, Washington, for a wonderful three-year tour.

At Fort Lewis we were quartered in a semicircular row of five officers' homes familiarly known as the "Goldfish Bowl" or "Snoopie Loop." The houses faced on an impressive monument to the World War I dead of the Ninety-first Division. The monument, with its sculptured soldier and nurse, was greatly admired by the grownups and a constant source of amusement to the children, who vied with one another to see who could make the monument look the funniest. They draped the soldier and nurse with the most irreverent of caps, scarves, and jackets. They painted mustachios on both figures. In all they had a field day until the post commandant, Brig. Gen. A. T. Smith, ordered a halt, by issuing orders that any child found on the monument would suffer severe punishment. Wayne relayed the orders to the children with firm emphasis.

Wayne was accustomed to obedience from the children, and usually got it. He was dumfounded, therefore, when General Smith called him into his office and said, "Clark, your children were climbing the monument at 4:30 yesterday afternoon."

In a most unmilitary manner, Wayne said, "I doubt it, sir."

But at home Wayne was even more surprised when he asked Ann and Bill if they had been on the monument and they admitted it. Wayne demanded to know why, and Bill, with the best of all little-boy logic, explained, "Well, we look at it all the time out of our bedroom windows," and Ann added, "We wanted to do it, we had to."

Wayne was angry and, if anything, General Smith was angrier. "I want you to punish those children, Clark," he ordered. That night Wayne announced that the children would be kept away from the movies for one whole week, which meant the matinee on Friday and the matinee on Saturday. Those were extremely important occasions to the children on the post. They were like a party, and all the youngsters just had to go. For a child today that was like having television cut off for an entire week.

Later the general asked Wayne what punishment he had meted out. Wayne's first reaction was that the general was going beyond his authority in asking, but rather than make an issue of it, he replied, "Sir, I denied their movies for a week."

The general said he didn't think that was much of a punishment, certainly not enough to match the offense of climbing on his monument. Wayne replied that if he knew how important movies were to the children he would realize that the punishment was pretty severe. General Smith, who had no children, realized from the tone of Wayne's voice that he had exceeded his authority, because the matter was dropped right there.

Army regulations for the most part are designed to maintain

64

discipline by clearly defining the authority of a senior officer over junior officers, but they also define areas in which the senior officers have no authority at all—and the upbringing of children definitely is one of those.

Wayne always was close to our children. He enjoyed fully the wonderful relationship that can be achieved between a father and his children. Evenings were happy times in our home because Wayne so enjoyed relaxing and playing games with Ann and Bill. One of the favorites was marbles—and they played for keeps. Great, long, lanky Wayne would sprawl out on the living-room floor with the two little children and shoot marbles. As Ann recalls it: "He loved winning our marbles away from us—and usually did." Of course Wayne kept the marbles only for the duration of each game and the next night Ann and Bill would be back on the living-room rug with the same old marbles they had lost the night before.

I was not particularly happy one night when Wayne gave Ann and Bill their weekly allowance and then suggested maybe it was time for them to learn to play poker. They agreed. Wayne won back all their money. Neither has been much interested in gambling since then as far as I know.

Wayne taught the children to fish, and to love to fish. He took them on long hikes through the woods. And he taught them to enjoy stamp collecting just as he did.

We dug our roots deep in Fort Lewis and in Washington state. In memory it seems to have played the most important part in our lives of any of the prewar Army posts. Ann and Bill were growing and Bill had his first dates. Years in the Army had made us both more a part of it and of the many service groups connected to it.

My mother spent more time with us at Fort Lewis than she had at previous posts, and through her we got a permanent tie to the Seattle area. Mother received a letter from an almost-forgotten cousin, Maude Griffiths, who was living in Washington state, and at Mother's suggestion we invited Mrs. Griffiths and her husband, Tom, to visit us at Fort Lewis.

The Griffiths then insisted that we visit them at their summer home on Camano Island, sixty miles north of Seattle in Puget Sound. We did and were entranced. We gloried in the view from their hilltop home, a view that stretched across the Sound to the snow-capped Olympic Mountains far beyond, and knew that we had found our own one-spot-on-earth.

We all knew it at once. It was one of those things people don't have to talk about. The beauty was overwhelming. And for Wayne it was a glorious place for his favorite sport, fishing. The children, too, loved the island. They climbed the cliffs, raced on the beach, rowed out into the Sound, and dug clams in the low tide.

Only our two dogs dissented that first day. They teamed up in a four-dog fight against the two Griffiths dogs. The fur flew. Conversation was impossible. Once Wayne had to push two of the fighting dogs down the steep hillside to break their holds.

In the excitement Bill and Ann began chasing each other, and Bill slammed a plate-glass door so hard it shattered into a thousand pieces. Ann tumbled down a hill that was almost a cliff, and only the underbrush saved her from harm.

And I, quite unmotherlike, sat back like a spectator and simply enjoyed the excitement, which for a while took on the wilder aspects of a rodeo. I always blamed the salt air and the exhilaration of finding such a spot for the complete and unseemly abandon of the Clark family that day.

After that inauspicious beginning we visited the Griffiths on Camano Island as often as we could get away from Fort Lewis. And the Griffiths always welcomed us and urged us to come back, despite the shambles we made of their place on that first visit.

For the children it always was a picnic. Maude had the delightful custom of making pies for anyone who would pick the wild blackberries and raspberries to fill them. And always we marveled at the scenic beauty, with Puget Sound as the front yard and the distant mountains as a backdrop.

Today Wayne and I and Bill each own property on Camano. It is part of the Clark family way of life, the one place in all the world that is our own. And when we drive to it from Stanwood, Washington, these days we drive across a beautiful new bridge that has replaced the rickety wooden span that used to connect the island to the mainland. The new bridge is named the General Mark Clark Bridge.

It was at Fort Lewis that Ann and Bill quit being children and got into the problem-filled era of the teens. Their outside interests became increasingly important; their dependence on the home became less and less.

We got a foretaste from Ann before the children actually entered their teens. She had a part in her school play. I spent weeks making her costume and she talked of nothing else. Wayne and I were certain she had the lead role because it all seemed so terribly important to her. Finally the costume, over which I labored long in the making, was ready and so was Ann, as happy as any ingénue in her first real role. Wayne and I had caught some of her excitement and eagerly we went to the school to watch our Ann perform. Something was wrong. We couldn't even spot her in the first act, and I knew that no matter how much she was made up, I would be able to tell at a glance the costume I had made. The second act wore on and on and still we could not spot our Annie. Stage fright? Sickness? But no, almost at the end of the second act, and the play, our daughter marched proudly on stage, stiffly presented a wand to the Fairy Queen and self-consciously walked off stage, without a word. The theater just wasn't Ann's forte. The paint brush was, and today she is doing extremely well with it as a portrait artist in California.

Ann suddenly grew up at Fort Lewis. I didn't really notice, or didn't want to notice, until she forced the fact on me. She did it as gracefully as she could. "I don't want to hurt you, Mother," she said, oh so gently, "but please don't make any dresses for me any more. They are beautiful, but they do look like loving-hands-at-home."

Another part of my life had ended. I no longer had a little girl.

I didn't have a little boy, either. He was all the way up to the stage of buying corsages for his dates. He arrived at Fort Lewis still a smudgy little boy who had to be told to wash his face and hands. But soon he was preparing for his first dance. Everything

67

was set and I was about to drive him off to call for his date when Bill stopped suddenly with a panicky, sick look in his face. "I've forgotten a corsage," he said, "and she'll be mad because all the girls get them."

He still was too close to the little boy to have lost his feeling that Mother could fix anything, and although he didn't say it I knew that he expected me to perform his miracle for him right then and there.

It was much too late to go to a florist. But one look at his young face showed me I had to perform his miracle for him. Fortunately for me, who so wanted him to keep faith in me, there was inspiration —a little tarnished, perhaps, but not bad. In the refrigerator was an orchid I had worn several nights before. There was a rush and a bustle. Then there was disappointment. The edges were brown. Then there was more thought and the scissors were brought out quickly and the brown edges trimmed off with great delicacy. A large tired orchid had become a small but acceptably fresh one. We had saved the day, I thought, until Bill's face got long again and he said, "We haven't got a box and I have to give it to her in a flower box."

My heart went out to him. He so wanted everything to be just right, and so wanted to avoid mistakes on that first dance date. I had to solve this problem for him, too.

The solution was makeshift but adequate. "Carry it in wax paper," I said, "and then pin it on her, Bill. She'll like it better that way."

And he did. As I chauffeured those two youngsters to their first dance date, Bill pinned on the orchid. And his girl, wearing the only genuine orchid on the floor that night, was the belle of the ball and Bill had happily survived his first dance without a mistake.

CHAPTER FIVE

FORT LEWIS ITSELF WAS A GAY PLACE IN WHICH to serve, even though Wayne was being loaded down with increasingly heavy duties. He still was a major, but a very senior major indeed. The Army was promoting its people so slowly between the two World Wars that men often were given jobs according to seniority instead of rank. And Wayne had begun his Army career at West Point more than twenty years before.

At Fort Lewis, while still a major, Wayne planned and implemented the first full-division amphibious training exercise the American Army ever had. He was G-3 of the Third Division, which meant he had charge of Plans and Operations. In that job he trained the entire division for the assault landing on the beaches at Monterey, California. This experience stood him in good stead later because through it he began a correspondence with Brig. Gen. Leslie McNair. General McNair was intensely interested in amphibious warfare and the development of its techniques. He wrote Wayne many letters, and although the two men never had met before, they became good friends. That friendship became professionally important to Wayne later when McNair called him up to work on Plans and Operations for the whole Army.

Social life at Fort Lewis was most informal. I think that was because of the wonderful huge crabs that were so abundant around Puget Sound. They were so good that the majority of us just didn't think of serving anything else, and when you served a crab dinner it had to be informal.

We would set an enormous tray on the table, overflowing with tender cracked crab. Empty bowls were placed on the table to take the discarded crab shells. A tossed green salad, garlic bread, carrot sticks, olives, and celery completed the main course.

Most hostesses on the post always served the same cracked crab dinner and nobody ever complained. We simply did not compete with one another in regard to the main course. But we did compete on desserts. That was the only part of the meal in which one hostess could outdo another and we all tried our very best. It became a game for the hostess to keep her dessert a secret, even from her husband, until the final moment.

Wayne and the other husbands always tried to break that secret. Wayne took particular delight in peeping into the hostess's kitchen and refrigerator to find out ahead of time what dessert she was serving, and when he was successful he would whisper the word to all the other men at the dinner.

One of Wayne's favorite companions on these dessert hunts was Lt. Col. Dwight D. Eisenhower, fresh from the Philippines where he had served with General MacArthur. One hostess took care of these two dessert hounds one night. They searched and searched, but their reconnaissance brought them nothing. They didn't find a clue. Finally when dessert was served, everyone roared with laughter at Ike and Wayne. The hostess had let the rest of us in on the secret. She had hidden the dessert in her neighbor's kitchen next door.

Ike and Wayne had been friends since West Point days. Ike was two years ahead of Wayne at the Academy, but they got to know each other well during the summer encampment between Wayne's first and second years. Ike was a cadet officer of Wayne's company. At the end of the summer Ike asked Wayne if he would like to live in one of the eight barracks rooms over which Ike had supervision at West Point. Each of the cadet officers had charge of the men in a certain number of rooms and they tried to pick men they liked. Wayne accepted and the friendship blossomed.

Strangely, the two men were in the Army twenty years before they served together again. In the interim they exchanged letters occasionally, and Ike fed Wayne stamps he was eager to get for his collection. It was the period of the "first flight" stamps, and Ike was in a fine position to send Wayne these prized one-issue stamps. Every time there was a "first flight" from the Philippines to somewhere in Europe or Asia, Ike would mail Wayne a letter aboard the plane and would always enclose a note with news of himself and mutual friends.

One day Wayne received a letter of a more serious nature. Ike had been doing staff work for General MacArthur in Washington and the Philippines for a long time and thought he should get in some troop duty. At that time the Third Division was one of the two full divisions in the American Army on active duty, and Ike asked Wayne whether he could help get him a troop assignment when he reached the division. As G-3, Wayne could help, and did.

Then came more letters. Ike wanted to know what kind of housing he could expect and whether there were good school facilities for his son John. The assignment came through for Ike and he was given a battalion in the Fifteenth Infantry Regiment. He no sooner arrived with Mamie and John than the whole division went south to Monterey for summer maneuvers. Ike didn't really have time to meet the commanding general, Maj. Gen. Walter Sweeney, before he rushed off to Monterey.

General Sweeney loved poker. During maneuvers he insisted that a game be arranged nearly every night. And he named his Plans and Operations officer, Mark Wayne Clark, to arrange the nightly session. He had two rules. First, there must be at least five in the game and preferably seven. Secondly, he didn't want any strangers in the game. He wanted his own staff officers.

One night two of the regulars left camp to go into Monterey city and Wayne just couldn't find enough men to fill a table. He was still scratching his head, trying to think of somebody, when out of the darkness came the general's call: "Clark, where's the game?"

Wayne shouted back: "Several have gone into town, sir, and I don't think we have enough."

Then came an inspiration. "We could make it, sir," he called, "if you don't object to a new officer."

"Who is he?"

"Col. Ike Eisenhower of the Fifteenth, sir."

"Can he play poker?"

"I think so, sir—and I know he has a wallet stuffed full of money, sir, because I saw it this afternoon."

That did it. Ike was welcomed warmly into the staff poker game, even though he was a regimental officer, a sort of "outsider" to the general.

He soon answered the question of whether he could play poker. By the time the game broke up his wallet was a good deal fatter than it had been at the beginning. He not only had all of his own money, but a lot of that of General Sweeney, Wayne, and the others in the game.

And next day General Sweeney eyed Wayne coldly and asked, "What do you mean bringing a ringer into the game?"

Later that same summer, after some hard maneuvers, the general lent Wayne his automobile so that Wayne and Ike could go into Carmel to relax on a twenty-four-hour leave. Ike and Wayne played golf all day on the beautiful Pebble Beach course. As always, Ike was in perfect physical condition. He was especially trim because of the hard weeks of campaigning in the field during the troop maneuvers. He still had some of his sandy hair left, although it was thinning even then.

Wayne, too, was in top physical condition. Each was eager to expend some energy at play on the golf course, and Wayne was particularly eager because he had a brand-new set of woods that he wanted to try. He learned quickly, however, that the new woods didn't help much. Golf just wasn't his best game. He was a tennis player and a swimmer, but no great hand at golf. Time after time Wayne whirled those beautiful new clubs at the ball with a powerful swing. And time after time the ball would dribble out twenty yards or slice into the rough. To make matters worse, Ike laughed and said something like "Let me try one of those clubs to see whether they or you are to blame." And each time Ike tried one of Wayne's new clubs he got a beautiful drive, long and straight down the fairway.

All that summer Ike and Wayne worked together very closely. Ike was full of ideas about how to fight a war, and used his battalion to test his theories. Wayne told me, "That Ike always is trying something new. He wants to experiment. I think he is using that battalion to test every rule he ever read in the book."

Actually, after years of staff work with Gen. Douglas MacArthur in Washington and the Philippines, young Lieutenant Colonel Eisenhower seemed to be determined to cram a lot of troop experience into that one summer.

Although Ike and Wayne had been good friends for twenty years, I did not meet the Eisenhowers until they came to Fort Lewis. The first one I really got to know was young John, who became a close friend of Ann and Bill. I got to know John quickly when the Eisenhowers moved to Fort Lewis because we had him over for meals several times while Mamie and Ike were moving into their new home. We knew it was too much to try to get settled and cope with a small boy too, so we took John off Mamie's hands for a few hours.

After the Eisenhowers got settled we went to their home often for cracked-crab dinners and they came to our house for the same thing. That is, it was cracked crab during the first three weeks or so of each month. The last week of the month was different. By that time nobody had any money left for crab. The gaiety subsided just before each pay check as we were brought face to face with the high cost of living. Any parties held then were quiet affairs. Usually it would be necessary to serve only a dessert and coffee and then to go to the post movie. The show would end early, we would say good night in the theater lobby, and everybody would be home by 10:30.

Budget worries led me into my most weird experiment with a dress. I reached the stage where, budget or no budget, I just had to have a new evening gown. My birthday was close and Wayne took me into Seattle to shop. We studied all the windows, carefully seeking the best lead, and I was lighthearted and gay in anticipation.

Wayne stopped short at one window. I was puzzled. There was no evening gown on display. What they had was a nightgown, a wonderful one, but still a nightgown. It had a floral design, with lace, and a wide elaborate sash, and was quite elegant. But it was a nightgown. It was frivolous and beautiful and expensive.

Proudly Wayne announced "I want you to have that."

My heart sank. I protested: "I thought an evening dress . . ."

But by that time Wayne had me by the arm and was marching me into the shop.

There was no denying him that day. When we came out, the box with the nightdress was under his arm and he was beaming with pride, so pleased with himself that he had bought me something nice that I no longer had the heart to remind him that what I needed was something to wear to dances, not to bed. It would have been a futile reminder anyway, because after he paid for that nightgown we no longer had enough money for a dress.

At home I tried on the nightgown and paraded before my mirror. I began to catch some of Wayne's enthusiasm. It was something, and it looked grand. I began to dabble with the idea that maybe, just maybe, it could be worn as an evening gown. Perhaps it would look good over that periwinkle-blue slip of mine.

It did, too. That year I wore it to party after party, with assurance and success. Then one night I had to relegate the gown to the bedroom where it belonged. I was feeling at my very best that night, until a major's wife, quite innocently and without malice, said thoughtfully, "Do you know, that neckline is exactly like one my mother has on a nightgown."

The need to scrimp and save at that time also led to a Thanksgiving turkey with only one drumstick and one wing.

It all began when Jane Howard and I took a long ride in my automobile one day in November. It was a scrimp-and-save trip to a farm to load up with fresh vegetables at low prices. Jane and her husband, Edwin, then a captain, were lifelong friends of ours in the Army.

On the way home we spotted a turkey farm. There were hundreds of plump turkeys behind wire fences, turkeys gorging themselves and fattening for the holidays.

Like most other Army wives, we had been worried about the cost of a Thanksgiving turkey. The market prices were very high, and turkeys were costly even at the commissary at Fort Lewis. Jane and I had but a single thought. We would buy our turkeys live and save lots of money. The prices were right, much lower than market or commissary prices. Or so it seemed to us. And it was such fun to pick out your own turkey, live. Jane picked her favorite and I picked mine and the turkey farmer went after them. There was an exciting chase with the gobblers and hens racing around and raising a great ruckus.

At last the two turkeys were rounded up, their legs tied together tight, ready for delivery. The farmer put them in my car, and Jane and I took off for home, mighty proud of ourselves and the money we would save.

We were a good way toward home when a disturbing thought hit us. How would we kill the turkeys? Neither of us had ever done anything like that before. We recalled pictures of people carrying a turkey and an ax to a log and chopping off the turkey's head. That was what we would do.

Then there was another problem. Jane said, "Let's kill them in your garage."

I had the same misgivings she did so I said, "No, let's do it in your garage."

There was no meeting of minds whatever, so we decided to flip a coin. I lost. The experiment would be in my garage.

We dragged the squawking turkeys into my garage, got a log from the firebox and a hatchet, and set down to work. The ensuing half hour was pretty awful. The turkeys made a frightful racket. Jane and I added our screams. It was quite a struggle. And it was quite a mess. We literally hacked the birds to pieces.

Then there was another crisis. Would the birds be cleaned in my kitchen or Jane's? We flipped a coin and I lost again. It would be my kitchen.

For some hours we plucked and plucked our birds. There were feathers everywhere. If anything, the kitchen was more of a mess than the garage. Then came the big letdown. What we had after all our struggles were two of the scrawniest-looking birds I had ever seen. Those turkeys which had seemed so fat and nice when they strutted about the farmer's yard were skinnier and tougher-looking than anything anyone would buy at the market.

And to top it all off, I had to serve my turkey minus one drumstick and one wing. The others had been lost in the battle of the garage!

It was at Fort Lewis that I first had the privilege of meeting one of the finest gentlemen I have known—George C. Marshall. He was a brigadier general then, in 1937, in command of the Vancouver Barracks near Portland, Oregon. He came to Fort Lewis for summer maneuvers. We had just arrived at the post, and our furniture was still en route from the East. All we had in the house were a few boxes we used as chairs and some newspapers spread on the floors to keep them clean.

General Marshall took all this in stride. He had been in the Army a long time and there was no need to apologize or explain, but beyond that he went out of his way to be gracious and show us that he understood. We chatted for a little while, some of us sitting on boxes and others on radiators, and then all of us, the general, Wayne, Bill, Ann, and I, piled into our car and went to the Grey Goose Restaurant for an enormous steak dinner. I'll never forget the price, either. It was $1.25 for more steak than anyone could eat.

My husband had frequent conferences with General Marshall because the latter commanded one of the infantry brigades of the Third Division of which Wayne was Plans-Training Officer, and Wayne flew down to Vancouver Barracks frequently to discuss these problems with him.

General Marshall was shy and unassuming, and stayed that way even when he rose to the highest place in the Army during the war years and to high civilian rank in the government after the war. But once he knew people and dropped his reserve with them, he was a most warmhearted and considerate friend. At Fort Lewis he visited us often, every time he came up from Vancouver Barracks. And each time as he was preparing to leave the post, he made it a point of dropping by the house to say good-by to me. He would stand at the front door, his hands behind his back. I would say, "Do come in, general," but he would smile and shake his head and say no, there was no time and that he had to leave right away.

Then hurriedly, almost with the embarrassment of a little boy, he would bring his hands out from behind his back and somewhat self-consciously give me a box of candy. This little tableau was performed each time General Marshall completed a visit to Fort Lewis while we were there.

Shortly after General Marshall began visiting us, we suggested that he bring Mrs. Marshall because I so wanted to meet her. Arrangements were made and a date set. But family trouble intervened.

Bill was a Boy Scout then, an active one working for the Eagle badge he later won. On a hike in the woods with other boys someone suggested they play Tarzan in the tall pine trees. Bill always was a climber, so he scampered up into a treetop and began doing all the tricks he could remember from the Tarzan movies, swinging from the limb of one tree to a limb of the next. He remembered one trick too many, though, leaped for a branch he couldn't reach, and fell hard to the ground.

His friends had to half-carry him home. He was running a fever. I hurried him to bed and called the doctor. There were apparently no broken bones and there was no concussion. The doctor couldn't quite understand the fever, which persisted, and after another visit he suggested we call a specialist. X rays were taken, and the specialist made a long examination. But there were no signs of broken bones, no concussion.

For several days the fever persisted, and it was a high one. The doctors were baffled and we were distraught. Then something did break. Measles! Nobody could have been as happy as we over a case of measles in the house. We finally knew what was wrong with our boy and knew it was something that would be cured without too much trouble. Apparently the hard fall had jiggled the measles to life.

We thought of Mrs. Marshall's impending visit. It was fortunate we did because, although we did not know it at the time, she had never had measles. She bowed out of that visit graciously.

The Boy Scouts and Girl Scouts took up a good deal of our attention in those years. Not only were Bill and Ann members, but Wayne was a scout committeeman. His job was to examine scouts for merit-badge tests. Boys are creatures with one-track minds and their business, to them, is much more important than anybody else's business can be. So when a boy was ready to take his test he showed up at our front door, no matter what time of day or night and no matter whether we had a houseful of guests or were eating dinner. The boy simply had to take his test, and he couldn't wait. Sometimes I was exasperated by these untimely interruptions, but Wayne was always tolerant and gracious with the boys and I had to admire him for it. And I couldn't really blame him, either. Those boys were so happy and eager and expectant when they thought they were ready to win another merit badge that it would have been cruel to make them wait.

So many scouts came in the evening when he had guests that it became something of a stock joke among our friends to quote Wayne as saying, "Excuse me, please, I have to help these youngsters climb the ladder of scouting." He always said it, just that way, with a great big grin.

In the summers Bill went to a Boy Scout camp about fifty miles from Fort Lewis and Ann to a Girl Scout one thirty miles away, and we visited Bill one Sunday and Ann the next. Each was in the heart of the pine forest. One Sunday at the Girl Scout camp, fire broke out in the woods. Forest fires are a problem all along the West Coast, where in some places the law has the power to round up men on the street and rush them to the forest to fight the blaze.

Everyone fights those fires because they endanger the homes and lives of whole communities.

It was late in the afternoon when the nearby fire started. Most of the visiting parents had already left for home, and those remaining crowded all the girls into their automobiles and drove them to the safety of the beach, well beyond the reach of the fire.

The men stayed behind to fight the flames, which were spreading rapidly on the wind. Wayne fought the fire until his clothing was all but burned off—a new Sunday suit! He was so exhausted and had breathed in so much smoke that he was taken to the hospital tent, where he was revived and treated for burns. Fortunately, no one was injured seriously and the fire was brought under control.

Three of the units where the girls slept were destroyed, but the efficient counselors quickly righted the chaos. The scouts finished their allotted time at the camp happily and without further mishaps.

Fire caused great embarrassment to Bill in his scouting. The Boy Scouts of Fort Lewis spent a weekend at American Lake. It was real camping. They pitched their own pup tents and were to cook their own food. Saturday night it rained and Bill's tent leaked. His clothes were soaked, but he knew how to take care of that, and the following morning strung his clothing on a line outside, building an open fire beneath them to dry them out. They all burned, of course, and when he sent me an S.O.S. for replacement clothing Sunday morning, all he had to wear was his bathing suit.

It was also the rainy season when Bill was working for his merit badges to become an Eagle Scout. It was so rainy, in fact, that the counselors agreed that boys trying for their merit badge in cooking could take their test indoors, in their own homes. Bill rubbed his sticks and started a fire in our fireplace and began to cook. The smoke from his fire rolled out into the living room in great billows, chasing the rest of us upstairs. He stayed with it, though, with great tears rolling down his face from the smoke and with steak fat splattering all over him, the hearth, and the carpet. After he earned his merit badge, I told him I thought I should get some special kind of award for my cleanup job afterward.

Bill was not the only member of the family who was out in the woods at every opportunity. His father spent every hour he could tramping in the mud fishing. Nothing made Wayne happier than an afternoon in the open with his rod and reel. Sometimes his hobby made our home look like a fisherman's shack. His fishing gear would turn up in the most unlikely places. There was a time he came back from fishing and stretched his lines out to dry in the guest room. He strung them from side-wall light fixtures to dressers to door-knobs. That evening we had dinner guests and I quite innocently told the women to leave their wraps in the guest room, not know-ing about the fishing lines. The first woman into the guest room was caught under the chin by a fishing line and fell flat on the floor. There was no difficulty making conversation that night!

The big event of the year at Fort Lewis was the Army Day dis-play of clothing, weapons, heavy equipment, rations, mess gear, and all the other things our Army needed to support itself and fight in a war. The festivities were capped always by a review. The main display was in the big gymnasium. There, a 75-mm artillery howitzer was put in place and covered with wire. Wayne and I were asked to cover the whole thing solid with daffodils, so there would be a floral float to add beauty to the display of army equip-ment. Literally thousands of daffodils were provided for us, but we could not go to work until the last possible moment. If we put out the flowers too early, they would wilt and we would have a very sorry-looking display.

We started working late and didn't finish until after midnight. We were completely exhausted and about to go home for as much rest as we could get before the big day dawned when a colonel and his wife appeared to make a survey of the displays.

The colonel's wife withered us with a glance at the gun. "I think that's perfectly hideous." She set her jaw and declared, "I won't have it!"

Now one of the protections the Army gives its officers and men is that they do not have to take orders from anybody's wife, no matter how high the rank of the husband. The great majority of Army wives know this, and when they want an officer or enlisted man to do something for them, they request it and never give an order. They know that if they are reasonable in their requests and their attitudes they probably will get what they want. Nobody but a fool is going to antagonize the wife of a superior officer if it can be helped. But the officers and men have the right to refuse to comply with requests or demands from officers' wives, and if the demands are unreasonable a Regular Army man who knows his rights and privileges will refuse.

Wayne knew his rights and privileges. "I'm sorry," he said, "but unless your husband orders the caisson dismantled, I'll not dismantle it."

When it became obvious that the colonel was not going to oblige his wife by ordering us to tear down the display, Wayne continued, "It remains as it is and I think it's beautiful."

The flowers did stay in place and most people seemed to like them.

I have mentioned before difficulties with wives of senior officers, like the woman who accused my children of making anonymous telephone calls and the one who criticized my wedding silver and almost broke my heart. These were events which left sharp memories. But it must be made clear that they were isolated frictions that ran counter to the over-all pattern of my life in the Army, a life enriched by the most pleasant of relations with so many of the wives of officers both senior and junior to my husband. The rule was consideration among the wives, and the few who failed to follow this rule of conduct stood out in the memories of all the rest of us.

Bill became interested in public speaking at this time and began to win prizes in school competition. We were at Fort Lewis when Hitler marched into Poland and World War II began. For Army families, that event created a particularly tense situation for we all knew in our hearts that our husbands and fathers might now be taken from us. We had known that all along, of course, because the business of the Army is to fight and Wayne was in and of the Army. But we could feel easier when there was no war anywhere than after our friends in Europe became embroiled in a death struggle with a dictator bent on world conquest.

And Wayne wouldn't let us forget. History was in the making and he insisted that the children know about it, keep up with it. Young as they were, he had them listen to certain radio commentators and news broadcasters so they would realize what the world was moving into. The one commentator Wayne never let us miss was Lowell Thomas, and it was through his voice we learned so much about the war raging in Europe. The climax in this radio course of training came with the British evacuation of Dunkirk and the tremendously moving speeches of Prime Minister Winston Churchill.

Against this background Bill worked on a speech for the Washington State High School declamation contest. His subject was "Why I Am an American . . . What I See in the United States." He won the state championship. We always felt that he was helped to win it because of the fact that Wayne had insisted both he and Ann listen to those radio broadcasts and learn what it meant to be an American in a world on fire with war.

CHAPTER SIX

THE YEAR 1940 WAS AN ANXIOUS AND CON-
fused one for Americans. Some clamored for neutrality in the war
with Hitler. Others saw the war as our war and advocated anything possible to help Great Britain which, after the fall of France,
stood alone against the Fascist nations. In Washington, President
Roosevelt proclaimed that the United States must be the "arsenal
of democracy."

And in Fort Lewis and every other Army post in the land,
Army families asked when, not if, their husbands and fathers would
be called to fight. Little time was wasted with speculation of
whether the United States would get into the war. That was not
for the Army to decide. Professionally the Army people had to do
their utmost to get ready to fight if they were called. Emotionally
the families of the Army people had to steel themselves for the day
their loved ones would be called, a day everyone felt would come
all too soon.

Rumors of war were on everyone's tongue. We studied the newspapers and listened to every radio broadcast to try to find clues as
to whether America would be in the war soon or late. It was a
dread thing to live with day in and day out. We tried hard not to
think about the fact that in all of America's wars, the Regular Army

83

took the highest percentage of casualties of any group, that the men from West Point, the Citadel, V.M.I., and the other military schools, the regulars who came up through the ranks or from ROTC, were the shock troops who led the way and held the line during the difficult period while the civilian army was being built up to bring the full power of America to bear for victory.

Things were moving in the Army. Promotions were coming through. Wayne was boosted to lieutenant colonel on July 1, 1940, and almost simultaneously orders came through from General Marshall for him to report to the War College in Washington, D.C. General Marshall was Chief of Staff and he wanted Wayne at the War College as an instructor.

There were all sorts of rumors that the War College was about to be closed. Whenever the United States gets into a war, the schools like the War College and the General Staff School at Fort Leavenworth are closed so the officers assigned there as instructors and students can get into active service in staff and troop duty.

The War College was one of the choice assignments in the Army, and to instruct there was a mark of distinction every officer wanted on his record. There had been a difficulty in Wayne's assignment, however. While Wayne had eagerly accepted General Marshall's first suggestion, word came back from the general that the personnel people had reported Wayne long on staff work and short on troop experience and felt he should be assigned to troop duty. Wayne immediately answered that he didn't know who had studied his record but that he believed he had a truly balanced experience of troop and staff duty and enclosed his record to prove it. He added that, of course, much as he would like to go to the War College, he would be happy to stay with troops and continue the kind of work he had been doing at Fort Lewis for three years with the Third Infantry Division.

There was a long lapse, and then came the message from General Marshall that Wayne should report to the War College as an instructor.

Wayne was elated. We had all our furniture packed, crated, and shipped to Washington via the Panama Canal. We booked passage for ourselves through the Canal and then loaded the car for a drive to Camano Island, where we would spend a few days at our cousins' summer home. Before departure from Fort Lewis we handed the key to our house to the Quartermaster and checked out.

At noon we were in Seattle, right downtown, passing the Olympic Hotel. Wayne said, "Turn on the radio, Renie, and get the twelve-o'clock news." I did and the first news item we heard was from Washington, announcing that the War College had been ordered closed. Wayne pulled the car to the curb, switched off the motor, and said, "I guess I'd better make a telephone call."

I had an empty sunk feeling and said to my husband, "We have no more home than a jack rabbit, have we?"

He went into a drugstore and telephoned Gen. Walter Sweeney, our commanding officer at Fort Lewis and our very close friend. The general was a good-natured, hearty Irishman who was able to size up a situation at a glance.

Wayne told him about the news broadcast and said he didn't know what he was going to do but did know that he wanted his house held for him at Fort Lewis. "We turned in the key forty-five minutes ago," Wayne said, "and sure would appreciate it if you could keep the Quartermaster from giving it to anyone else until we get back."

General Sweeney roared with laughter. "That house is yours as long as you want it."

Wayne welcomed that, of course, so we backtracked to Fort Lewis, where Wayne sent a message to General Marshall, and then to Camano for our holiday.

Wayne sent a full explanation to General Marshall, telling about the news broadcast and stated he would await further instructions. General Marshall replied in a couple of days with a message that Wayne always said was "pure, classic Marshall." He wasted no words and explained none of the unanswered questions. He just messaged: "COMPLY WITH ORDERS."

Wayne complied.

85

He didn't get the answers to all those questions until he arrived in Washington where, according to his orders, he was to teach at a school that was already closed.

In Washington Wayne got one of the big surprises of his life. He and twelve other younger officers had been hand-picked to serve on a General Staff. Gen. George Marshall was the commander, Gen. Lesley McNair his Chief of Staff. Wayne was head of the Plans and Operations Section, the G-3. The General Staff was set up in the War College buildings, so the orders for Wayne to report for duty at the War College had been technically accurate.

Wayne felt that he had been singled out for the job by General McNair, who was a rising star in the Army. McNair had started as a captain in combat in France and came out of World War I a brigadier general. At the end of that war, when the Army announced that all officers would revert to permanent rank, McNair took the star off his shoulder and replaced it with the leaves of a major, four ranks down. But in 1940 he was a brigadier general again and a very big man in American planning for the war that seemed inevitable.

General McNair was not in Washington when Wayne arrived. He was north, in upstate New York, on maneuvers. Wayne had been told to report to General McNair at the War College, but decided that it would be better to go up into New York and meet him there. None of Wayne's gear had arrived, and General McNair left Wayne a note that since he didn't have a sleeping bag or other camp equipment available he had better wait at the War College.

Wayne borrowed and begged rough-weather gear, including a raincoat several sizes too small for him, the sleeves of which ended just below his elbows. Then he took off for the maneuvers.

General McNair was most happy to see that Wayne had decided to join him on maneuvers and said, "Look, Clark, we have three more days of this and I want you with me every minute of them."

They had never met before but they had corresponded a good deal about the Third Infantry Division amphibious exercise and the landing on the beach at Monterey. McNair was intensely interested in amphibious techniques and during those three days on maneuvers he asked Wayne every possible question about the Third Infantry exercise.

In Washington we lived within the grounds of the parklike Army War College, long since renamed Fort McNair. The house was especially roomy and comfortable, with long porches both upstairs and down for Washington's hot summer evenings.

War was such a threat, such an everyday fear, that the family seemed to draw closer together. We enjoyed the little things. On those hot summer nights we would sit, the four of us, on the porch upstairs and watch the lights of the cruise boats floating down the Potomac to Mount Vernon. Sometimes when it was terribly hot, all four of us slept on that porch upstairs, falling to sleep lazily, still conscious of the lights of the river boats and the gay music that was played on their decks.

War or no war, the children were growing up faster. Ann was in junior high school in Washington, and soon it was her turn for that first dance date, that very big event for her. She even got a pair of high-heeled shoes, along with her first long dress. How she treasured these first new things! She wore them the night of her first dance date, and she also wore her first corsage that night. As I gazed at my baby girl, so fast growing up, I had a sick feeling in the pit of my stomach. The day would soon be here when she would be married and gone! Her date arrived, polished, well groomed, and just a bit uneasy. Ann made her entrance, starting at the top of the stairs. All of us, including her young date, looked up with admiration as she started down those stairs. She was so young and pretty and fresh and poised.

But the high heels were so strange—the dress so long. One heel caught on the stair, and Ann came tumbling down, all the way down, and landed at the feet of her young boy friend. I held my breath but it wasn't necessary. The poise was not mere veneer. Ann looked up at her boy and grinned, the kind of grin her father would use to work out of a silly situation like that one. The boy grinned too and helped her to her feet. There was a little delay while we checked to see if she was hurt and then to see if her dress was torn or her hair in need of repair. Everything was all right and she swept out of the house on the arm of her date, a little over-cautious about those high heels but once again the poised, fresh girl she had been at the top of the stairs.

Ann was a spirited girl with just a touch of the tomboy in her. That probably was due to her effort throughout childhood to keep pace with Bill. We got a scare once at Fort Lewis, for instance, when she came home bruised and hurt from a tomboy exploit that failed. She climbed a tree in the center of the mule corral and tried to drop onto a mule's back and ride him away, like the cowboys in the movies. She landed on the mule's back, all right, but was bounced to the ground immediately as the startled animal took off fast.

At the War College she tried something from which she got a good scare. Ann and some of her girl friends got peculiar enjoyment from climbing through the window of the Officers' Club after hours and sitting in the darkness talking. They would sit in the big, empty parlor, enjoying the luxury of the heavily overstuffed chairs and lounges. One night they found all the windows locked. The girls put their heads together and decided they would fool the club management next night by planting one of their number in the club at closing time so she could open a window after everyone left.

Ann volunteered. The club was in a big colonial-style building right on the Potomac. The dining room, bar, parlors, and kitchen were on the first floor, the ballroom on the second, and a small room on the third. The small room opened onto the lattice-work rafters that were above the ballroom.

Before the club closed Ann hid in the attic on the third floor. She watched the club lights go out one by one. The last light was switched off and she heard the door latch shut. Then she heard something else, much closer at hand. Her little hiding place seemed to come alive with moving things. The things seemed to be leaping from the rafters. A faint light glimmered through the window on the stair landing. It caught silvery threadlike things that twitched and moved in the darkness.

They were the whiskers of rats.

Ann fairly leaped down the stairs. She was certain something leaped after her. She made it to the ground floor. She got her hands on the lock of a window. But it was like a nightmare. Her hands just couldn't move fast enough, it seemed. Finally, after what seemed an eternity, Ann got the window open and jumped outside, breathless.

Her girl friends heard her story. Never again did they think of using the Officers' Club as a meeting place.

Raised on Army posts, Bill always was fascinated by the military life. As he said, "I always loved soldiers, real or toy." So I guess his decision to go to West Point just grew. Wayne and I talked about it often, and decided that neither of us would put any pressure on Bill to go to the Academy. We wanted him to make his own decision. Gradually it came to be understood between Bill and Wayne that Bill would go to West Point.

It was a Clark family tradition to go to the Academy. Wayne's father was a graduate with the class of 1890. Wayne was a member of the class of 1917. And now Bill was trying to equal his father's record of entering before he was seventeen years old. That was not all good. Wayne was just enough younger than the other men in his class to be left out of athletics. At seventeen he couldn't compete with men three to five years older than he. But with the war coming on and with Wayne almost certain to be out of the country, we wanted to arrange Bill's entry before it was too late and I would be left with the whole job of getting some congressman to appoint him.

Bill was enrolled in Sullivan's Prep School in Washington to get ready for West Point and was doing fine, particularly in mathematics. His father, meanwhile, had to find someone to appoint him.

We spent a good deal of time on this task. We were so anxious to get Bill set in West Point. It was a little difficult for Army officers, who have no political ties or influence until after they reach high command, to arrange West Point entrance for their sons. The fact that so many sons of West Pointers do go to the Academy is due, I think, to the great desire the officers have to send their sons there and to the work they do to get the appointments.

In the midst of these efforts, General Marshall sent Wayne to a congressional hearing on the removal of Japanese from the West Coast. Wayne was chosen because he was familiar with the Coast and knew a little of the problem. Wayne was to represent General Marshall at the hearing, and was given strict instructions to telephone the general as soon as the hearing was concluded.

Young Henry Jackson, a representative from Washington, also was at the hearing, and since Wayne then considered Washington our home state, he struck up a conversation with the young congressman. The upshot was that they lunched together that day and Jackson gave Bill the right to compete for Jackson's appointment to West Point.

When Wayne finally returned to his office, very late, he found several messages to call General Marshall. He did without further delay, and found he was on the hot seat.

General Marshall wanted to know why the delay, why no report, what happened. Wayne said, "Nothing much, sir, except that I got an appointment to West Point for my boy."

The general answered coldly, "I didn't send you up there to work on an appointment to West Point."

It all worked out fine, however. Bill won the competitive examination and Jackson's appointment to the Academy.

Jackson was—and is—one of the finest young Americans we have known. We were so happy in 1954 when he became United States Senator from Washington, which had been our home state more than any other. We had our property on wonderful Camano Island, and we loved the beauty of the Northwest.

Our admiration and affection for Henry Jackson were based far less on the fact that he appointed Bill than on the things he did later. Those things showed the kind of American he is and how seriously he considers his obligation as an elected representative of the people of his state. After the war started, Henry enlisted, with the request that he be assigned to Wayne's Fifth Army in Italy. He would have gone to Italy had not President Roosevelt, alarmed by the number of very fine men who were leaving Congress to fight for their country, decided they were more needed at home and could better serve their country in Congress than at the front.

The President ordered all congressmen who had enlisted to return to Congress and ordered their enlistments canceled.

Jackson came back from the Army with an idea. As far as I know, he is the only congressman who ever had this particular thought. He wrote to Wayne and said that for the duration of the war he wanted Wayne to name a soldier from the Fifth Army to fill the one West Point appointment Jackson was authorized to make as a congressman. Wayne selected the finest combat soldier he had in Italy, and the boy made a fine record at the Academy.

With war raging in Europe and threatening America, much of the fun and humor seemed to go out of our lives. We didn't really feel we were different people, but we were, just as all Americans of that period were different from what they had been before. Life when threatened is stripped to fundamentals. We cherished each little family pleasure, each moment of joy with our children, all those evenings watching the river boats from our porch and listening to the music that came from the Potomac.

There were some mishaps, of course, but they didn't have the wonderful silly flavor of those of bygone years. Our dog, Pal, ate the bottom from the new and gorgeous mink coat of Muriel Thurber, wife of a colonel and a good friend of ours. Pal had never chewed any of my old fur coats and we tried to joke about how he knew quality, but it was a lame joke. Muriel was most gracious and assured us the coat was insured so there would be no loss. But the time just wasn't right for humor.

Mother had come to live with us at the War College after she developed a heart condition and the doctor told her to take things easy. She had been alone in Muncie for many years after Father died in 1926, just about the time Ann was born. She was a great boon to me in those anxious pre-Pearl Harbor days. I had studied rug weaving and had made a hobby of copying the patterns of famous Persian rugs that hung in museums in New York and Philadelphia. During those troubled times this hobby, which kept my fingers busy, was a great solace. Mother helped by reading to me, hour upon hour, while I wove those rugs.

It was customary in those big old houses at the War College for the husband to use the downstairs bedroom and bath as his study. In that way students and other officers could enter the office directly from a side door without disturbing the rest of the family. It was a most satisfactory arrangement and everyone on the post used it as an officer's study. But when Mother arrived, with doctor's orders that she was not to climb stairs, Wayne was kind enough to give up his downstairs study so she could live there and would never have to climb to the second floor.

Mother was not able to halt all her activity, even in view of the doctor's orders, so she organized a Sunday-school class for the children of the officers and enlisted men at the War College and conducted it each Sunday morning in our home. Mother Clark was living in an apartment in Washington then, also alone since the death of Dad Clark, and our two mothers spent a great deal of time together and became close friends.

Another important person entered our lives at the War College. That was Sgt. Bill Cheney, the Negro soldier who joined us there and stayed with Wayne as orderly all through Italy and Austria and well into the postwar years.

In the fall of 1941, Wayne was promoted two grades to brigadier general, the biggest mark of achievement in any officer's career. The first star is the big one, the one for which friends send wires and flowers and the one for which the officer throws a champagne party. We did and it was a wonderful one. We were particularly honored because Wayne skipped a grade. In all my husband's Army career, he never wore the eagles of a full colonel on his shoulder.

Whenever we could get away during these days of danger we took an outing, anywhere across the Potomac into the open, woodsy country of Virginia, so close to the city and yet so rural in those days. There came a Sunday when we were invited into Arlington County for Sunday lunch and a tramp through the woods afterward, just the kind of happy holiday we loved so much. It was late in the year, but the day was perfect. Heavy jackets and sweaters gave us all the protection we needed from the chill of the final days of autumn. Our hosts, Capt. and Mrs. Edwin B. Howard, knew how much we enjoyed walking, so they planned the day to include a hike in the woods that came right down to the back of their comfortable home.

Wayne had been working so hard on his training job that I was overjoyed that he was able to get away to stretch his long legs and breathe deeply the clean, crisp air of the woodland and feel again the spring of soft forest soil beneath his feet. This was what he loved so much, the main reason for his being such an ardent fisherman and hunter, and I was glad that his work had let up enough to permit him to break away from his desk if only for one afternoon.

He was never more gay. The fatigue from all his confining work seemed to evaporate in that clean wood air. He strode out ahead of us, his long strides carrying him swiftly down the forest paths. And he whistled as I had not heard him whistle for weeks and weeks. It was a whistle of sheer carefree joy with life and with the fact of being alive.

Suddenly there was a disturbance. Someone was running through the woods with reckless abandon. There was an urgency in that run and we heard whoever it was crashing against underbrush and pushing aside low-lying branches long before we saw him.

Finally the runner, a next-door neighbor of the Howards', came into view, breathless and so agitated I knew in my heart this was no ordinary disturbance. My first thought was of the children.

"Pearl Harbor . . ." he gasped. "Bombed. . . . It's war!"

All my fears were wrapped up in those terrible words, and all my life seemed to come tumbling down with them.

All I remember of that mad race back to the house and our car was that Wayne ran so terribly fast I had a frightful time trying to keep up with him. His long legs covered the forest paths with giant strides. I don't even remember if I was crying as we ran through the woods as though in a nightmare, although I do remember that there were many tears later.

When we got to the house, panting for breath, Wayne already was in the car, starting the motor and looking back and calling for me to hurry.

The whole Army and Navy must have been in Virginia that day and received word at the same time, for the highways, the fine, modern roads built for high speeds, were jammed that Sunday afternoon with men rushing back to their duty stations. We moved at a snail's pace. The ride out had taken us less than half an hour. The ride back took two full hours.

The men in the cars around us during that unbelievably slow ride did not look like Army or Navy men at all. They were in hunting jackets, sports jackets, sweaters. Frightened little children fussed, and the one thing that marked the men and women was the stern, tight look of their faces. Many of the men rode alone. They were the men whose families were left behind in their homes in Virginia, where so many of the service people live, the men from Alexandria, Falls Church, Arlington, Sleepy Hollow, Mount Vernon, Fairfax—the George Washington country. Each little place had a story of Washington and what he had done when he visited or worshiped there.

Few of these men had been ordered back. The call had gone out for all men to report for duty, and had been radioed, but in the years that followed most of those men remembered only that they had heard Pearl Harbor had been bombed. That was order enough.

The stories of that day have become legend. Men dropped golf clubs on tees and greens and never swung a club again for years. Men reported for duty in Washington wearing golf clothes or gardening clothes or sports clothes and didn't have time to get into uniform until late the next day.

Wayne gave me a quick kiss when we arrived at his War College office and I hurried home to the children. I did not see him again all that night or all the next, long day. When he finally did come home, exhausted, he already had the look of war upon his face, like all the others I saw dragging themselves to their homes for a short, troubled rest.

The pressure was unbelievable on all those men charged with the duty of meeting the most awesome threat yet made against America. Wayne was G-3 in charge of Plans and Training for the Ground Forces. As such he worked in an office adjoining that of General McNair, who, Wayne often told me, was one of the greatest soldiers in the American Army. The relationship between the general and Wayne was particularly close. For one thing McNair was a ground soldier who believed the war would be won on the ground. And then there was the fact that McNair was hard of hearing. This made conferences somewhat difficult for him and frequently he sent Wayne to represent him at meetings. Many of these were held in General Marshall's office. McNair relied a good deal on Wayne, not only to report back what was said, but also to present McNair's ideas on various problems.

McNair went to the more important meetings himself. Wayne said that the general might have missed some of the statements made at these conferences but that he was so keen he could almost read the minds of his fellow officers and follow their thought by picking up a few key words here and there as they talked.

After Pearl Harbor, Wayne said he spent hour after hour discussing the future with McNair. Wayne told the general that it was certain large forces would be put into the field ultimately and that when they were McNair was the logical man to command the ground forces. If and when that happened, Wayne said, he wanted to be sure to go along and not stay home with a staff job. McNair was about sixty years old then. He looked at his Plans officer, and said, "We will have troops in battle, but I am too old. This will be a young man's war. You are more apt to be the commander than I."

To Wayne that was unbelievable at the time, but McNair was right and the younger men were given the command posts in the field. It was ironic and tragic that General McNair himself was killed in July of 1944 while inspecting the battlefields. The tragedy was compounded for the McNair family on the other side of the world. Within a week after the general was killed, his son, a colonel and chief of staff of the Seventy-seventh Infantry Division, was killed by a Japanese ambush on the front lines of the battle in the jungles of Guam.

These were the kinds of tragedies all Americans feared when the grim news came from Pearl Harbor and finally we were caught up in the war that spread around the globe.

Everything was moving so fast I didn't even have time to sit down and think what all this would mean to our future. The most wonderful era of my life was over, never to be recaptured. I knew in my heart that never again would the four of us be together as a family in the same way we were before the bombs hit Pearl Harbor. And I knew, too, that so far we were luckier than many, for the casualty list from Pearl Harbor itself that very first day carried irreparable heartbreak for over three thousand American families, and there would be more, oh so many more. I prayed that it would not happen to our family—a selfish prayer, perhaps, but one I am sure was uttered that night by every wife and every mother in the land.

Things moved so swiftly I could hardly keep up with them. In April, General McNair pinned the two stars of a major general on Wayne's collar. Only a few days later I went out to the airport to say good-by to Wayne, who was off to England with Eisenhower for a quick survey trip. The Air Corps sent Gen. Hap Arnold and Col. Hoyt S. Vandenberg along on that same flight.

The first trip to war lasted only three weeks. In May, Wayne and Ike returned to Washington. But only a day or two later Wayne was named commanding general of II Corps, assigned to permanent duty in the European War Theater. I was fortunate in one thing. Duty kept him in Washington for another six weeks and it wasn't until June 23, 1942, that he left me "for the duration."

The strain, the fears, the deep, basic, primitive disturbance were terrible to bear.

The children were old enough to know what it all meant. Bill was seventeen, Ann almost sixteen. Like so many scores of thousands of American boys, Bill wanted to get into the fighting. He vowed that he would enlist. We argued, of course. Wayne explained to him in great detail how much more he could do for his country if he continued his education and went on to West Point.

"Your chance will come later," Wayne used to argue, not dreaming how quickly it really would come in Korea, where Bill was wounded so badly.

Ann remembered the war monument at Fort Lewis.

"I am going to war in the Red Cross," she declared with girlish, almost childish, determination.

Even Pal, our black cocker spaniel, seemed to sense the change Pearl Harbor had brought into our lives. He dogged Wayne's footsteps all over the house, in a way he never had done before. When Wayne sat down Pal would leap into his lap and snuggle, and if Wayne set him down on the floor, he would bounce right back into Wayne's lap, as if he knew Wayne was going away.

On a rainy morning, dark and gray, Bill and I went with Wayne to the airport from which he was to leave for that strange, menacing war whose course and ending and tragedy none could foresee. There he joined Ike for the flight to England. It was like a dream, frightening and unreal, to think that in a moment or two Wayne, whom I could see and hear and feel; Wayne, who was standing there with his arm around me; Wayne, who was grinning and trying to give me a final word of cheer, would step into that airplane and be lost to me, gone from my sight and touch for nobody knew how long.

Ike said good-by and left Wayne, Bill, and me standing alone in the rain, trying so desperately to think of something meaningful to say, something that could be treasured as a parting memory. Nothing came and finally Wayne kissed me and was gone. Bill and I turned to walk toward the automobile. But a figure came hurtling through the rain, out of the mist. It was Ike, trying to do just a little more to help me keep my chin up, kissing me once again and saying, "Don't worry about Wayne, I'll take good care of him." And then they were gone.

Everything fell apart. Immediately after Wayne left, I went home and cried. It was one of the few times in my married life that I had wept. Ann soon entered Marjorie Webster College, a boarding school in Washington. Bill went to West Point right away, and for the first time since they were born I was alone, completely and utterly alone. It did me no good to keep telling myself that hundreds of thousands of other American wives and mothers were alone that day, too, because of the same war. I sympathized with them, but that did not take the bitterness from my loneliness, just as nothing could take the lump of loneliness out of their hearts.

Even Sergeant Cheney left me. He stayed behind when Wayne left and was most unhappy about it. Here he was, a soldier, and here was a war going on, and what was he doing? Helping a woman around the house! He didn't like it and wanted desperately to join Wayne. Word came for him from England only a few days after Wayne left. He was sweeping the kitchen when I told him Wayne wanted him to report and that his orders were ready. He dropped that broom right where he was and took off, leaving the broom on the unswept floor behind him.

Mother and I seemed alone in that beautiful big house at the War College in Washington in which my own little family had spent its final months and weeks and hours together. We still were a family, but I knew in my heart we never would live together again under one roof, never sleep on a porch and listen to the music of the river boats together. Bill would visit, Ann would go to college and then probably marry, but they were on their own, grown-up, and no longer dependent upon me for all those little things they once had needed me for. I missed even the chores of cleaning up after them, of patching their clothing, bandaging cuts, settling their fights. A twinge of guilt swept into my mind when I remembered how often I had been cross and irritated with them when they cluttered a room with toys or turned the house into a bedlam of noise. How I longed for that bedlam as I sat in that empty house which no longer seemed beautiful to me and which no longer was mine! Another Army family had been assigned our quarters and I had to find an apartment in Washington "for the duration"—as everyone described the weeks and months and years of dreadful waiting for a war to be won.

Almost everything was packed. Grand old Cassie was a great

help. Cassie was a Jamaican, and never did we have a more loyal servant. She was good clear through. She came to us while we were at the War College, having advertised for a job. I answered her ad, and she became a part of our household, even a part of our family.

Cassie was big and heavy and troubled with arthritis, but she worked so hard and understood so much that she was a great comfort to us always. Together on that sad day Cassie and I worked to dismantle the house which had been such a wonderful and happy home. Together we took the pictures from the walls, the drapes from the windows. Everything that had made this house a home had to come down. The furniture and packing cases were all downstairs, awaiting the moving van.

There was just one more room to do. Bill was the last one out of the house before me, and his room still had to be done. Slowly I climbed to the third floor where he had lived by himself in a room that hid all his young secrets. I entered the room and a terrible nostalgia swept through me. It was unchanged from yesterday and all the other yesterdays when it had been his own little retreat. He had taken his toothbrush to West Point and little else. I opened his closet and reached in to begin taking out the boy things hanging there.

Then the dam broke. The tears that had not come in all those nightmarish days from the time we heard about Pearl Harbor, that day so long, long ago when we were hiking so happily in the woods, came now in torrents. I cried with abandon, huddled there on the floor of Bill's closet. I cried for the world and for myself . . . for the boy who would leave West Point only to go into the Army and never to live with me again . . . for the girl who would be grown, ready for her own full life without me when this time of trouble was over . . . and for the husband who already had left for the war itself.

I'll never know how long I wept. It was the kind of cry that blots out all else, that is independent and apart from reality, that creates a little era of time all its own. But soon or late I was not alone. Someone else was in the room, kneeling with me in the closet and holding great comforting arms around me and whispering gently and softly and with great sadness and understanding into my ear. It was Cassie, heavy, slow, old Cassie, who never before could climb those steep stairs to the third floor because her knees were arthritic and would not carry her there without great pain.

She patted me and cried with me and spoke solacing words that came from the heart of the great sadness of her people, and finally my grief and loneliness were spent and we went downstairs together into the kind of unknown that only war can bring.

War made me a visitor to my own children. I thought it best for Ann to be a resident student at Marjorie Webster College in order that she could become a real and full part of the school and get to know her classmates in a way that would have been impossible if she had been living at home. Often I visited her at the school, and most Sundays when I was in Washington she would come to my apartment for early dinner. Those were happy Sunday afternoons when Ann trooped in with a few girl friends, afternoons that brought life and laughter and youth to the apartment that was so lonely too much of the time.

All through the war Wayne bombarded me with questions about the children. He, like almost all other men at war, seemed to have a real need for every scrap of information he could get about his loved ones, though he often tried to mask this need with good humor. Once, for instance, he asked what Ann was studying. I wrote back: "Art, swimming, tennis, horseback riding, and such things." Wayne asked by return mail: "Who is Art?"

As often as possible, I went to West Point to see Bill. He always seemed to welcome my visits, but I never was certain whether it was because he was glad to see me or because I always took him to the Thayer Hotel and bought him a big steak dinner.

Bill was becoming quite grown up and had his share of the condescension boys get toward their parents after they leave the family hearth and go out on their own. He wrote to his father in Italy once about how well he was doing at West Point, and added that Wayne seemed "to be doing all right, too," against the Germans.

Bill was genuinely proud of his dad, but fearful that people would think he was trying to get by on his father's coattails. Bill showed this one night when we were together in New York for an evening and had a ringside table for dinner at the Plaza. Hildegarde was singing and from time to time she added an intimate touch to her show by asking people to stand up at the microphone with her and tell a little bit about themselves. Bill, all dressed in his cadet's uniform, was a natural for her. She couldn't miss that uniform as she looked around the room for someone to invite to the floor.

Bill was eighteen, with all the mixture of pride and shyness, sensitivity and boldness that any normal eighteen-year-old boy has. Hildegarde asked his name. At first he tried to get by with a diversion. "I'm a cadet from West Point," he said. Hildegarde said, "Yes, but what's your name?" He tried to put her off but she persisted. At last he said, "I'm Bill from West Point."

He was no match for Hildegarde, of course. She kept after him. "You must have a last name," she said; "what is it?" He struggled a bit more and asked her if it wouldn't be all right to just let it go as "a cadet named Bill." She said it wouldn't, so he said he was "Bill Clark."

By this time Hildegarde must have sensed something, for she asked, "Who is your daddy?" Bill mumbled, "M. W. Clark." Hildegarde pressed the point. "What does your daddy do?" she asked. Bill said, "Oh, he's overseas."

"Oh, what is his rank?" asked Hildegarde.

"Well, I guess he's a general now," said Bill.

"How many stars does he have?"

"Three."

"What do the initials 'M. W.' stand for?"

"The 'W.' is for Wayne."

"Your father isn't General Mark Clark by any chance?"

"Well, yes ma'am."

Hildegarde gave Bill an American Beauty rose, a great big kiss, and a very red and embarrassed face. Then she handed him a carton of cigarettes and asked if he smoked.

"No ma'am," said Bill, "but my mother does."

He came back to our table with his face still beet-red with

embarrassment despite the friendly calls and applause he was getting.

Those rare outings with Bill in New York were some of the most pleasant times I had during the war. I always planned so much for those evenings, and counted on them desperately to break, in part at least, the never-ending loneliness of the war years.

CHAPTER SEVEN

WAYNE'S FIRST TRIP TO WAR WAS A SHORT one. He was back in Washington in three weeks. Actually he and Ike had flown to England only to make a quick survey of the situation and begin to formulate plans.

But if his first trip to war had been short, his first return home was even shorter. The day he arrived back in Washington, Wayne was told he had been named commanding general of II Corps and was headed for England on permanent duty.

I implored Wayne to write at least once a week, and felt I had to because he hates to write letters. He assured me most solemnly that, no matter how busy he was, he would. To make doubly sure, I cornered Sgt. Kenneth G. Merrill, who served Wayne as secretary, when he came to the house to help Wayne pack.

Sergeant Merrill was a man with a robust sense of humor. He also was a man with a keen eye for the ridiculous, and something struck him as being most ridiculous when I insisted that he make sure Wayne write me at least once a week.

He broke out into a silly grin, tried to hold it back and then roared with laughter. I asked him what was so funny, and his laughter became hysterical, uncontrollable. I kept after him until he finally broke down and admitted that during the past several days Wayne had dictated a batch of letters to him for me, dated a week apart and spread out over the next three months. The letters were all signed, sealed, and addressed, and little tags were clipped to them so the sergeant would know when to mail each one. I saw to it that those letters were destroyed promptly.

War does much more than separate families physically. It breaks the bonds of common experience and confidences that are built up in any successful marriage. For eighteen years Wayne and I had shared every experience, every hope, every dream. We laughed about the same things and worried about the same things.

But in war there is a thing called security. The men are out on the biggest adventure of their lives, a terrible adventure from which so many never return, but because of security they cannot even tell their wives what country they are in, sometimes not even what continent.

Shortly after Wayne's arrival in England he was made commander of Ground Forces under General Eisenhower. In that job he was an important intelligence target for the Germans. If they knew where he was they could go far toward deducing what the Allied Armies might do. So he had to be especially careful about what he told me in his letters. He no longer could share with me the intimate details of his plans, his work, his hopes, his fears.

Later, much later, he was able to take me over the battlefields and reconstruct for me in his own words the campaigns he fought, the dreams he dreamed. He was more fortunate than most soldiers in this, because although so many would like their wives to visit their battlefields with them, only a handful ever have the opportunity to go back and relive for their wives the time of their terrible struggles.

The continuity of our common experience as husband and wife was broken during the war, however, because of separation and security, and I knew nothing of his big moments while they were happening.

I knew nothing of the details of the breath-taking assignment General Eisenhower gave Wayne in the fall of 1942. Ike called Wayne into his office in London one October day and said it had been decided that a small group make a landing in French North Africa preparatory to the big landings we were planning. And such preparatory work!

Wayne was to fly secretly to Gibraltar and there board a submarine with a handful of carefully selected officers and make a landing in a rubber boat on a North African shore controlled by Germans and patrolled by their police. The details read like a dime spy thriller. The submarine was to travel submerged from Gibraltar, through enemy waters most of the way, arriving at the appointed spot under cover of darkness. Arrangements were made for a signal light on shore, in a dormer window of a house which was supposed to be the residence of Frenchmen devoted to the fight against the Nazis. Assigned to the hazardous mission with Wayne were Brig. Gen. Lyman L. Lemnitzer, head of the Allied Force Plans Section; Col. A. L. Hamblen, our shipping and supply expert; Capt. Jerauld Wright of the United States Navy, who had been our Navy liaison man since TORCH was started; and Col. Julius C. Holmes, a former State Department officer, who headed up our Civil Affairs Branch of the TORCH plan. They were all Americans. But some British commandos went along, too, to help in the boats and to guard.

The mission was undertaken and everything worked according to plan until the submarine arrived off the African coast. The signal light was not visible. It was a frightening moment. What had gone wrong? What should be done? The decision had to be made on the spot. Radio silence was imperative. Finally the sub had to be submerged for safety because dawn was breaking.

All that day and until after midnight there were conferences on that submarine, tense, tight conferences in which each man realized that his life might depend upon the right answer to the problem. Finally, after midnight, the light appeared in the window. Wayne decided to go on in.

The seas were rough that night. The rubber kayaks were catapulted into the waves from the submarine and some were dunked. Finally they made the house, and the Frenchmen who were to rendezvous with them were there. These negotiations with the French would have been difficult enough in a quiet diplomatic chancellery. They were frightful under the conspiratorial atmosphere of the hostile coast. The Vichy government was operating in Southern France, also trying to get control of the French fleet which Admiral Jean Darlan still had under his command in Africa. Wayne's job was to win at least neutrality from this fleet and from the French ground forces if and when a landing was made.

The talks were interrupted. Someone had spotted footsteps on the sand and told the police. Word was flashed to the house that the French police were on their way. The Americans hid in a wine cellar. Robert D. Murphy, from the American Consulate in Algiers, and the owner of the house, Mr. Teissier, stayed upstairs and pretended they were having a drunken party.

The police still were suspicious. They looked almost everywhere, in the closets, under the beds. But they didn't lift that trap door. Finally they left, but unconvinced. It was decided that despite rough seas, an effort should be made to get back to the submarine. The first effort failed as the rubber boats capsized in the surging surf. Wayne had stripped down to his shorts and shirt just in case he had to swim. He even took off his money belt with several hundred dollars' worth of gold. He lost his gold and his pants when the kayak capsized.

The men got back to shore and hid in the woods until nearly dawn, when they made their second try to reach the submarine. This time they were successful and started back for England and safety.

The mission had been accomplished. They had obtained the invaluable information necessary to the success of an Allied invasion.

I had been given a hint that something was in the wind, something dangerous, but had no clue as to what it was.

The word, when it came, came from General Marshall himself.

106

Throughout the war years General Marshall as Chief of Staff was a great comfort to the wives and families of the officers he knew personally. Despite the terrible burden of responsibility and his work as Chief of Staff of one big war in Europe and another in the Pacific, he always tried to find the time to pass along word of the officers to their families. He made me and many other wives feel that our Army had a heart and soul and that our husbands were something more than mere numbers dropped into the slot for which their training fitted them.

Just about the time that Wayne left on his hazardous mission, General Marshall telephoned me at my apartment. He told me only that I was not to be too concerned if I didn't get a letter from Wayne for a little while. That was all. I was given absolutely no clue. A million questions popped into my mind. The very tone of General Marshall's voice made me realize that something big, awfully big, was in the wind. But the tone of his voice also let me know that I could ask every one of my million questions without getting a single answer. I had been told all it was intended for me to know, and I simply thanked General Marshall for his consideration.

A few days later he telephoned again. This time he told me the whole story—that the terrifying mission was completed and successful, and Wayne back on friendly soil. Then, after giving me all sorts of details about the mission, General Marshall said very seriously I was to reveal the story to no one. He specifically mentioned my mother, who was with me in Washington; Wayne's mother, who was close to us; Ann, and Bill.

It was a small bit of torture for me to restrain myself from shouting from the rooftops about Wayne's adventure. I was so proud of him. And I was so happy that he was back and safe. But I couldn't breathe a word of it to a soul.

General Marshall made it very clear that it was a secret that simply had to be kept, adding that it had not yet been decided whether the story would be made public ever. I didn't try to figure out why. All I could think of was that I had to keep this great big proud story locked up in my heart, secret even from my own mother and my own children. It was most difficult to keep from blurting out the whole thing to my mother, there in the apartment with me, but I didn't.

Fortunately for me I didn't have to keep silent very long. The day after General Marshall told me the story, it was released to the world.

I was so excited and thrilled. But I no longer had a cozy, quiet, peaceful apartment in which to live. From that day on, privacy was one of the most difficult things for me to achieve.

Although the story, as told to me by General Marshall, thrilled me to the core, it was not until some time later that I fully realized what a tremendous emotional experience it was for Wayne. He is not given to overdramatizing himself or his experiences, but this one really got him. He showed it in a letter given to his aide to be delivered to me only in the event that Wayne did not return from the submarine trip. It was later Wayne sent it on to me. It was perhaps the most sentimental letter he ever wrote me.

The letter said:

Darling Sweetheart—
I am leaving in twenty minutes on a mission which I volunteered to do when it was suggested that a general officer do it.

If I succeed and return I will have done a fine deed for my coun- and the Allied cause. Of course you know my life is dedicated to military service and now that my opportunity has come for that service I go forward proud of the opportunity which has been given me.

If I do not return know that I loved you and our Bill and Ann. Only one request I make. You have been an angel on earth to me— continue being that and do everything you possibly can for our Allied cause. Only in so doing will you find solace, and only by all so doing, will Victory be won.

God bless and keep you.

Wayne.

Shortly after the submarine trip to North Africa was splashed over the newspapers and while people were still talking about it as one of the more melodramatic personal exploits of the war, Mrs.

Roosevelt invited me to the White House for luncheon. There was a fairly large guest list, so large that Mrs. Roosevelt, the gracious and accomplished hostess, carried a lightweight little stool with her so that she could move about the room freely and sit down with each of the several groups and join in their conversation.

When Mrs. Roosevelt joined our group, she told me she had met Wayne at a dinner in London on the night after his return from the submarine trip. The trip still was a secret then, and in addition to Wayne, Ambassador Winant and Mrs. Roosevelt were the only ones there among all those well-informed people who knew about it. Mrs. Roosevelt said she had been impressed with the way Wayne kept his secret that night. Not only did he not mention it, but Mrs. Roosevelt said she had noticed particularly how poised and at ease he was. No one in the room who did not already know about the North African adventure could possibly have guessed, she said, that he had done anything more exciting than desk work for months.

Wayne and his companions on the North African trip learned enough to convince them that the landing could be made according to the plans being developed in London and that the French, by and large, would assist the Allies to land. At least, Wayne later told me, he found out what French elements in the Army, Navy, and Air Force would oppose the landings.

The war was stepping up, the Army getting bigger and stronger. In November, Wayne participated in the landings in North Africa and Ike flew to Algiers and pinned the three stars of a lieutenant general on Wayne's shoulder in a ceremony at the airfield.

Each time Wayne did something himself, like the trip to North Africa, or each time his Army won a new victory, the newsmen and photographers would flock to my apartment to try to get a story and pictures. Wives were good copy in those war years. I saw as few of these newsmen as possible. For one thing I wasn't fighting a war. I didn't like publicity in the paper. Like so many wives of generals whose names were daily in print, I felt it was the woman's place to remain in the background as much as possible. It was difficult. The press were a fine, considerate group but they had a job to do, an assignment to carry out, and in devious ways they would catch one unawares. One evening there was a knock on the door and I was surprised to find a photographer there, asking for permission to get a picture story of me. I was surprised because newsmen were supposed to be stopped short of my door. I never did learn how this man got my apartment number.

He was a real character. He brought me a present to try to win my favor. As soon as I opened the door in answer to his knock he thrust a great wet package at me, saying, "Mrs. Clark, I brought you some lobsters." There were four of them, all alive and squirming.

The photographer knew his business. He talked so fast and so persuasively and with such a pleasing tone to his voice that I let him in. But I didn't want the live lobsters. I explained I was going out to dinner that evening and that I thought it would be better if he took the lobsters home. I went into detail. In my tiny kitchen I didn't even have the utensils needed to prepare the lobsters nor a pot large enough to boil them in. He had no interest whatever in the lobsters, of course, and to change the conversation and get on with his job of getting a picture of me, he agreed quickly, and I put the wet package on the kitchen floor so it wouldn't mess up the house.

Then I answered his questions and he got his story and pictures and took off, leaving the lobsters which I, too, forgot until after he had gone. When I remembered, I went to the kitchen and tried vainly to stuff the package, lobsters and all, into my garbage pail, but it was too small. By this time I was running so far behind schedule that I had to rush to get dressed and away to keep my dinner appointment. The lobsters were still on the kitchen floor.

Hours later I returned home, tired and ready for bed. I went to the kitchen for a glass of water, not even bothering to turn on the kitchen light.

Something cold touched my foot.

I froze with fright. For an instant I could not imagine what had grabbed me. Then I remembered. The lobsters! They had worked through the paper wrapping and were crawling all over my kitchen floor. I turned on the light and the kitchen seemed to be alive with those horrible crawling things.

Interviews and photographers were the easiest of the things we wives faced in the war. For me the hardest was making speeches. Bea Patton, wife of the colorful and brilliant Gen. George Patton, worked on me for quite a while before she persuaded me to make speeches to sell bonds. I had never spoken to an audience in my life, and the very thought of it sent nervous chills down my back. But Bea kept after me and finally I agreed to go with her to a big meeting in Boston.

There were hundreds in the audience and it looked like thousands to me. Bea went on first, and that did me no good. She was an accomplished public speaker, assured, effective, and smooth. As I listened to her polished delivery I became more and more convinced that I had made a mistake, that I would at best be a flop and at worst make a fool of myself. Minute by minute as Bea continued I became more and more frightened. I wanted to run, faint, anything but stand up before that audience, which by this time looked to me like a mob of hungry wolves waiting to devour me.

I was well prepared. That speech was so well memorized I could have delivered it backward—in my living room with no one to hear. But I might just as well have never given it a single reading. My name was called and people applauded and somebody literally pushed me forward from the row sitting on the stage. I stood looking out into that sea of faces and my mind went blank. I couldn't remember a single word of that speech.

But I did have the written speech with me, clutched in my hands. It was a precaution against which I had been warned. Speakers speak, they don't read, I had been told. A few notes maybe, but not a written speech, not a text.

All this I had to ignore when the applause died down and it was up to me to do something. I did. The fun and humor came back into our lives right there in public, with all those people to see.

I couldn't read without my glasses. My glasses were in the purse I held in one hand. The speech was in the other hand. I shifted the purse to my left hand, which held the speech, and fumbling around inside the purse with my free hand, I got the glasses all right, but had difficulty getting them out of their case, an operation not designed for one hand.

It seemed I was using up an awful lot of time and that everyone in the audience must think this a weird performance, so once I got the glasses free of the case and the case back in the purse I tried to put the glasses on too fast.

They tangled in my veil. I tried to yank them free. Veil, hat, and one earring fell to the floor.

It was so terrible and so ridiculous and I had made such a fool of myself that I got a little hysterical. I laughed. I laughed right in the faces of all those people. To me they will always stand out as the kindest people in the world. They laughed too, with me, not at me. Somehow the friendly, sympathetic spirit of their laugh broke through my hysterics and put me on an even keel. I was able to begin to talk.

The first thing I said was that I was scared to death, an unnecessary explanation of the obvious if there ever was one. Then, almost defiantly, I tore up my speech before their eyes and in my own words, unrehearsed, told them why I thought they should buy war bonds. It was far from being a creditable performance. In fact it was a poor speech, hesitant, ill-phrased, and pulled together loosely. But I think the people understood, sympathized, and were friendly. I may not have helped the bond drive, but I don't think I really hurt it too much that afternoon.

That night Bea Patton took me in hand. She talked to me for hours. Forget self—think of your audience and subject. Be relaxed, else the people listening won't be, and so forth. She convinced me I should continue to make speeches. Without her guidance and inspiration I never would have made another public talk.

As it was, I talked five nights a week for nine months in 1943, nine months in 1944, and five months in 1945. It was a roadshow, a new city each night, a one-hour talk in each city.

Bandleader Glenn Miller was in our bond-selling team, alone, without his band. It was a strange thing. With his band behind him Glenn Miller was poised and in complete command of his audience when he talked. But on stage alone, without that band behind him, he was nervous. It was as though a necessary prop had been removed. Often before his speech he would tell me how nervous he was, and perspiration would stand out on his forehead as he spoke and his hand would shake as he reached for a handkerchief to wipe his brow.

Glenn also missed his wife terribly on those trips and often would say how he wished he had been able to bring her along. Regardless of his inner feeling, he always gave a fine talk, and his kind, sweet nature communicated itself to his audience. People all loved Glenn Miller.

Once I asked Glenn why he appeared on stage alone, without his band and without his wife in the wings to cheer him on. He replied that he felt everyone should contribute what he could, the best he could, to the war effort; when he was asked to make speeches to sell bonds, therefore, he could not refuse. Actually his timidity before an audience helped sell bonds, for it made him speak so simply and so sincerely that he had a tremendous appeal.

I didn't mind the speech making after I got used to it, but I didn't like living out of a suitcase month in, month out. After a while the whole thing was as familiar as a stuck phonograph record.

One night, for instance, after I had been on the tours for about two years, I was to appear before several thousand students at a large coed university. The university president sat next to me and introduced me. By this time I had been introduced something like 350 times and had developed the bad habit of just not listening. I paid no attention at all to what he was saying and didn't even notice when he finished.

The president, fully expecting me to rise and take his place at the rostrum, backed to sit down, missed his direction, and sat in my lap!

The students roared with laughter. But the president rose to the occasion by telling the students, "You see, I make mistakes, the same as you."

CHAPTER   EIGHT

THE WAR CRASHED ON. IN THE LATE SUMMER of 1943 the United States Fifth Army which Wayne commanded stormed the Italian beaches at Salerno to begin the grueling and costly march toward Rome, a march that wasn't over until early June of 1944. Wayne never told me so in so many words, but I believe the capture of Rome was the high point of his military career. At least on our garden wall in Charleston, South Carolina, today is a big bullet-pocked blue and white metal sign that says ROMA. The sign was the one Wayne stopped by as he crossed into the city limits of Rome. The city authorities later gave it to him as a reminder of the Fifth Army's day of triumph.

But like any soldier in the midst of history and great events, Wayne was troubled occasionally by more normal little concerns. He wrote that he found some drawbacks in high command position. He had a trailer which for a long time was his office and home while he campaigned in Italy, and when things were quiet some of his staff officers would sometimes drop around in the evening to spin yarns or relax at cards. But after he got high rank Wayne wrote to me: "The more stars a man gets, the more lonesome he becomes." He complained that "they used to come around in the evening, but they don't any more." Then I got to the punch line: "I wish, Renie, you would send me Pal."

The question of Pal had come up before. In North Africa after he got his third star, Wayne had dabbled with the idea of having the cocker spaniel sent over from Washington but rejected it. This time, however, Wayne was serious. He wanted that dog.

To me, the little black cocker spaniel was the one living bridge I had with the family, with the happy days before the war. He was my constant companion when I was not on the road trying to sell bonds. He also was a comfort to my mother, alone in the apartment while I was on the road speaking. But Wayne's plea was irresistible and I agreed to part with Pal.

Almost immediately the sting of the impending loss of Pal was wiped out by overwhelmingly joyous news. Wayne was coming home for a few days to report his plans for a spring offensive. For the first time in almost two years I was to see him again. Every woman whose loved one went to war knows the thrill that comes with word that her man is returning home.

The flight Wayne made to Washington in April of 1944 was his first trip home in just short of two years. It was a secret trip. It had to be. If the Germans had learned the commanding general of the Fifth Army had flown home to talk with the President and the Chief of Staff, they would have been forewarned to get ready for something big.

It was such a secret trip that the landing was timed for the early morning hours, about 3 A.M. at Bolling Field, the military air base across the Potomac River from Washington. General Marshall sent an aide out to meet Wayne. No other military man was there. No high-ranking officer was permitted to go out to welcome Wayne because the Army wanted his movements to be as inconspicuous as possible.

The Army and General Marshall still had a heart, though. The general arranged for me to be at Bolling that early morning. I was all dressed up in my very best suit, as fluttery as a schoolgirl. Under General Marshall's instructions, I sat in the back of a closed automobile, staying out of sight so that there would be no chance for anyone to spot me. In wartime the Army was most sensitive to the gossip that spread through the service clubs and snack bars about the comings and goings of generals and their wives.

The big plane landed and Wayne was rushed to the car. I was a little shocked. He looked so thin and tense and tired. And he looked haggard. I had never seen him look like that before. His face, usually so full and handsome, was drawn tight and hard. He wore his olive-drab field shirt and trousers, his combat boots, and the green scarf which had been adopted as part of the uniform for the men of the Fifth Army headquarters.

It was overcast and chilly that early April morning and when the door was opened for Wayne to get into the car a cold blast of air came with him. But a remarkable thing seemed to happen to him in the car. It seemed, as he sat back beside me, that I could almost see the strain and tenseness leave him. He was home. And in my way, I felt I was home, too.

Who can recall the words of such reunions? I can't. I know we said nothing at all about the war. I know that he wanted to learn all he could, all at once, about the children, about his mother, about my mother, and about me.

And I know the words did not come to us in the old easy manner. There was a strained sort of strangeness between us, something neither of us had ever experienced before, not, at least, since that first blind date so terribly long before.

It was so difficult to bridge the gap of those two long years of separation. We even were a little self-conscious with each other, a little timid. That was not too surprising, and I have heard others say they went through the same experience when their husbands returned from war. After all, we had been oceans apart, literally and figuratively. Our separation was not only geographical but mental, for he had experienced things and dealt with things I could never know about or fully understand.

There were no tears, and as we talked about the things dear to both of us, the strangeness wore off and was replaced with a wonderful happiness and relief from the tension of war and separation. We lived neither in the past nor in the future. We merely grasped the present, minute by minute, the blessed present for which we both were so grateful.

The car whisked us to General Marshall's house at Fort Myer on the other side of Washington in Virginia. Fort Myer was not too far from the Arlington home where Wayne's parents lived when we first met. I thought of that as we rode from Bolling Field.

In the morning, with great secrecy, Wayne was driven to the Pentagon nearby. He even was spirited inside through a secret underground entrance and was taken to General Marshall's office in a private elevator. Every precaution was taken to limit the number of people who saw Wayne on that trip.

The conferences were important. General Marshall had asked Wayne to fly to Washington for consultation before the offensive was renewed to join the Fifth Army troops on the southern front with those who were bottled up at Anzio. Wayne had been given three or four days' notice before the flight, but the final decision had been left up to Wayne: if the battle situation became critical, he would not have to fly home.

What General Marshall and the President wanted was firsthand word on the chances of the Fifth Army's capturing Rome before Eisenhower attempted the cross-channel invasion of France. Wayne told me later that the President and General Marshall were agreed that if the Allies could capture Rome before France was invaded, it would be a big morale boost for Eisenhower's forces and the French people, and might also chip away a bit at the German troop morale in France and the enthusiasm of the French collaborators.

Wayne showed the President and the general his full plans for the campaign against Rome. As it turned out, the Fifth Army captured Rome two days before the invasion of Normandy, but that was almost two months after Wayne's secret trip to Washington.

In Washington everything was so rushed and businesslike I hardly had time to see Wayne alone. I felt quite sorry for myself, left out and neglected for this war business even when Wayne was with me. For a while I felt he might just as well have been in Italy for all the attention he was able to pay me.

But General Marshall made me feel ashamed of these thoughts after the conferences were concluded. He gave Wayne a few days off and the Army sent us to the Greenbrier Hotel at White Sulphur Springs, West Virginia. The government had taken over the hotel for use as a hospital, and the Army felt Wayne could spend a few days there without being detected.

It was a wonderful break in the loneliness of the war. Mother Clark was with us and so was Ann, and we had a private cottage in the beautiful green grounds of the hospital. Bill couldn't get away from West Point and my mother was temporarily in the hospital and unable to join us.

Wayne and I had wonderful talks together planning for the future. Wayne said he thought it would be good to retire and devote as much time as he could to fishing. We talked about Camano Island and how glorious it would be to settle into the quiet life there.

While we were there, Wayne borrowed some golf clubs and played a little on the fine Greenbrier course. The course was in good shape, tended by Germans from a nearby prisoner-of-war camp, but it had been a long time since Wayne had played. And that caused a little incident. Some of the German prisoners were working on the green of a water hole when Wayne reached it, and they stepped off the green to let him shoot.

The first drive went into the water.

So did the second and the third.

The German prisoners roared with laughter.

When Wayne came back, he said, simply, "I'm sorry I took those guys prisoners in Italy."

For those short days at White Sulphur Springs there seemed to be no war. That was something far away and unreal, something we tried so hard to put out of our minds for just that little while. But this pleasant time was broken by a call for Wayne to fly down to South Carolina alone, to talk with President Roosevelt at the home of Bernard Baruch. Mother Clark, Ann, and I went back to Washington, and when Wayne returned, there was more

My mother and I. Taken in Muncie when I was twelve.

At the wheel of our old Buick in Indianapolis with Ann and Bill in the back seat.

Ann and Bill in Indianapolis in 1933.

Wayne in front of our house at Fort Benning, 1924.

*This is probably our most famous picture. It was taken at the
Chicago Airport on Wayne's return from Europe, May 30, 1945.
(International News Photo)*

Wayne and I on the train leaving Vienna on our way to Moscow, 1947.

TOP RIGHT: *Ann and Gordon, Fort Monroe, 1952.*

BOTTOM RIGHT: *Bill and Audrey, just married, New Orleans, 1954.*

In Rome, 1948.

The family together in San Francisco. Ann and her husband on the left; Audrey and Bill on the right.

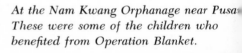

My arrival in Tokyo in a pouring rain.

At the Nam Kwang Orphanage near Pusa: These were some of the children who benefited from Operation Blanket.

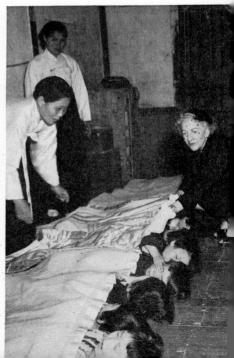

Wayne's and my good friend
Yoshi with her grandfather
at tea at our house in Tokyo.

Yong Dong Po, Korea. Wayne
being greeted by Col. L. H.
Ginn, while I talk to Gen.
James Van Fleet, commanding
general of the Eighth Army.

This got to be a familiar routine for Wayne and me. Here we are landing at Saigon.

business waiting for him. General Marshall wanted Wayne to meet secretly with a few carefully chosen members of Congress.

After that Wayne was permitted to spend twenty-four hours with me in my apartment. He was a virtual prisoner there. General Marshall stage-managed the whole thing. Wayne was taken to the Kennedy-Warren Apartments, where I lived, in the morning. He entered through a basement door in the alley. A Secret Service man, who had taken over the elevator from the regular operator, rushed Wayne up to my apartment and made certain no one else saw him. Once inside the door, Wayne was a prisoner, under strict Army orders not to leave that apartment. No visitors were to be allowed, and under no circumstances was he to answer the telephone unless I first made certain it was General Marshall or one of the few others who knew he was in town.

Finally the time came for him to leave, and the same precautions were taken to keep his departure secret. This time I was not permitted to go with him to the airport and we had to say our farewells in the apartment. As I look back, the extra hour we could have had going to the airport does not seem like much, but at the time it loomed like a terribly important thing I was losing. Like every wartime wife, I treasured each fleeting minute that I could steal my husband from the war.

And now I was more alone than ever. For this time Pal went with Wayne, flying to Italy with him in the airplane Lt. Gen. Ira Eakers had lent Wayne for the flight. Through the rest of the war Pal was with Wayne constantly, sitting at his feet when he worked at his desk, riding with him in the open jeep, scampering around him when he trudged through the Italian mud on foot. Pal has long since gone, but we have a new Pal now, a golden cocker spaniel, and the new Pal, like the old, goes to work every day with Wayne and sits in his office all day. That's where he wants to be. The few times Wayne left him at home, he was a fussy, crabby dog, not nice to have around the house at all.

The new Pal came to us when we were in Japan and lonely for a dog. We wrote to our dear friend Ansel Robison who owns the House of Pets on Maiden Lane in San Francisco asking him to ship us a cocker puppy. He did and this is our present Pal No. 2.

After Pal No. 1 flew off to Italy with Wayne I felt quite good about my sacrifice. I felt that I was lucky to have been able to help Wayne just a little bit by giving up something he wanted very much, something I greatly missed.

I felt good, that is, until I saw a picture in the newspaper. General Marshall was trying to inspire interest in the Women's Army Corps to encourage enlistments. He asked his commanders all over the world to do what they could to publicize the WACs. He suggested that the commanders have their pictures taken with some of the women already in uniform and overseas, and so Wayne had himself and Pal photographed with a WAC secretary.

It happened that General Marshall telephoned me the very day I saw that picture. I told him about the picture and said jokingly:

"I gave up that dog because Wayne said he was lonely. I don't mind Wayne helping the WACs with their publicity. But General, I don't see why Wayne's secretary has to pet *my* dog."

I can still see that picture—that WAC petting my dog, with Wayne sitting nearby. I still don't like that picture.

With Wayne back in Italy, I returned to the dreary wartime routine. The bond-selling speeches were resumed. There were happy Sunday afternoons with Ann and her friends. There were the trips to West Point to see Bill and the visits we had together in New York.

One of these I shall never forget. *Oklahoma!* was the smash hit on Broadway. With a great deal of effort I arranged to get two seats for it on a night that Bill could get permission to leave West Point. There were precious little time on those trips. He would arrive in time for dinner and would have to board a train about an hour after the theater.

But spending an evening with Bill always was a bright, happy break in the bleak years of my war loneliness. This night we met in New York and I took Bill to a big steak dinner. It was a gay meal and we both bubbled with happiness. Then to the theater and a frightful shock. The friend who got the tickets for *Oklahoma!* for us had done his very best, and it was quite a feat to get tickets for that show that year. But at the theater we discovered to my dismay that the best the friend had been able to do was to get one ticket for one side of the house and another ticket for the other. Instead of enjoying *Oklahoma!* happily with my son, I had to sit through it alone, separated from him by what seemed to be at least a thousand people. After the show we did get together, but by then there was just time to rush off to the railroad station and put Bill on the last train for West Point.

To me one night was the symbol of the war years for the wives left behind. It was New Year's Eve, December 31, 1943. I gave a dinner party in my apartment in Washington for thirteen other women whose husbands were overseas, many with Wayne in Italy. Included at the party were the wives of Generals Lesley McNair, Richard Moran, Edwin Howard, and Al Gruenther and the wife of Colonel Coburn Smith, among others.

I had been subjected to social failures before, but never really one like this. Part of the failure was mechanical. I prepared a chocolate ice-box cake and covered it with whipped evaporated milk. Whipping cream was impossible to obtain during the war, but the evaporated milk seemed a good substitute and everything looked lovely when I put it in the refrigerator.

But it didn't look lovely when I took it out. I was horrified. The whipped milk had melted and my lovely chocolate cake, looking messed and a little dirty, was floating in it.

That was but a minor part of my failure, however. The war, the mood, the loneliness created the real failure. We all had thought it would be so nice to be together to see in the New Year—or so it seemed on the gay, happy afternoons when we made our plans.

The party started off gaily enough, just as we thought it would. We all tried so hard to be brave and to cheer up one another. After all, that was what the party was for. But somehow, as the evening wore on, the spirit went with it. Almost as soon as dinner was over, one woman made a self-conscious excuse and left. Then another and still another bowed out as gracefully as possible. It was painful because nobody wanted to hurt anyone's feelings that night, but each woman was brimful of memories, tender memories, that fairly forced her to get away from her friends and be alone. As the hour of midnight grew closer each of us felt less like having a party and more like having a good cry.

By midnight I was alone. The lights were dimmer so I didn't notice the half-empty dishes and the cluttered buffet table. I sat in a chair by the window and looked out across the city. But I didn't see the city. I saw other New Year's Eves and other rooms and Wayne following that grand old custom of elbowing and pushing his way through the crowd to reach me in time to give me the traditional and wonderful Happy New Year kiss just at the stroke of twelve.

Wayne's letters helped me keep my chin up. Although he hated writing letters, he did a good job during the war, when he felt he had to. He couldn't write of his plans or much about the course of battles, but he gave me the chitchat, the little things that helped me build a picture of how he lived and how he was and felt.

He liked to write me about people I knew. There were a whole series of letters about Sgt. Bill Cheney, the good soldier who had dropped his broom in my kitchen and never stopped to pick it up when he was told he was going to England to join Wayne. Cheney served Wayne faithfully and loyally all through North Africa and Italy, and Wayne often wrote about him and his problems. Once Cheney knocked on the door of Wayne's trailer late at night to ask help in a problem. The story unfolded in a series of letters.

That first night he told Wayne that he had just received a letter from the War Department. The Department said its records indicated there had been overpayment of his allotments.

Wayne went to work on the problem. For one thing, he was extremely fond of Cheney. For another, he welcomed a chance to work on a problem that was different from his regular routine. The War Department asked why he should not repay the government. Wayne helped Cheney prepare a reply which, although not satisfactory, would put the whole matter in litigation and delay the evil day when Cheney had to pay up.

Cheney was unfamiliar with the word "litigation" and asked what it meant. Wayne told him that litigation meant delaying the reply as long as he could.

Another letter told me what happened. Cheney took Wayne literally. He stuffed the letter in an Italian mail box he found smashed and lying by the side of a road.

That did it. Within three months Cheney got a second, and very harsh, letter from the War Department. Cheney went to Wayne again for help. Wayne was stuck completely this time and had to tell Cheney that "the day" had arrived and he would have to pay back the government. Cheney was crushed—and broke. But soon afterward Wayne wrote that he had promoted Cheney to master sergeant.

Wayne never would admit it, probably, but I have always been sure he promoted Cheney so he could get enough of a pay boost to pay off his debt to the government.

CHAPTER NINE

I N THE SPRING OF 1945 THERE WAS A MARKED change in Wayne's letters, a happy change, for it seemed that he was writing from a conviction that victory was close at hand and that the war would soon be over. He never said just that, but there were two things about his letters that gave the tip-off. For one thing there were fewer letters during the last weeks before the German surrender. At first this annoyed me, but gradually I came to realize that he was so busy in the final cleanup days of the war that he just didn't have time to write.

Then the tone of his letters and the things he talked about changed. His final war letters were filled with talk of the future, of Camano Island, retirement, and fishing. He began to ask more questions about what I wanted to do when he came home, and I knew he felt the time of home-coming was not far distant.

His happier mood could have been due to his personal success within the Army. In quick succession in the winter of 1944 and the spring of 1945 he was given signal honors. In the winter he was made commanding general of the Fifteenth Army Group, which meant all the ground forces of all Allied nations in Italy. In the spring he got his fourth star, the insignia of a full general. Wayne's chief of staff, Al Gruenther, pinned the four stars on his collar.

But I did not think this personal advance was the cause of his more happy and optimistic mood. It seemed to me certain that Wayne felt the war in Italy was just about over.

The newspapers, too, carried strong evidence that the Germans were through. Allied armies everywhere were crashing through German lines and chasing German troops faster than ever before.

Wayne's letters during this period were brief, hurried notes. He apologized and said he was frantic with work. He asked me if I would be happy living on Camano Island, away from city life, apart from friends, out of the social whirl that had become such a big part of our lives in later prewar years.

My heart was light with hope from those questions. I wrote that I would be happy, overjoyed, to live anywhere he desired, to do anything he wanted to do, even if that was only to go fishing. "I will be blissfully happy," I wrote him, "if only we are together."

Then came a note from Wayne which plunged my heart once again into the depths. Wayne said that once the fighting was over in Europe he would request reassignment to the Pacific if the war was still going on there. He explained as considerately as he could that he had thought it over carefully and felt he should go— that he wanted to go. To me that sounded like beginning a whole new war all over again. I had followed the Pacific war news in the newspapers and through the radio, of course, but with my husband in Italy I had paid far more attention to the European side of the fighting. From a family viewpoint—and I suppose all wives must view war from a family viewpoint—I couldn't see that Wayne had any responsibility for the war in the Pacific and, selfishly, felt he had no business even thinking about it.

Then came the great news. On May 3, 1945, the Germans in Italy surrendered. Prepared as I was by Wayne's letters, I still experienced such great feelings of joy and relief that I thought my heart would burst.

I was alone in my apartment when I heard the first word on the radio, but bedlam broke all around me almost before the announcement was completed. The telephone began to ring and it never stopped, day or night for days on end. Friends called just to talk and laugh and share their joy with me. Reporters called for interviews. Photographers clamored for pictures. It was all wonderful and joyous and busy and exciting, but it became more than I could take. I had to get away. Gen. and Mrs. Robert Daniels, those fine, considerate friends, saw the strain and finally broke it. They urged me to go with them to West Point to "see our boys." We did. It was soothing to get away from the victory bustle of Washington and reach the quiet of the little town on the Hudson. Bill was happy for Dad and for his country, but I seemed to detect a little touch of disappointment that he had missed the war.

And always, during the bustle in Washington and the quiet of West Point, there was the nagging fear that Wayne would go out to the Pacific to serve under his father's old friend, Gen. Douglas MacArthur, in another war that most people in Washington thought was going to go on for another year and a half or so.

But then came joyous news again. Wayne was coming home. The war in Italy was won and the War Department ordered him to fly back to the United States to attend a victory celebration in Chicago. He had lived in Chicago as a small boy and had gone to school at Highland Park nearby. Wayne selected a group of Fifth Army veterans, mostly from the Chicago area, to come back from Italy with him for the celebration.

There was one fly in the ointment this time. Shortly before Wayne returned, he wrote that during the war years he hoped I had saved some money. He wondered how much. Would it buy a house if he retired? Wayne had sent me a most liberal allowance all through the war. He needed next to nothing in the field so most of his pay came to me. Perhaps he had the idea that I had been able to save most of it.

I knew he could not realize how much it cost to live in the United States in wartime, how prices of everything had soared since 1942. I had to explain to him most carefully that Ann's private school cost a considerable amount, that Bill wasn't a little boy any more and that I had to send him money now and then,

126

that the apartment cost a good deal and that food prices were very high, compared to prewar levels.

I had to explain, too, that I had put away quite a lot of money in a separate savings account so that it would be there when we had to have it to pay accrued income taxes for the years Wayne had been away. There also were the government bonds, the war bonds, that I bought regularly and that had to be counted as savings even though they didn't mature for ten years. All this I explained to Wayne most carefully.

After the celebration in Chicago we went to West Point for Bill's graduation. There Wayne handed Bill his diploma and his commission as a second lieutenant in the United States Army. It was a proud day for both of them, and for me. That little ceremony at West Point, with a father being permitted to bestow honors on his son, seemed to me to typify the sentimental values that mean so much to fighting men. I have found not only in my husband but in many other officers with combat experience a great deal of sentiment—and a noticeable and, I think, praiseworthy lack of shame about the expression of it.

Wayne and Bill had not seen each other in the whole time that Bill was at West Point, not since Wayne had gone off to war in 1942, more than three years earlier. They decided to spend that first night after Bill's graduation alone together. They went to New York and had a big steak dinner and talked and talked.

The one part of that conversation Wayne will always remember came at the end of the evening just before they went to bed. Bill, who was twenty and an officer in the United States Army, looked seriously at his father and said, "Gee, Dad, you *have* matured in the last three years since I saw you."

After the Chicago celebration and the reunion with Bill were over, it was my turn to have some of Wayne's time. Mr. and Mrs. Charles Davis, family friends from Muncie days, now living in Chicago, offered us the use of their fine home in Palm Beach, Florida. It was the off season and everything would be quiet and peaceful, just the way we wanted it.

We flew down to Palm Beach to begin our four-day holiday.

The house was in perfect order as the servants were on duty all year round, even in the off season. The government supplied us a sedan and a jeep and we were all set.

One evening while we were lounging around the house Wayne suggested we go for a ride. "Let's not take the sedan," he said; "let's take the jeep and I'll drive." It was so warm and balmy that a ride along the beach in an open jeep sounded like just the thing, and off we went. I was wearing slacks and looking, I guess, like the cartoonists' idea of the typical American tourist. Wayne wore his o.d. trousers and shirt but without insignia.

We got some popcorn and put the bag on the seat between us. Finally Wayne took off his cap and put it in his lap.

It was delightful to drive along the beach in the evening air, eating popcorn, laughing, joking, and once again forgetting the hated war.

But something else intervened to break the spell of our little idyl. It was a siren. I don't remember ever hearing so harsh a sound.

The next sound we heard was the screeching brakes, as a Military Police jeep pulled us over to the side of the road. The MPs alighted and walked over to our jeep.

"You've got a government vehicle and a dame in it," the toughest of the soldiers snapped. "Let's see your trip ticket."

In the Army, of course, nobody is supposed to drive a military vehicle without a trip ticket that says who gave the authority for the use of the jeep. The soldier was being very thorough and went on to ask for Wayne's driver's permit—another military paper Wayne should have had.

He had neither permit nor trip tricket, of course. But he did have his four-star overseas cap on the seat beside him. He popped it on his head quietly, but fast, while the MPs were digging in their jeep for the forms on which they planned to charge Wayne with every violation in the book. They got the forms, turned back to us, and stopped dead in their tracks, openmouthed.

Four stars!

Before he could think, the first soldier, who had done all the talking, blurted out, "Good Lord!" and then, really frightened, slapped a hand over his mouth. He made a valiant effort to recover what he could from a bad situation by saying, "I didn't recognize you, sir."

Wayne smiled at the boy's predicament and said, "You're on your toes. I'll commend you to your commanding officer."

The MPs seemed doubtful of that promise, but were happy enough to get away from Wayne.

Next day Wayne did call their commanding officer and commend them. "Please tell them I called you," Wayne said.

Later the commanding officer called back and reported, "I wish you had been here to see those lads, sir. They were scared stiff when I called them in. They thought they were going to be torn apart for arresting you. They were completely floored when I told them of your commendation."

It was so much easier to part with Wayne after this visit than it had been the year before. This time he was not going back to war. And, more than anything else, this time he was not going to be away from me for long. Unless, of course, he went out to fight the Japanese.

I kept telling myself he wouldn't. I kept telling myself they needed him in Europe or maybe he would retire, but that he would not go out to fight in the Orient.

Bill went with Wayne on the flight back to Italy. Bill was a second lieutenant on leave, a disgruntled young officer who got his commission just too late to fight in Europe.

But he still was eager. Somewhere he got the idea that General MacArthur planned to send the paratroops into Japan in the first part of the anticipated invasion. Bill thought if he could get into the paratroops he would have a good chance of getting into combat. So he volunteered for paratroop duty and after he returned from his leave in Italy went into training.

Wayne's letters from Italy had a new kind of importance for me after the fighting was over. I opened each new letter with a special type of anticipation. For one of those letters was going to spell out my future, our future. There were two possibilities.

Either he would retire and we would go fishing on Camano Island or he would go to the Pacific and I would stay on in my lonely apartment in Washington. I knew those were the only two possibilities because they were the only two Wayne had talked about.

But there was a third and completely unexpected possibility, and that was the one that came true. It would be neither Camano nor the Pacific, but Vienna. Wayne wrote that he was to be United States High Commissioner there.

And the happiest line of all was that as soon as the War Department gave the green light and dependents were permitted to join their husbands, Ann and I would go to Vienna to join him. Three-fourths of the family, at least, would be together again, a joy for which I had not dared to hope back in the uneasy days of 1942 when our home was broken up by the war.

My happiness at the end of the war and the certainty of rejoining Wayne was a tainted one, however. My mother, who had been such a comfort and solace to me through those dreary years of the war, was desperately ill in a sanitorium in Washington. By midsummer of 1945 she no longer could recognize me when I visited her.

Then came an invitation for a reunion with Wayne under the most exciting and romantic circumstances. The Brazilian government invited us both to Rio de Janeiro as guests of the state during the national holiday to welcome the first Brazilian combat troops back from Italy, where they had fought under Wayne in the Fifth Army. General Marshall gave me all the details of the trip and urged me to go. I wanted to go very badly to see Wayne, for it was a chance to be with him much earlier than I had hoped. But I didn't want to leave Mother and hesitated to make the decision. I asked her doctors for advice, and Ann, Bill, and General Marshall. Each one urged me to go. The doctors pointed out that Mother no longer recognized me and that there was nothing I could do to help her. They all said my place was with my husband.

At last I decided to accept the Brazilian invitation. General Marshall arranged for me to fly to Miami in his own airplane.

Officers met me there and took me to dinner and then out to the airport to board a C-54 transport plane at 10 P.M. to continue the flight to Rio.

All the planning was precise. The Brazilian government had arranged the schedule so that I would arrive at Rio ten minutes after Wayne. Together we were to take part in the tremendous welcome Brazil had scheduled for its returning soldiers—the first Brazilian soldiers ever to go overseas to fight for Brazil. The Brazilians are a romantic, sentimental people and they wanted to share in the moment that Wayne and I were reunited, the moment when we met for the first time since the war was won. They wanted to see us together, out in the open at the airport, when we greeted each other.

But the best-laid plans often go awry. The C-54 flying me from Miami lost a motor in the middle of the night. We were forced to land at Atkinson Field, Georgetown, British Guiana. A new motor had to be flown down from Miami and I was a whole day late reaching Rio.

Under any other circumstances I would have welcomed the chance to spend some time at Atkinson Field, and in memory I now cherish that brief interlude which was so foreign to anything that ever happened to me before or since. The Air Corps commanding officer was a bachelor. I had never met him before but he was most considerate and thoughtful. He moved out of his little hut in the wilderness, a hut that was set high upon stilts, native fashion, and let me sleep there. At dawn I was awakened by the beautiful songs of myriads of jungle birds.

As it grew lighter I stood by the window watching those exotic birds with their gorgeous plumage fly among the trees and strut along the rich ground. It was real jungle. Monkeys abounded. I was fascinated to watch them play and listen to their constant chatter.

The motor arrived from Miami and was installed in our airplane and my jungle idyl was over, none too soon for me. Wayne was at the airport at Rio when my airplane landed. Brazilian dignitaries were flanking him on both sides. And behind them were hundreds and hundreds of the curious, whose interest had been whetted by the newspaper stories of my delay in Georgetown.

I always shuddered when photographers took pictures of our reunions during the war. To me those first moments belonged to Wayne and me and nobody else. Certainly the emotion was far too deep to be the subject of a public spectacle. But in Rio that day there was no way to avoid it. The people were on a holiday and were sentimental and this was part of their great day they were not going to miss. I knew what was going to happen, although not in precise detail. Wayne is so tall and strong that whenever he hugs me I either lose my hat or have it knocked out of place and pushed down over one ear or something. The pictures always were ludicrous, but Wayne never cared and the people in Rio, like the people everywhere else, were most understanding.

After the show we put on at the airport we were taken to the beautiful Government House where we were to stay. There were flowers everywhere. Even in my bedroom suite the bedspread was made of orchids, little living wild orchids fastened together in a great coverlet that reached the floor on both sides of the bed. I was so thrilled with my orchid bedspread, but when we returned from dinner, it was gone. I was a little disappointed and never did find out what happened to it. The next day I told Wayne: "Maybe they need it for another visitor later."

We loved Rio. We went boating in the harbor, which certainly is one of the most magnificent in the world. From the boat we felt the full flavor of the beauty of that gently curving clean, sandy beach for which Rio is so justly famed. Never had I seen such an abundance of tropical plants and flowers of such varied and delicate colorings. And the birds, the wonderful birds, filled the air with their songs.

The home-coming festival for the Brazilian troops was a thing to remember always. There were fireworks. There was street dancing. There was music. Brazilians told us it was one of the biggest celebrations in the history of their country, a country which loves celebrations.

The troops arrived by surface transport and formed ranks to

132

parade through the city. Wayne has reviewed many parades but said he never witnessed one like that. Each soldier stayed in line until he saw someone he knew—and no longer. As soon as a soldier saw a familiar face—a mother, a father, a girl friend, a wife— he quit the national celebration to begin a private celebration of his own. It was sheer bedlam, but the happiest, gayest bedlam I ever saw. There was something of an ancient flavor to this home-coming parade, something basic and something admirable. These Brazilian soldiers had done their duty for their country on the battlefields of Italy. Neither they nor the Brazilian populace thought that they owed the further duty of parading in ranks through Rio to put on a show for the home folks. They were willing to help with the parade, but not to the extent of passing by their loved ones.

The crowd was in the same mood. I doubt if any parade ever was held under more difficult conditions. The mothers and wives and sweethearts crowded into the ranks. Sometimes the marching soldiers had to buck their way through a whole sea of crying, laughing, happy feminine faces. As I watched I could understand better the way these people had reacted to my reunion with Wayne at the airport.

From Rio we flew to São Paulo in Brazil for some more re- ceptions and reviews and good-will work. It was there that the long-anticipated and long-feared cablegram arrived. It was from Mother Clark. My little mother had passed on. Mother Clark was most kind. She told me in the cablegram that my mother had not even known I was away, couldn't have known if I had been by her bedside. That helped a little to ease my feeling of guilt.

The cablegram was delivered in the early evening while we were dressing to go to another official dinner. Wayne had to go, but he told me I could stay home and he would make excuses for me. The Brazilians, of course, would understand. They are as sensitive to grief as to joy. I was glad to be left alone in our room, alone with thoughts of that remarkable, wonderful woman who was my mother.

Wayne flew to Vienna to assume his new duties as High Commissioner of Austria, I to Washington. We had no idea when Ann and I would be able to join him. There were complications. He had a big house all ready for us and could have given us the word to go on over. But he wouldn't because he said it would be taking undue advantage of his command position. He said he would not let us go to Vienna until he had enough housing available to permit many of the other wives and families to join their husbands on occupation duty there. And he emphasized that we would not leave the United States until he could open houses for the families of enlisted men as well as officers.

So I went back to my waiting. Bill was at Fort Benning in Georgia, just about ready to leave for the Pacific with the paratroops. Orders actually came through for him. He was to leave late in the third week of August.

As a mother I had no sympathy at all with his eagerness for combat. And on August 14, when word came that the Japanese had surrendered, my heart sang. I was so relieved and happy when I realized there was no war for my son that I picked up the telephone and tried to call him.

The lines were jammed. It wasn't until next day that I was able to reach him. When he answered the telephone, I blurted, "Bill, isn't it wonderful news about Japan?"

He was sour. "What's wonderful about it?" he asked. "I could slit my throat. My whole career is ruined. There's no future in the Army now for a second lieutenant who never got into combat."

If he had been closer I might have tried to spank him. But I realized that he was just like any number of other ambitious young men in the Regular Army, men eager to get a chance to put some good combat experience into their early record.

With our plans for moving so indefinite, we decided Ann should go on with her school work. In September she went to Bloomington to begin her sophomore year at Indiana University. We decided she would stay there until we got word to go to Vienna.

But then came a terrible night. Bloomington telephoned me in Washington. Ann had pneumonia. There was a flu epidemic. All the Bloomington hospitals were crowded. Ann could not stay in her sorority house. The best solution would be to move her to the general hospital at Camp Atterbury, sixty miles away. An ambulance would take her all the way. Would I approve the move? Of course I approved, and then asked a thousand questions. The answers were guarded, inconclusive, the kind that frighten the wits out of people. I so wanted Wayne, so needed his strength and calm good sense. But all I could do was send him a cablegram about Ann. Then I booked passage on the first available airplane and flew to the Middle West.

As soon as I arrived at Atterbury I rushed to Ann's bedside. She was flat on her back. But she looked wonderful. There was no sign of sickness in her face nor in her manner. She was cheerful and we had a good time chatting away.

The Army gave me a neat little cottage on the hospital grounds so that I could live close to Ann. I stayed there almost three weeks. I knew Ann had recovered from pneumonia and wondered why they did not release her. But nobody told me anything.

Finally one morning I was called in for consultation. I went into the room and found five doctors awaiting me. They were terribly solemn, so stern and somber that I got panicky. One of them broke the fearful news.

"Mrs. Clark," he said, "your daughter has tuberculosis. We five have agreed it is necessary she be taken immediately to Fitzsimmons General Hospital in Denver, where we handle all our tuberculosis cases."

We at once boarded the train for Denver. There the tests on Ann began all over again. They went on for two months. In Vienna, Wayne was frantic, and it seemed to me he demanded a full report every day. Only later did I learn how distraught he was.

Wayne had a long talk with Eisenhower in Vienna about it. Ike visited Wayne in Vienna shortly before he left Berlin to go to Washington and become Chief of Staff. It was a farewell visit. Wayne told Ike about Ann and he said if the doctors decided Ann had to stay at Fitzsimmons for any great length of time he was going to go to Denver to be near her. He told Ike he would retire if necessary.

Ike assured Wayne that would not be necessary and said that

if Wayne wanted to be transferred to the States where he could see Ann often, the transfer would be made.

But then a strange thing happened. The doctors in Denver came to me with puzzled expressions on their faces. They said they had given Ann every test known to medicine. Every test was negative. She didn't have a trace of tuberculosis. I felt like singing for joy. I didn't, but I did something perhaps even better. I bundled Ann up and took off with her for Miami, where we had a three-month fling together, celebrating her health.

At last Wayne sent word that we could begin to get ready to join him in Vienna. The thrill I got was like a small repetition of the thrill that came with word of the German surrender almost a year before. As long as Wayne and I were apart, the war didn't really seem over to me.

CHAPTER TEN

A SMART ALECK ON MY HUSBAND'S STAFF IN Vienna once pinned the title "Operation Henpeck" on the movement of wives to Austria to join their husbands after the war. Wayne accepted that title as the official code name for the operation and I was never quite sure whether I should forgive him for that. Since he never did tell who it was that first suggested the name, he himself has never been completely free of suspicion in my mind.

But in April of 1946 I didn't care what they called it, just so long as Ann and I could join Wayne in Austria. The job of cleaning up after the war was far from finished, but it was complete enough to permit the Army to issue the order that wives could join their husbands.

I was only slightly miffed by the "Operation Henpeck" title, but I was deeply resentful, as always, of the official Army description of all wives and children as "dependents." I never resented a word so much as I did that one. I had always felt I could stand on my own two feet and that word "dependent" never failed to gall me. But even that was but a minor annoyance when viewed against the great, all-encompassing fact that Wayne and Ann and I would be together again and that Bill would be close by. Wayne had his job as United States High Commissioner in Austria and his home in Vienna. Bill was on duty in Austria with the famed Forty-Second Rainbow Division under Maj. Gen. Harry Collins and we would be able to see him when he was on leave.

Ann and I got all our orders and clearnces. We packed. We closed the apartment. We rushed to New York to catch our transport, the S.S. *Thomas Berry*. It was the first transport load of wives and children for Germany and Austria, and it was packed. The passenger list was made up almost wholly of excited women and children going to join their husbands overseas.

It was on the *Berry* that I suddenly realized how deeply I was steeped in the ways of the Army. My close friend on that trip was Marge Sullivan, wife of then Brig. Gen. Joseph P. Sullivan, Wayne's old classmate at West Point and close companion down through the years. It was Sully who told Wayne how to take a short cut through the redwood forests from Monterey to San Francisco the day Ann was born. Sully was on Wayne's staff all through Italy and stayed on Wayne's staff in Austria and later at Fort Monroe, in Tokyo and at the Citadel after they both retired from active duty.

Marge was new to the Army when we boarded the *Berry*. She and Sully had been married shortly before the war began and she had not lived on Army posts. She had lived in Detroit and had helped her first husband run a newspaper in nearby Mount Clemens. Marge knew nothing of Army life and regulations. She learned the hard way.

As she boarded the ship she was asked for her orders and medical "shot record." She was nonplused. Then she remembered that before she left home in Detroit a lot of papers had been given to her, but she explained, "I didn't know what they were for and I threw them away. They didn't look important."

The port authorities were exasperated. The war had been bad enough for them without having to be inflicted with a lot of women who didn't know the importance of all those papers the Army prepared so carefully. But while Marge didn't know the Army, she knew people and had a convincing way of talking and a more convincing smile. Things were patched up, a little irregularly, but enough to permit her to board the *Berry*. The officers in charge winked at regulations and gave Marge new orders and a new shot record.

With all that fuss and bother Marge got a headache. A few hours out of New York she asked me, "Is there a doctor aboard?" I said, "Of course," and we went to him. The doctor gave her some pills. It was the first time Marge had ever been to an Army doctor, and before I knew what she was doing, she had opened her purse and was offering to pay the man, who was so surprised he had a difficult time explaining to Marge that during the trip all medical services for "dependents" were to be on the Army.

We "dependents" had to share crowded quarters aboard the *Berry*, but that didn't dampen our enthusiasm or excitement. The trip itself probably was the most thrilling experience in the lives of any of us. Our husbands had come through the war alive. We were joining them after so many lonely, fear-filled years. With such treasure at the end of the rainbow, who cared about crowded quarters on such a quest? We were more than gay, we were hilarious.

And we did what we could to help one another. Marjorie Clay, wife of Gen. Lucius B. Clay, who was in Germany, more or less looked after the women going to join husbands in his command, and I did the same for women going to Austria. Because of Wayne's rank, I had the only suite on the ship. I learned almost as soon as we got aboard that while I had my own bath, all the other women had to line up and wait their turn to get into the community bathrooms. I passed the word to the wives going to Austria that they and their children could use my bathroom any time they wanted, and soon my suite began to seem like Grand Central Station.

There were many old friends aboard. Some were wives of men on Wayne's staff in Italy and now in Austria. The tables in the dining room were for eight, and the wives of the men on Wayne's staff just filled one table. We ate every meal together. Besides Marge Sullivan, there was Jane Howard, at whose house Wayne and I had been on Pearl Harbor Day. Her husband, a captain then, was Brig. Gen. Edwin Howard by this time and was serving with Wayne in Austria. Alice McMahon, wife of Maj. Gen. William McMahon, who was with Wayne, was aboard with her lovely daughter Alice Mary. Marguerite Tate, whose husband was Brig. Gen. Ralph Tate, was with us and so was my old friend Jean Smith, wife of Col. Coburn Smith. Jean was one of the veterans of my ill-fated New Year's Eve dinner party for lonely wives. With Ann and myself that made a jolly eight at our table, and we spent almost all our time together aboard the *Berry*.

Few of us had been to Europe before and there was a great deal of talk about how we would live, what we would do, and what nice things we could buy. We would see a new land, live in homes our husbands had secured and "settled" for us. There would be servants and an easier life. Our homes would be furnished and ready for us. This was not going to be an ordinary change of post. There would be no curtain tailoring for any of us, no penny pinching to make ends meet. We had left most of our own things in storage back home and each of us knew she would walk into a home fully furnished and just ready to be lived in.

All day and at every meal we chattered and chatted about the new life opening before us. We planned and dreamed and hoped. For myself, I never had such a satisfying, concentrated, and extended session of daydreaming as I did on that ship.

All in all, it was such a happy voyage that it seemed no time at all before it was over and the ship was pulling into the dock at Bremerhaven. It was all tremendously exciting: so many people on the docks, straining to catch a glimpse of American women; in the distance, the special railroad trains waiting to carry us to all parts of Germany and Austria. Special telephone lines were strung to the ship so that many of the wives were able to talk with their husbands waiting in distant cities.

The women left the ship in groups to board the special trains. Because the train to Austria was the last to leave, we were the last to debark and did not leave the ship until late afternoon. That one day aboard the motionless ship seemed longer than all the rest of the trip. On the dock a tin-pan German band played most of the day. It drew quite a cry from those of us still aboard the *Berry* when it played "Don't Fence Me In."

Finally the call came for us. We walked in a group directly from the ship to our special train and began the last lap of the journey into what looked like a big and exciting adventure. It was a happy, exhilarating ride into the future. The excitement rose after the train crossed the border from Germany into Austria. That was the final landmark on the long, long road out of the loneliness that settled on us so many years before when America got into the fighting.

But in addition, Austria was festive as Germany had not been. There was a celebration at every stop. Bands played and flags waved and children sang and people danced. Huge bouquets of flowers were presented to us at each station stop. In the evening there were torchlights, more flowers and thousands of people, many wearing the colorful costumes of old Austria. I knew in my heart that Wayne had arranged this for all us wives, that it was his way of welcoming us. It was overwhelming. It began to seem a little too much. It was, as we went eastward.

The date was April 30, 1946. I knew I was in Austria but I didn't know the chopped-up treaty divisions of the country and didn't know we had entered the Russian zone. And in my excited state of mind it was a long time before I remembered that the next day was May Day and realized that here was a May-day Eve celebration in which all the people were participating by order of the Russians.

At Salzburg, several hours before we reached Vienna, Bill boarded the train to join Ann and me and we were overjoyed to see him and to have the chance to talk with him and throw questions at him. We hadn't seen Bill for almost a year, not since he left the States in the summer of 1945 to joint the Forty-second Division in Europe. Bill seemed glad to see us, too, but it was an effort. He had been on maneuvers and was completely worn out. He was hardly able to stay awake long enough to get on the train and say hello. Then he fell asleep and slept all the way to Vienna.

At each stop some of the women left the train to join their husbands. The reunions were difficult to watch. There were many tears of joy. Sometimes there was a strangeness, a little formality and self-consciousness. I found myself feeling like an intruder, seeing things that belonged to the eyes of the families only, not to a stranger like me. I felt that I and all the other strangers who witnessed those greetings somehow spoiled those precious moments for the happy young people. But I also felt a sense of joy that these young Americans were back together again and able to be happy again for the first time in ages. It had been three or four years for some of them.

There were so many touching scenes. Little children did not know their daddies, could not remember their faces. It had been almost a year since the fighting ended, but once in a while a look of shock and surprise flashed through the eyes of a young wife when she saw the mark and the lines of war etched in the face of her husband. The boyishness some of the wives looked for could no longer be found. But perhaps the greatest of all happiness is that which comes when trouble is over, and there was great happiness at every train stop.

Finally, at 1 A.M. of May 1, 1946, the train reached Vienna. Wayne was at the station, tall, lanky, and grinning from ear to ear. On a leash he had our cocker spaniel Pal. The crush of the crowd did not inhibit my greeting to him, or his to me. My hat went sliding about my head, as usual, but I didn't care about that, either. We were together and meant to stay together. We each felt that as we embraced. This was no stolen holiday at White Sulphur Springs, Palm Beach, or the home of the Chief of Staff, no little island in time. This was real and permanent and forever after—or so I thought then.

Wayne rushed me home to the villa just outside the city. It was an impressive and comfortable Old World home with large grounds which, in the darkness, gave only a hint of their beauty. I remember thinking as we drove up to the door that I would have flowers and trees around me in Vienna.

Late as it was, the people who worked in the house and on the grounds were lined up to greet me. They bowed deeply, their faces wreathed in smiles. There were six, including the yardman and the handy man who tended the furnace and fixed things around the house. Most wore the colorful Austrian country costume, which gave the whole thing a touch of musical-comedy atmosphere. Later I found they all were fine workers. Each was so poverty-stricken and had suffered so much during the war that he was more than willing to work his heart out just to be in an American home where he knew there would be good food and lots of it and where he knew he would be well cared for.

In the months that followed I was to learn just how far they would go to serve me, and I learned it to my chagrin. I was shocked and embarrassed to learn through an incident how dependent I had become upon them. The incident could have appeared trifling, but to me it was a real shock.

I had dropped a piece of facial tissue and asked my maid, Augusta, to pick it up. As soon as the words were out of my mouth I realized how ridiculous I was acting, and to what a ridiculous habit I had fallen into. It was such a luxury to have servants after doing all my own cooking, scrubbing, and cleaning in Washington during the war years that I had gone completely overboard.

I was so disgusted with myself after the incident of the dropped tissue that I vowed never again to become so completely dependent upon the help of others.

But this introspection was far ahead of me that night that Wayne first led me into our home in Vienna. As we entered the house three dogs bounded down the great staircase growling at me. Pal had immediately known me, but to these three I was a stranger. The others were Mike, a police dog that had been with Wayne since North Africa, a dachshund, and a nondescript mongrel. I was surprised to have these dogs growl at me in what I already considered my own home. When I asked Wayne about this ungracious growling, he smiled broadly and said, "They haven't seen a woman in four years."

Every light in the house was blazing to make it cheery for me. That was a mistake. Before we even began to look around, the fuses blew, every one of them, and the house was plunged into blackness.

There was a scurrying around by match light until somebody located a flashlight and handed it to Wayne. That was the way I first saw my new home—by flashlight. Wayne took me from room to room. They were high-ceilinged and heavily paneled, and by flashlight they looked very eerie and strange.

Finally we finished our tour and went up to the bedroom. There were dozens of packages which seemed to fill the place. May 1 was Wayne's birthday and these were his gifts. He had kept them wrapped so that I could be there to share his surprises when he opened them in the morning before breakfast.

But where were my bags?

Wayne's face dropped. He called his aide. No, the aide didn't know where they were. In fact, nobody could be found who had even thought of them at the station, and they were still there.

I looked at my husband with the four stars and a whole victorious war behind him and wondered out loud how he had managed to command a whole army if he couldn't even get some luggage home from a railroad station. Of course, it was a teasing, playful wonderment I expressed, because who could really be upset by anything on a night of reunion like that?

I soon found out who could. It started shortly after I fell asleep, when I was awakened by a scratching noise somewhere. Now a strange sound in a new house is much worse than the same sound in an old, familiar house, and I sat up, wide awake.

Finally I located the noise. It came from one of the larger of Wayne's packages, a big one wrapped in brown paper and set beside my bed. But the noise stopped and I slipped off to sleep again. Then the noise resumed and once more I was wide awake and a little frightened. I awakened Wayne and asked him whatever could be in that package. Wife or no wife, reunion or not, he wanted his sleep, and grumbled that it doubtless was a package of cheese and the mice probably were having a meal.

That did it. What woman can sleep with a bunch of mice eating cheese beside her bed? Not this one, certainly. I may have had a few winks from time to time during the rest of that night, but no more.

144

Next morning Wayne began to unwrap his presents. When he came to that big box of noises I scurried to the far end of the room. If mice were going to leap from that box I wanted all the space I could get between them and me. Wayne seemed to be enjoying the whole thing, though, and took his time unwrapping the box.

He uncovered not mice and cheese but two of the most lovely canary birds anyone could want to have.

A big, perhaps the biggest, part of Wayne's job in Vienna was to negotiate with the Russians. There were negotiations about everything that happened in Austria, for under the surrender arrangements the United States, the U.S.S.R., Britain, and France had equal voices in making the rules of the occupation and in carrying them out. Before I ever left the States, Wayne had written to me about his troubles with the Russians. He said that after the first few days of meeting with them it was perfectly apparent that they would cheat and lie and do almost anything to avoid living up to their solemn pledges.

My first brush with the reality of all this came that very first day in Vienna. Nobody had yet coined the phrase "cold war," but everyone in Vienna already had the feeling of what that phrase would come to mean.

I saw the Russians. It was May Day. Their soldiers marched. They goose-stepped almost like Hitler's Nazis, and they marched with bayonets drawn and forward. It seemed that at any moment a Russian soldier would jab his bayonet into the man ahead of him. One misstep would have done it.

That night there was a May-day dinner, and Marshal I. S. Konev, now Deputy Minister of Defense in Moscow, was host to the British, French, and American officials in the city. It was all terribly elaborate and crowded. The Russians had two bands playing for the huge throng. The women wore their best finery and the men were resplendent in dress uniforms, their tunics covered with decorations they had won in the war. There were only a few Russian women there, since few of the Russian officers had yet brought their wives to Vienna from the Soviet Union, nor did they later.

The party was in the great palace that the Russians had for

their headquarters. I could not help thinking how strange it was to go to a party given by the people who claimed they were revolutionaries and leaders of the masses, only to find it was the closest thing to an old-fashioned story-book royal ball I had ever seen. There were tremendous bowls filled with caviar. Vodka was everywhere, and so were Russians to make sure everyone drank his fill and perhaps a little more. And there were fish of every kind, "dead fish" as Wayne called them.

We were conducted first to a great hall where Russian singers and dancers were to perform. It was a thrilling show. The Russian men stirred us with their rousing folk songs, and then the dancers came on with swords, which they plunged into the wooden floor. Splinters flew and the swords were left quivering like struck bow strings, as the dancers whirled and stamped around them, leaping and twirling to the exciting Russian music.

Konev had an excellent dinner served. There were lobsters, shrimp, beef, lamb, veal, salads, dessert—and more "dead fish." The Marshal was a genial host, and he and Wayne seemed to be on friendly terms—at least for the moment.

After dinner we got one of the Russian movies which guests at Soviet functions almost invariably must sit through. These are propaganda movies produced to show the glories of the Soviet Union, not primarily to entertain, and the one we drew was the recent Soviet film of the Russian Youth Movement. There was no plot, of course, and no professional actors. The movie just showed how the Russian Youth Movement was organized and what it did. We saw Russian boys and girls in mass calisthenics. We saw them camping, studying, discussing political problems.

Konev sat with Wayne and me and was as proud as he could be. "Nowhere in the world," he said, "are people so trained and organized."

I don't think Konev had any idea how that would sound to Americans devoted to the idea that the less regimentation the better, not even after Wayne said rather pointedly, "I hope someday you can see the way we raise our children in America."

Vienna, gay Vienna, was a dreary place in those days. When we arrived, there were few stores open in the city. War had ravaged the once-beautiful Austrian capital. Then came the Russians to loot and pillage. Soldiers of four nations—Britain, France, Russia, and the United States—were billeted in the larger buildings that still stood in usable condition. For the Viennese there was next to nothing.

The Viennese had to do anything to try to get food. I remember the fine, cultured woman who came to see me one day, at home. It was no small job for a Viennese to reach me, because security considerations made it necessary to screen all visitors carefully. But this woman was obviously all right. She entered my room proudly, and my eyes bulged out a little. On her arm was draped the most magnificent white ermine coat I ever saw anywhere. Indeed, that ermine was the reason for her visit. With just a trace of hurt pride in her voice, the woman told me she wanted to trade the ermine for cigarettes, food, and sugar. She asked for quite a lot of food and sugar, particularly, but her price was ridiculously low when compared to the value of that astounding fur.

As a woman who likes a bargain as well as the next one, I was sorely tempted. But as the wife of Gen. Mark Wayne Clark, I had to turn down the trade, even though it hurt. Wayne had issued strict orders that anyone caught bartering with the Austrians would be shipped home immediately. It had to be that way. We didn't have enough ships on the ocean to carry all the PX supplies that would have been needed to fill the great consumer-goods void in all the occupied areas like Austria, Germany, and Japan and the war-torn countries like France, Italy, the Philippines, and China.

Many Austrian women tried to make trades with me. I could have returned home one of the most bejeweled and befurred women in America if bartering had been permitted.

Vienna was a pitiful city. It seemed to be a great sea of poverty and misery and hunger, with the Allied troop-barracks areas standing out as little islands of plenty. High wire fences enclosed all the barracks areas, and in the summer hungry Viennese walked by the barracks and looked through the fences to see the troops of the conquerors eating on long tables set outside in the barracks grounds. The soldiers' tables were provided with good, nourishing food. It made my heart ache to observe the crowds pushing forward to a vantage spot close to the high iron fence, thrusting their hands out for food which the soldiers always gave to them, frequently doing without to share more than generously.

It must have been a trial for the Austrians to see our bounty, the same kind of trial a little boy has when he pushes his nose against the candy-store window and knows he hasn't a penny to spend. For the Austrians had terrible difficulties getting food in those days. There were ration distribution points instead of stores, and the Viennese used to crowd around four or five deep struggling to get what little their ration books called for before it was all gone. It was a common sight in those days to see beer-loving Austrians pedaling bicycles miles and miles to pick up the one bottle of beer that was their weekly ration.

The Austrians made a real effort to try to beat their way back to some semblance of good living. Gradually work began to open stores that had been closed for several years. Marge Sullivan and I were invited to the opening of Stone and Blythe, the most fashionable dress shop in Vienna and, before the war, one of the finest in all Europe.

It was winter, a cold winter. There was no heat in the store, which was so frigid that the women clerks wore their heavy coats while they worked. Neither was there electricity and at about 4:30 in the afternoon, when the winter darkness descended, the girls had to light candles.

The famous Herr Adlemuller showed what few wares he had. Most of the racks and showcases were empty. But Herr Adlemuller had such a reputation that many of us wanted him to make dresses for us. He was prepared for that. He had soft pencils and sketchbooks handy and designed dresses to our order, before our eyes. Later, when we returned for fittings, it was so cold that goose bumps puckered up our skin while we changed clothing. Marge and I were happy to read in 1955 that Herr Adlemuller was doing well again and that he was commissioned to create the costumes for a noted opera star.

Another famous Austrian was of great help to our family on a personal basis. He was Sergius Pauser, one of Europe's great portrait artists. Pauser taught at the University of Vienna and was one of the recognized modern masters. But that winter of 1946 there could be no art classes at the university. The people were too poor, too busy trying to find food and trying to keep alive to be able to spend money and time to study art. Besides, the university building itself was full of holes and could not be heated.

Through her studies Ann was familiar with the work and worth of the master and sought him out. He recognized her as a serious student of art. Arrangements were made for him to give her private instruction. The artist and the young girl met regularly in the eerie atmosphere of the ruined, almost deserted university building. But Ann was so excited about the help Sergius Pauser could give her that Wayne and I were happy and did what we could to help. The main thing that could be done was to make that drafty old schoolroom, part of which had been bombed out, a little more comfortable. As American High Commissioner, Wayne did not feel justified in rebuilding a room just so his daughter could study painting. But he did feel that it would be all right to buy an old potbellied wood-burning stove and set it up in the room. To this day Ann says that the work she did with Pauser was of the greatest help to her in developing her ability to paint.

Wayne was powerless to provide enough food and drink for the people of Vienna. But one thing he could do, and did. One of his first projects was to get plans under way to repair the once-magnificent Opera House which had been destroyed during the war. He knew how much the Viennese loved their music and their opera and he wanted to give them at least that.

It was wintertime before Wayne took me to an opening performance at one of Vienna's many theaters. The company was quite good. The first-night production was well chosen, a long-time favorite of the Viennese, Strauss's *Die Fledermaus*.

It was thrilling to witness the return of opera to Vienna and to see the Viennese revel in the pleasure of hearing the work of their own Waltz King played once again in the opera house that held so many memories. The memories were warmer than the opera house that night, though. It was really an old barn of a place and it was not heated. The chill of winter swept through it almost unchecked, and it was biting cold, even though every seat was taken and people were sitting shoulder to shoulder. Wayne and I were in a box. It was so cold I wore several sweaters, galoshes, and my heaviest coat. Wayne wore GI longies under his uniform.

But in their happiness the Viennese seemed to ignore the cold—or perhaps it was always cold for them that winter, in their homes, in their offices, wherever they were. At any rate, they were ecstatic that night, rising to their feet and waving and cheering and shouting, "Bravo!" in a mighty accolade for the singers. It was a moving sight. Wayne was pleased. "Maybe," he said, "we helped them forget their troubles for a little while anyway."

In the summer we went to Salzburg for the opening of the Music Festival. Again the emphasis was on the beloved Johann Strauss, whose music always seems to mean so much more to the Austrians than that of any of the other masters. At Salzburg his "Blue Danube" seemed to be the dominant theme.

We had a box at Salzburg, too. That time heat was the problem. It was stifling and I was dripping with perspiration. And then the spotlight hit us, with its intense heat, and I felt I must have looked like a boiled lobster to those people who stared up at us.

Music is so much a part of the life of Vienna. The first Christmas we were there the famous Vienna Boys' Choir came to our house to sing carols. We looked down on those beautiful faces and invited the boys in for hot chocolate and cookies. Such things were unheard of luxuries to the Viennese, and the boys were so profuse in their thanks that we felt we had given them a little Christmas pleasure they would long remember. They seemed almost as happy to see our decorations as they were to sip the hot chocolate, for Vienna had no Christmas decorations that year. The ones we had in our house we had bought in Switzerland several weeks before.

From the vantage point of Austria, Switzerland was like an oasis in the desert, a war-made desert of desolation and want. Here there was little electricity for lights or fuel for heat. The people of Austria had few jobs as many business houses were closed. Food was terribly scarce, clothing just could not be had.

Wayne and I arranged to have milk shipped from Switzerland to Vienna so that children and old people in hospitals could have at least that. We also wrote to many friends in the States to send CARE packages and old clothing, anything that would help even in a little way to alleviate the suffering of the Viennese.

In those early days our forces in Austria and all other occupied areas were forbidden to use American Army food and clothing to relieve civilian needs. Later those regulations were relaxed a bit, and in addition America began sending great shiploads of food for the people. It was absolutely necessary for America to do something about the food situation. Not only were the Austrians subsisting on an average of about 1,500 calories a day, but the problem was being aggravated by a constant stream of people fleeing from the Russians.

My heart ached to see the misery at the railroad station where the refugees arrived and sat, bewildered, hungry, and cold. Few had a definite goal. All knew from what they were fleeing. Only a handful knew really where they wanted to go. There were Poles and Jews and Balts and Czechs and even Russians in that unhappy crowd. They came into the United States zone in open boxcars and many had to stay in the railroad station for days, seeking shelter in those same boxcars.

Wayne ordered temporary shelters built for refugees in Vienna and provided blankets and food. The blankets and soup-kitchen meals the Americans were able to provide really gave many of those frightened people the best living conditions they had known for years.

But the refugees could not be kept in Vienna. It was too close to the Russian zone. The fear of the Russians was still upon them as long as they remained in Vienna, and there always was the danger of kidnaping by the Reds. So Wayne had them moved back to the American zone of Austria, far from Vienna and far from the Russian zone, as swiftly as he could. For many that meant moving by American air transport for the trains were a little risky. As in Germany, the American Army train that linked the American zone of Austria to Vienna had to run through Russian territory. For a time there was trouble on that train. Russian soldiers boarded it frequently. Some were drunk and almost all were troublemakers. They tried to molest American women. They stole baggage. Finally, Wayne put American armed guards on the train with orders to shoot if necessary. One MP found it necessary, shooting and killing a Russian. Marshal Konev screamed in Vienna, demanding retribution and making all sorts of threats. But Wayne yielded to nothing, and the Russians quit boarding our train.

The problem of the struggle with the Russians was dramatized for me through personal contact with a story of heroism and tragedy. It started in September of 1946 when Wayne and I flew back to the United States for a brief visit. We went to the Hotel Hershey in Hershey, Pennsylvania, for a holiday. There, in the great dining room, the headwaiter approached us as we ate. He said his name was Hartman, that he was an Austrian and that he had family trouble. His brother, he said, was in the Russian zone of Austria and was sick and not getting enough to eat.

"Please, General and Mrs. Clark," he said, "when you go back to Vienna, please try to help him."

Wayne said he would do what he could but that the problem was most difficult and he could not promise anything.

"Please, sir, take this and use it to try to help my brother. It is not much, I do not have much, but it might help some," Hartman said and handed Wayne an envelope. Inside was five hundred dollars in cash. Wayne protested, saying he could not take the money because he could not give any guarantee that he could help Hartman's brother. But the headwaiter said, "No, I want it this way, it must be this way." Wayne took the money.

Back in Vienna, we gave the money to an officer in Wayne's headquarters and Wayne told him to try to make it useful to the sick man trapped in the Russian zone. He also said efforts should be made to get the man and his family out to the United States zone.

Our plan, as requested by Hartman in Hershey, was to try to smuggle small food parcels to his brother each week. Our channel was the anti-Communist underground and the agents working for American intelligence in the Russian zone.

Because of our personal connection with the case, we kept close watch over the project. The brother lived in a small town on the route used by American supply convoys between the American zone and Vienna. The underground and the agents organized things beautifully. The small food packets were dropped at specified points, picked up and delivered to Hartman. Agents who worked on the railroad did much of the work and got us word from the little town. We learned that the man was suffering from tuberculosis. We learned also that the food packets were getting through and that they were a great help to him and his family. Finally the underground and the agents went all the way, smuggling the sick man and his family out of the Russian zone and into Vienna, where we were able to take care of them. The man himself was given the best treatment available, but the ravages of the disease had taken too great a toll and after some time he died.

My main interest in Vienna was to try to get food for the people. I did all I could to stimulate interest among Americans in the CARE package program and the response was gratifying. The packages rolled in. The job then, on our end, was to distribute the packages to the best advantage. Everybody in Vienna needed food. We had to find the ones who needed it the most, so we combed the city, seeking the poorest of the poor.

Santa Claus is a great tradition in Austria, just as in America, and we wanted to keep his legend alive for the children. I got the idea of having Christmas parties for children at the mess halls each Christmas Day. It was great fun for both the children and the American soldiers. We served the children cake, cookies, and hot chocolate. In each mess hall a soldier dressed as Santa Claus distributed little toys to the kiddies. It was a small thing, materially, but I thought a very big thing spiritually. Certainly, as I went from mess hall to mess hall on Christmas Day, I felt that any effort we had put into the project was more than repaid by the smiles and laughs of happiness of children who had been cheated of so much of the joy of childhood.

CHAPTER ELEVEN

EVEN BEFORE ANN AND I GOT TO AUSTRIA WAYNE
dreamed of planning a trip to show us the Italian battlegrounds where
he had fought his great campaigns. After we arrived, it seemed as if he
could hardly wait for an excuse to whisk us off to Italy so that he
could show us around and try to give us an understanding of the war
he fought. He got us to Italy before the end of 1946.

The tour he took us on was one of the highlights of my life, and of
Ann's too. For there in Italy our general, Ann's father and my husband, showed us something of the life he led in combat, made us
understand better than ever before what war meant in general and
what it meant to him in particular. He took us over the battlefields
where he and a truly great staff planned the campaign later won by
the officers and men of many nations. Standing on those battlefields—Salerno, Anzio, Cassino—we literally trembled as he told
the details of the terrible fighting, the stories of the tragedy of war,
the travail of command, the heavy toll of decision.

It was a privilege few wives get and I always have been grateful
that Wayne, in this and later trips, wanted to share with me these
haunted memories of the war. I thought I had followed the war so
closely that there was little more for me to learn, but standing on
the beach at Salerno or in the well-kept American cemetery outside

Anzio or looking at the ruins of the Abbey of Monte Cassino I found that I had known nothing, really, of the fear and hurt and uncertainty and terrible fatigue that go into the make-up of battle.

Wayne tried to keep the tour from being too emotional. He joked once, for instance, "I'm going to take you to Florence to prove to you that I was writing about a beautiful city and not a beautiful blonde."

But that tour of the battlefield, which to me was my husband's battlefield, had to be emotional. On the beach at Salerno, where the United States Fifth Army had crashed ashore and suffered so many losses, Wayne got a misty look in his eyes and talked as though he was living again that harrowing day when a German counterattack almost pushed some of the Americans back into the sea. It took six days to establish that Salerno beachhead below Naples, six days of bitter fighting against crack Nazi troops who, Wayne said, seemed to sense that unless they held Salerno our Allied might would pour in over those beaches and eventually roll all the Germans out of Italy.

All the strain and worry of command seemed to come through in his voice as he recalled those days, and I had a better understanding of my husband's job than ever before. More than anything else, he talked about the men who had died on that beach, and he talked as though they were a weight on his shoulders, a weight that time might lighten but which nothing could remove.

Wayne took me by the hand and led me through the sand to the exact spot on the beach where the first boatload of troops hit the shore and led the first mass invasion of the Europe that Hitler had all but conquered. Wayne showed me how the men had landed, where they had taken cover from the blazing German guns which fired at point-blank ranges.

The reality of the thing came through as he talked, and the setting was there. This was not a war story told in a villa in Vienna or a comfortable apartment in Washington. This was the beach itself. Men had died here. Houses were still shell-wracked. Broken American and German tanks were rusting on the beach and in the wooded areas beyond. Hulls of ships poked out of the water off the beach.

Burned-out landing craft were toppled together crazily at the water's edge.

Wayne talked on and on. He told me why Salerno was the first landing on the road to Rome. It was the most suitable landing beach near Naples, he said, and the port of Naples was needed to supply the troops when they began their drive northward.

He showed me where he had lived in a clump of trees during and right after the Salerno fighting. He showed me where the troops took cover from the incessant barrage of German guns, where they had to fall back to the very water's edge, where they had to counter German infantry attacks. He showed me where the German defense finally cracked and where the embattled American foot soldiers finally made their gallant attacks to break out of the beachhead.

Wayne always had wanted me to understand what the Fifth Army had done, and why, and that day on the beach at Salerno I understood.

From Salerno we went to Naples, and Wayne was happy as a little boy. He was going to look up an old friend, a friend not only of his but of the whole American Army, or at least that part of the American Army that was in Naples.

The man's name was Giacomino. He ran a restaurant, a small place in 1943 but one that later became a hangout for American GIs. They flocked to his restaurant partly because his food was good but mostly because he loved them so much. Whatever he had he shared with American soldiers, any American soldier who came along. That was his way of expressing his undying hatred of the Germans and gratitude to the Americans.

Wayne had been to Giacomino's restaurant, too. He remembered where it was and that Giacomino and his family lived upstairs. We found him there. There was much embracing and celebrating. Giacomino insisted that we share one of his enormous dinners that night. We promised we would return, and did.

The whole neighborhood seemed to have crowded into his small home. The word that we were coming had spread throughout the block and the adjacent blocks, and Giacomino had called in old friends from distant neighborhoods, people Wayne had met during his wartime stay in Naples.

And Giacomino served a feast! There was *antipasto,* of course, a salad and a great fish on a big plate. Then he had boiled lobsters, followed by chicken and spaghetti and washed down with a never-ending flow of wine and champagne. Fruit and cakes topped off the meal, and Wayne was so happy and reminiscent that I lost some of my feeling that he had had it so rough during the war.

As we traveled about the city Wayne told me little stories, incidents too small in themselves to have been included in his letters during the war or in our talks after it, but necessary to fill out the color of his wartime life now that we were in Italy together and he was recalling so many things. He showed me the palatial villa which the Italians had selected to be headquarters and home for the commanding general of the American forces. It had belonged to the Royal Family and was a magnificent place. The military men pressed Wayne to stay in the villa at least until his Field Headquarters was ready and communications were working to the woods north of Naples.

Wayne told me the story. "When I moved into Naples after its capture," he said, "they took me to this place. I had only my aide and an orderly with me. It was impressive. It was the first house I had been in during the fighting in Italy. I'd always lived in my trailer, in the field. But, Renie, it was such a big house, and there were only three of us. I decided I couldn't take it. It was too lonesome. And I would be too out of touch with things. I got into my jeep and moved back into my truck in the woods, much to the consternation of my staff. They were not ready to do business in the woods and had hoped I would stay in that villa for a little while, at least."

I had a special thrill going to Naples. Secretly, within our family, we think of it as my city. The Fifth Army drove the Germans out of Naples on October 1, 1943. That was four days before my birthday. Wayne arranged by radiogram to have a birthday cake delivered to me in Washington with a message that he was "giving" me Naples for my birthday.

From Naples we went on to Anzio and the cemetery Wayne had dedicated so long ago, while the fighting was still under way. The memorial and park still were incomplete, but we were shown the blueprints of the plans for the permanent shrine to our American dead buried there.

Wayne was deeply moved. His eyes got misty and he had trouble controlling his voice. I had the feeling that he could never forget those Americans who had made the final sacrifice so that we could keep the blessings we hold so dear in America.

Flowers planted by the Italian people were everywhere. They indicated a loving care by the Italians for the final resting place of American lads who died fighting to break the threat of Nazism to Italy as well as to America. The flowers seemed to tell us that the Italian people still were grateful to America for their liberation from the German tyranny.

Then we went to the Anzio beach. Wayne told me how he had committed every American soldier he had into the battle of the Alban Hills in the latter part of May and early June of 1944. He said the Germans had thrown all their resources into the fray, and added: "It was like two heavyweight boxers slugging it out with Rome the prize. I was not sure which one of us would fall on our face first." The sadness descended upon Wayne again as he remembered the dreadful cost and fearful uncertainty of those days when it was touch and go whether any American could live within that cramped perimeter or stay on the beach.

From Anzio we went to Florence which, despite the scars of battle, still was a beautiful city, just as Wayne had said. We went out into the woods where he had lived in his trailer and where he had our dog, Pal, to ease his loneliness.

Wayne took me to look at the destroyed monastery of Monte Cassino. During the war when there was so much criticism of the bombing attack that destroyed this ancient seat of religious learning and devotion, I had defended Wayne hotly. I knew nothing of the reasons for the bombing then, but I was his wife and knew in my heart that the attack must have been the right thing to do or Wayne never would have ordered it.

But there on the scene I got a surprise. For the first time my husband got around to telling me the details of that action. He had protested against it. Every intelligence report from American sources said there were no Germans using the monastery. Wayne argued and pleaded. But the British were in command. Lord Alexander was Wayne's immediate superior in the field. Lord Alexander's headquarters directed the destruction of Monte Cassino. As time went on and as Wayne was given more and more responsibilities dealing with basic American policy, he found he had to carry out many more orders with which he disagreed.

Back in Rome we continued the tour to cover Wayne's war memories. We went to the gate through which he entered the city in his jeep and he showed me where the bullet-scarred sign ROMA had hung before the city authorities gave it to him as a trophy.

In our tour of Rome, Wayne took particular pains to show me how the city had been spared as much as possible and to tell me how he had ordered that every effort be made to avoid damaging unnecessarily this ancient seat of civilization. Combat commanders often have that problem. Their first duty is to safeguard the men serving them and to protect their lives. When a question arises that requires a choice between risking a man's life or destroying a building, the building goes. But within that framework, Wayne wanted to spare all of Rome he could.

Wayne told me again how Rome was the seat of his greatest disappointment in the war. The whole Army was keyed up when it took Rome. The ancient capital of Caesar was a symbol of superiority and there was exhilaration and eagerness to push on now that the Germans were on the run. Even soldiers who had to take the big risks with a rifle way up front began to feel that they had a better chance to live if they pushed on against an enemy in retreat than if they sat back and waited for the enemy to regroup and come charging back.

Wayne felt this most keenly and wanted to push on with his geared-up army of men who now were veterans who had tasted victory. He wanted to keep them moving. But the strategy called for other measures, and once again Wayne found himself at odds with the top planners.

The German army was a broken, retreating army. The Fifth Army was moving fast after Rome, right on the heels of the Germans. But immediately after Rome was taken, seven of Wayne's best divisions were pulled out of the Fifth Army and sent to camps where they were to get ready to invade southern France. Wayne told me that his Fifth Army, after losing those seven divisions, did not have enough power left to hit the Germans a blow that would destroy them. The fighting continued heavy, but with reduced power, the Fifth Army just was not then able to win the full victory that had seemed at hand.

Wayne protested from the field against the decision to strip his army of those seven divisions. Prime Minister Winston Churchill protested in London. Both Mr. Churchill and Wayne wanted to drive through Italy into the Balkans. Each feared that failure to go on and hit the "soft underbelly" of Europe would leave the Western Allies at a disadvantage after the war.

But others disagreed and their views prevailed. Wayne pressed on as best he could against a retreating German army which could have been routed. As it turned out, the Balkans had been saved for the Communists.

Occasionally the Fifth Army found Americans who had been stranded in enemy country when the war started. Almost all of them were in bad straits. They may have had money back in America, but they had no way to get it. Most of them had difficulty finding enough to eat. Wayne and the Fifth Army helped them with rations and occasionally one of these Americans would invite Wayne and some of his staff officers to dinner. Rarely could they attend.

Most of these invitations came from Americans who had money and who still lived in big homes, elaborately furnished. Wayne told me about a dinner he attended. "Our uniforms were a little rough alongside the fine evening clothes those people wore. In one home there was a dining room that looked as though it had been made for a movie set. It had crystal chandeliers and the furniture was unbelievably well carved and polished. But despite the splendid setting, the food was pretty bad. It was Spam, dehydrated potatoes, American-issue coffee, and Hershey bars for dessert. It was our own ration of food, of course, that we had sent to help the people out."

From a tourist's point of view the most enjoyable part of our holiday in Italy was the Amalfi drive along the Mediterranean. We had luncheon at Ravello on a veranda overlooking the picturesque sea so full of romantic images for anyone who ever read the Bible or heard any stories of Greek and Roman mythology. We drove on to Sorrento to board a ship for Capri, and later traveled to Milan where the great Arturo Toscanini was to conduct a concert in honor of my husband.

Wayne told me of his troubles with Italian opera during the war. From time to time in some of the captured Italian cities the people would rush work to restore their opera houses. The return of opera to these towns and cities was a great event and several times Wayne was invited to attend the opening. He is not an opera devotee and after the first soiree, at which he made his appearance and greeted the town elders and other dignitaries, he usually detailed a lanky officer to take over for him. In the darkness of the opera house it was not noticed that a shift had been made. "At least," Wayne told me, "I think I got away with it." In any event, he escaped sitting through the entire operas. He never did tell me whether the lanky officer who substituted for him liked opera or not.

But at La Scala, with Toscanini conducting in Wayne's honor, there could be no substitution. Fortunately for Wayne, Toscanini conducted symphonic works that night rather than opera.

On one trip we flew to Rabat in North Africa to meet Wayne's old and close wartime friend, Marshal Alphonse Juin of France. Wayne and the Marshal had been close friends ever since they met in the early days of the North Africa invasion. Marshal Juin invited Wayne and me to fly over to North Africa to visit him and Mrs. Juin. The Marshal then was governor-general of French Morocco. He met us at the airport with great pomp. The tallest Arabs that could be found were in the guard of honor, some afoot and others mounted on spirited, fine-limbed Arabian horses. The

Arab soldiers carried flags, banners, spears, daggers, swords. I felt as though I was stepping into the pages of the *Arabian Nights' Entertainment*.

Before we left Morocco I had even more reason to feel we had become part of the thousand and one tales. Marshal and Madame Juin had a dinner party for us that first night and we had made plans to visit the Sultan at his palace the next day. Wayne had warned me not to plan any shopping or sight-seeing tours because, he said, "We'll be tied up at the Sultan's." So while we were at dinner I blithely mentioned how much fun it was going to be for me to go into a real Sultan's palace for the first time.

There was silence. I looked around to see what I had done wrong. I felt as though I had forgotten myself and crumbled crackers in my soup or committed some other kind of horrible social error.

Somebody explained as gently as possible that no woman ever crossed the threshold or went through the gates of the Sultan's palace except those called to spend a lifetime in his harem. "Well," I said, just as confident as I could be, "tomorrow morning I'm going into that palace."

Everyone was too polite to argue, and anyway they knew they didn't have to. Next morning I found out in no uncertain terms that this Sultan would not break his rule for me or any other woman. I did not get into his palace. Wayne went on with the other men.

I learned much about palaces, though, while living with the Juins. They lived in one wing of their enormous and luxurious palace, and Wayne and I were in the guest wing that fingered out in another direction. The corridors seemed endless and in the daytime, with bright sunlight pouring in, they were fascinating. It was those corridors that carried me back into the *Arabian Nights*.

One night I read late and then went to look for the bathroom. When we were first taken to our suite of rooms great care was taken to point the way to the bathroom down one of those corridors. But that was by sunlight. At night the only light came from tiny overhead electric bulbs that gave little more illumination than a struck match.

It was a long way from our bedroom to the bathroom and the corridors didn't look at all as they did in the daytime. I got lost. I wandered down one corridor and up another. Finally, spotting one door that looked familiar, or seemed to anyway, I opened it. I was face to face with a huge Arab guard wearing long robes and holding an even longer spear and looking more ferocious than anyone I had ever seen in my life.

I panicked. I slammed the door in his face and ran. It was like a nightmare. And it was just as foolish because that Arab wasn't going to hurt a guest of the governor-general. He was stationed at an outside door to make certain no one got into the palace. But I couldn't think of those things. I simply ran, and when my slippers fell off I didn't stop to pick them up.

Somehow I found our room and awakened Wayne. He was no help at all. He thought it was a wonderfully good joke, and when I persisted in talking about the thing, trying to talk myself out of my fright, he said, "Oh, go to sleep and forget it, we have a busy day tomorrow." With that he dropped off to sleep, and I was left staring into the darkness, inventing all sorts of terrible noises.

After leaving the Juins, we went to Cherchel, and hand in hand we stood on the beach where Wayne and his party had landed from the submarine so long ago in their breath-taking adventure. Wayne led me to the house where he had met the French military men, and even led me down a short flight of dark stairs into the damp and musty wine cellar where he and the men with him had hidden with bated breath while the police upstairs searched the house.

Even in retrospect that fearsome adventure had made me catch my breath many times, and utter a quick silent prayer of thanks that my husband had lived through it and come back to me. But never had the danger and the risk seemed so real as when I stood in that wine cellar with Wayne and realized just how close those German policemen were to him that awful night.

CHAPTER TWELVE

⟨∽⟩ OUR TRIPS OUT OF AUSTRIA TO NEIGHBORING
countries always were exciting and interesting. Besides getting the
chance to see the battlefields on which my husband fought, I was
able to become familiar with historic places and with some of the
people my husband had known during the war years. When Wayne
was invited to Rome on an official visit, therefore, I was delighted
to go along. The Italians set us up in a suite at the Excelsior Hotel,
where Wayne had stayed overnight on several occasions just after
the liberation of Rome from the Germans, and in every way were
wonderful to us. We had a dining room in our suite and all our
meals were sent up.

Both Wayne and I are light eaters and enjoy small portions of
a variety of good foods, but the Roman dinner, while including excellent foods, included them in staggering quantities. We couldn't
begin to get through any of the meals. We feared, though, that if
we failed to make way with a reasonable amount of the food they
sent they would feel hurt. At one of these meals Ann and Marge
and Sully were with us, and the chef, an expert with *crêpes suzettes,*
sent us some of the finest we had ever tasted. But so huge were
the portions he sent up that none of us could make a dent in them.
After we had eaten all we could, therefore, and as soon as all the

waiters were out of the room, Wayne, Ann, Marge, and Sully ran out on our balcony and tossed out all the uneaten *crêpes suzettes*. I heard gasps and laughs on the balcony and rushed out in time to see a British army truck rolling down the street with our *crêpes suzettes* plastered along the canvas top.

Wayne should have learned from this experience, I guess, but he didn't. We visited Capri and had a villa on that magnificent pleasure island in the Mediterranean, where I never tired of looking out at that sea of aquamarine-colored water. The cook at the villa had worked for Wayne during the war and seemed terribly pleased to be able to cook for him again. He was a good cook, especially with desserts, which were so good we ate them against our better judgment. Usually we try to limit ourselves to simple desserts like grapefruit and honey, but no one could have resisted the tasty things that cook dreamed up for us.

He had one weakness, though. The biscuits he insisted on baking were like little rocks. They were frightful. Wayne didn't want to insult him by sending them back, so he tossed them out the window. As had to happen, the cook was standing on the terrace below our room, cooling off after completing his work on our meal.

The rocklike biscuits whizzed right by his nose.

For days afterwards that cook was cold and distant with us, an injured artist.

We had a set-to with another artist during that first trip to Italy. His name was Pietro Amnigoni and he was truly great. During the war the officers of the headquarters of Wayne's Fifteenth Army Group commissioned Annigoni to do a portrait of Wayne which when completed was to be presented to my husband.

It was a difficult process. Wayne was able to give Annigoni only a few minutes at a time for a sitting. But besides that, Annigoni was a temperamental kind of artist and didn't always feel like painting.

The Fifteenth Army Group officers took a proprietary interest in the picture and watched it closely as it developed. As Wayne's features began to emerge clearly on the canvas, one officer said Annigoni had made him look "gaunt" and another quickly punned that "there are twenty-seven German divisions between us and Florence and we'll all be gaunt if we're not careful."

The picture still was not completed when Ann and I first went to Italy with Wayne. Annigoni had completed Wayne's face and hands and the outline of his shoulders and arms before the war was over. But Wayne had had to leave his battle jacket with the artist so that he could continue to work after Wayne left Italy.

When Ann and I first saw the picture it was just about finished. Wayne took us to Annigoni's studio in Florence to see it, and we were shocked. This was not my husband or Ann's father. This was a man neither of us knew.

I said, "Oh, no," and Ann said she wouldn't have the picture in the house. Then Ann examined it more carefully, with an artist's eye, and became even more bitter. "If you bring that home, Daddy," she said, "I will cut it into four pieces and use the backs to paint new pictures."

Annigoni was crushed. Through an interpreter he told us: "I am devastated. I will destroy the picture."

Ann and I still did not like the picture. We suggested changes. "No," he said. He would slash the pictures—make no changes. We left him with it and forgot about it.

But the picture was to haunt us. Annigoni did not destroy it. Somehow it later was hanging in a hotel in Florence. There, Col. Jim Angleton, who had been with the Fifteenth Army Group, spotted it in the lobby, bought it immediately, and wrote to Wayne's former West Point roommate, Maj. Gen. William McMahon, suggesting that the picture be presented to West Point.

McMahon thought it would be fine to give the portrait to West Point and arrangements were made. By the time Ann and I heard about it the picture already was en route to the United States.

Ann was horrified. "We can't let West Point have that picture of Daddy," she said. "I'd rather have it hanging at home, where only we will see it, than have it at West Point for everybody to see."

I agreed. Under such pressure, from wife and daughter, Wayne had to agree, too. He wrote to McMahon and said he wanted the picture for his new home at the Citadel. It came and we hung it over the mantelpiece.

Then a strange thing happened. Every man who had been in the war thought it was a magnificent picture. They saw in that tired face, with its deep and compassionate eyes, the faces of hundreds of men, men who fought and feared and worried and struggled and lived life as no woman could know it.

Several artists have told us it is a fine portrait. Wayne thinks so too. Gradually, influenced perhaps by the reaction of others, I began to soften toward the picture. I still don't like it and I doubt if I ever will. It is not a picture of my man, the man I know and love. But I'm getting accustomed to it and appreciate its artistic qualities.

The last word we had of Annigoni was that he, out of all the artists in Europe, was commissioned in 1955 to go to Buckingham Palace and do a portrait of Queen Elizabeth. And somebody sent us a clipping from an Italian newspaper that said he appeared at Buckingham Palace wearing the old battle jacket that Wayne had left with him to help in completing his picture.

While we were on duty in Vienna, the occasional trips out of the country to Italy or Switzerland, Belgium or France, were welcome relief from the rigorous schedule Wayne had to maintain as United States High Commissioner. That schedule was so tight that we rarely had lunch or dinner without guests at our Vienna villa. Much of the time we had house guests and therefore company for breakfast, too. We enjoyed our guests, for many were exciting people who had done or were doing big things. Grace Moore came, as did Arthur Hays Sulzberger of *The New York Times*. The columnist Drew Pearson visited us and so did Juan Tripp of Pan-American World Airways. Then we had a number of congressmen and American diplomats at various times.

Our villa was perfect for entertaining. We had a swimming pool and a guesthouse which gave privacy to our overnight and week-end guests. In the summertime we entertained out of doors, in the garden which was brilliantly lighted.

We did enjoy entertaining guests, but we also enjoyed getting away by ourselves from time to time. In Vienna we had little or no time away from official functions or duties. Away from Vienna we could relax more.

One of our favorite trips was to Salzburg, the headquarters of the American zone of Austria. In 1945 it had been Wayne's headquarters for a time. He always said the Russians made him stay there while they completed the job of looting Vienna. In Salzburg Wayne had maintained his headquarters at Schloss Klesheim, the old Hapsburg palace which Hitler had modernized and turned into a luxurious guesthouse for the people who visited him at his Berchtesgaden "Eagle's Nest" retreat.

Hitler made the old palace luxurious with loot from France. There was silver service for a hundred people, and a table that would seat them. There were unbelievable treasures in painting, tapestry, rugs, vases, and carpeting. All or most were stolen from France.

One day we went to Schloss Klesheim with Gen. Emile Bethouart, French High Commissioner for Austria. The general was amazed. He had read about the German looting, but now he was seeing it. He wandered from one lavish room to another, wide-eyed. He knew each picture, almost, and most of the tapestries and rugs. As he wandered through the palace he would point to one picture and say, "That is from the Louvre," and to another and say, "That is from Versailles." He seemed to be meeting long-lost friends.

The furniture, too, was lavish—and looted by the Germans. When Wayne finally moved his headquarters into Vienna the Austrians insisted that some of the furniture be sent along to his new home. When I arrived I found that my bedroom had been furnished from Schloss Klesheim, and one part of that furniture I knew I just had to have. It was the down pillow on my bed. It was the softest, most comfortable pillow I ever had. When we finally left I asked permission to take just that one pillow home with me, and there has not been a single night since that I have not rested my head on it. Embroidered on the pillow case are the two words "Schloss Klesheim."

A few times Wayne was able to get away from the interminable negotiating sessions with the Russians to spend a weekend hunting in the Austrian Alps. We had a favorite place for that, an Alpine hunting lodge at Hinderstoder. Ann and I went with Wayne many times, traveling to the lodge by airplane or train and making the last lap in a jeep.

Each time Wayne went, he took cartons of candy bars and chewing gum and the townspeople, particularly the children, always thronged around the jeep when he arrived. They not only were happy with the candy and chewing gum, but pleased that their little village had been singled out by the American High Commissioner for his holidays. Sometimes the burgomaster would call a town ceremony to honor Wayne. On these occasions the burgomaster would wear the traditional leather overalls with short pants, and the Hinderstoder band would play gay beer-drinking songs.

The village fathers of Hinderstoder wrote to Wayne asking if he could replace the bells in their little church that had been stolen by the Germans during the war. Wayne in turn wrote to Cardinal Spellman in New York requesting his help. The Cardinal sent the money, several hundred dollars, and Wayne had the bells made and presented them at the church where all the townsfolk were gathered. It was the kind of fete day the people of Hinderstoder and the other villages had been enjoying for a couple of centuries, and it was wonderful to share their tradition-laden happiness.

As a special mark of honor for Wayne the townspeople dug up an American flag from somewhere and hoisted it to the steeple of their church. It must have taken a good deal of effort for them to get an American flag, and we felt so grateful and warm for this little thoughtfulness that we didn't have the heart to tell them that they had hoisted it upside down.

On those few and rare occasions that Wayne could get away, he used the hunting lodge as his headquarters for fishing and hunting. There were two guides, Knievaser and Baumschlager, who worked with Wayne in hunting expeditions that entailed a good deal of mountain climbing as well. They were excellent woodsmen and Wayne admired and respected them both. For Wayne the best sport was hunting the *Auerhahn,* a beautiful bird that looked something like the American eagle, and a most difficult bird to bag.

It was early spring when Wayne and Knievaser and Baum-schlager took off after the *Auerhahn*. The snow was still deep in the mountains, just the right time of the year for the *Auerhahn,* and the three men trudged off. They left about midnight and climbed several thousand feet up the mountain. They had to climb all night to get into position for the kill by dawn. Wayne said that a good part of the night he was pushing his way through waist-deep snow.

The guides had located the general whereabouts of the birds beforehand and knew where they were going. They led Wayne to just the right spot, following the song of the *Auerhahn*. Then came the crucial moment. The male *Auerhahn* can be caught only at dawn and only during the spring mating season. Only at that time does he perch motionless on a tree and send out his call to his mate, and, curiously, during a part of his call he is both deaf and blind.

The guides had to know his song well enough to know when to make the move without having to worry about frightening him off. They picked up the call of the *Auerhahn* a little while before dawn and led Wayne cautiously to the spot. Then they waited until the guide heard the bird go into his blind and deaf call to his mate. The guides leaped forward when they heard it, waving to Wayne to follow. They had to hurry because the best they could hope for was time for one shot. They went forward through the snow in leaps and rushes. Wayne's guides were good, and so was his aim. He got his *Auerhahn*.

The beautiful bird glided down the mountainside amidst a shower of flying feathers and fell so far down that a search party had to be organized to find it. The bird wasn't located until the next day, but an *Auerhahn* is such a prize that those mountain men would not quit the search until they found it.

Wayne had the bird mounted by the old man who once was taxi-dermist at the palace of Emperor Franz Josef. He also mounted the heads of deer and the chamois that Wayne shot in those mountain hunts.

Each time Wayne returned from a hunt he invited the guides Knievaser and Baumschlager into the lodge for a warming drink.

These two mountain men had great dignity. And, as with most Austrians, beer or wine was far more to their liking than the whisky Wayne served for a quick warm-up. They were always friendly, but always stern-visaged and serious and more conscious than we thought they should be about their "proper place." They never sat in our presence but preferred to remain standing, straight and tall. They took one drink, never more, and then bowed low and very formally and excused themselves.

The *Auerhahn* was the main prize for Wayne, one of the big thrills of all his many years as an ardent hunter, but he also had lots of hunting for roebuck and chamois, and all the trout fishing he could wish for.

When Wayne was successful on a hunt he would herald his return with the jeep horn long before he rounded the curve and hill that brought him within sight of the lodge. I used to tell him he acted just like a young fighter pilot wagging his wings or making the victory roll when he returned from a mission in which he bagged an enemy plane. But Ann and I enjoyed this playfulness, too, and when we heard that jeep horn we would rush from the lodge to watch Wayne drive up with a chamois over the hood or a long line of fish just ready for the stove. Then we would go into the lodge and stand by the roaring fire while Wayne and his guides warmed themselves with a drink.

In Wayne's study today he has a large number of hunting trophies mounted and hung on the walls. The ones from Hinderstode bring back the happiest of memories for me.

Love of hunting gave Wayne and Marshal Konev something in common. They never hunted together, but they talked a good deal about hunting and guns and dogs. In the beginning they were quite friendly. They visited each other and occasionally had a friendly drink together. Wayne decided that the best we could hope for with the Russians in Austria was some kind of compromise so he made a deliberate effort to establish friendly relations with Konev. He had a handsome hunting rifle made for the Russian marshal and sent it to him for Christmas. It had Konev's name engraved on it, along with the date of presentation.

The first time Wayne saw Konev after sending the Christmas gift was at a big reception on New Year's Day. Konev was pleasant but made no mention of the gun. Some weeks later they met again, but still Konev said nothing about the gift, and Wayne was beginning to get irked. He had heard nothing and couldn't understand it. Their third meeting after the presentation of the gift was several months after Christmas.

This time Wayne wanted an answer. He asked the interpreter to ask the Marshal if he had received the gun. Konev said, "Yes." That was all. No thanks, no nothing.

Wayne turned to the interpreter and said, "Ask him if he liked it." Konev answered again with the single word *"da,"* meaning "yes."

Wayne was no longer irked, he was furious. The color was rising in his neck, that old danger sign. Through the interpreter again he asked Konev, "Isn't it customary for people of the Soviet Union to express thanks for a gift?"

For the third time Konev replied with a simple *"da"* and nothing else. He was refusing to explain any further unless he was pressed. Wayne pressed.

"Well, why didn't he thank me?" Wayne asked.

The answer was a curt "You sent no ammunition."

Wayne was so mad he never did, either.

CHAPTER THIRTEEN

THE CONTRAST BETWEEN THE IMPOVERISH-
ment and need of the war-stricken Viennese and the plenty which
the normal world had to offer never struck me so sharply as it did
on a holiday we took to nearby Switzerland.

It was pleasant living in Vienna, of course. We received good
food which the Army shipped from the States to the commissary
and, indeed, felt no lack or need of anything until we left Austria
and entered a country untouched by war. There we became aware
of all the little things that even we did not have—things like fresh
milk, cream, chocolate, cheeses, fresh vegetables—things that were
hardly luxuries by normal American standards. In Vienna we used
powdered or condensed milk. I found I simply could not enjoy
coffee without real cream, or at least not enjoy it with condensed
milk, so I learned to drink it black. To this day I still do.

Our eye-opening holiday was in the wintertime. It was a family
holiday, or seemed so, since we now counted General and Marge
Sullivan as part of our family, and the five of us, Wayne, Ann,
Sully, Marge, and I, went to Zurich, to the Old Dolder Grand
Hotel. We went to the border of Switzerland on an Austrian train
and drove the rest of the way.

It was wonderful motoring through the snow-covered mountains. The whole scene was unreal, like a giant playground. Finally Wayne could resist no longer. He looked at that pure, clean snow and said, "Let's get out and play in that stuff."

We did. We frolicked in the snow like a bunch of ten-year-olds. We skidded and tumbled and laughed and screamed and threw snowballs. But it didn't take us long to realize we were not ten-year-olds. We were tuckered out, and we wanted a warm place to rest and something hot to drink. Our Swiss driver took us to a store nearby.

Inside, our eyes grew large. It was a combination grocery store and restaurant, and the sweet warm smell of hot chocolate immediately warmed us and whetted our appetites.

Sully was Wayne's Quartermaster and had charge, among other things, of food sent to the troops in Austria. It is a traditional joke in the Army that the Quartermaster eats better than anyone else. But we got all the evidence we needed that day that Sully wasn't holding out any goodies on anybody back in Austria. His eyes bulged just as far as ours when we saw all the great cheeses and fresh white bread and rich chocolate candy and all the other things we could not get in Austria. None of us said anything. We didn't have to. We just grabbed a table and ordered some of everything they had. We broke great handfuls from the long loaf of bread, gorged on cheese, and drank cup after cup of the rich hot chocolate, made with real milk and topped with whipped cream.

It was glorious while it lasted, but not so glorious afterward. Each of us overate that rich food, the kind of food we had done without for so long, and each of us paid with an upset stomach.

Ann went everywhere with us. She was a young woman now, and my treasured companion. She was making good headway in her art studies. Long before, when she was a schoolgirl, I had given up my efforts to interest her in the piano. She just didn't care for it, and I felt a little pang because I had studied music and, like all parents, had enough vanity to hope that my children would follow in my footsteps. But Ann's talent was with the paintbrush, not the piano keys. I would be untrue to my motherly pride if I failed to say here that Ann now is one of the promising young portrait artists on the West Coast and has won important recognition. But my pride is pale alongside that of Wayne's, when, in 1950, his little Annie did the art-work and maps for his first book, *Calculated Risk*.

Ann's work in painting led to what I am certain was one of the unforgettable days of her life. It was January of 1947. Wayne was called to London for the Council of Foreign Ministers which was discussing, among other things, a peace treaty for Austria. Wayne had been working in Vienna for almost two years in a fruitless effort to get an agreement with the Russians.

We had not been in London long before Winston Churchill asked us to come out to his country home, outside London, to spend the day. Mr. Churchill and Wayne had known each other during the war years and had been on the same side of many arguments about strategy. Notably, they had agreed that the best strategy would be to defeat the Germans in Northern Italy and drive on into the Balkans, a part of the area Mr. Churchill called the "soft underbelly" of Europe. Their efforts to win approval of this strategy failed, and Wayne, at least, felt that this failure had resulted in the troubles he was then going through in Austria. Wayne, of course, was fascinated by Britain's Great Man and Mr. Churchill seemed to like Wayne. They dined together many times at No. 10 Downing Street and spent weekends at Chequers when Mr. Churchill was Prime Minister during the war.

By January of 1947 Mr. Churchill was out of office for the time being and was living outside London at the estate the British government gave him when he went out of office after the war and which eventually is to be made a museum of Churchilliana. It was to this estate that Mr. Churchill invited us for a day. It was a miserable, rainy day which was spoiled further by the fact that Mrs. Churchill was in the hospital with a hip injury.

Mr. Churchill was devoting considerable time to painting and in his invitation mentioned that he wanted us to see his work. He knew of Ann's interest and specifically asked that she accompany us.

When we arrived at his home, he wanted to rush us off immediately across his garden and into the separate little house he used as his studio. Wayne and I were included in the invitation but it was plain to see that Mr. Churchill was concentrating his attention on Ann because he accepted her as a fellow artist and wanted to see her reaction. Despite the rain, despite the mud, despite anything, he just had to take us to that studio. Ann looked out at the mud and said in a wee voice, "But I have on high heels."

A little problem like that meant nothing to Mr. Churchill. "My wife has all kinds of shoes and boots," he proclaimed, and bustled Ann off to a closet. There he got down on his hands and knees and dragged out all sizes of walking shoes and boots and galoshes and tried them on Ann's feet until he got a pair that he was satisfied would keep her dry and comfortable. It was strange to see Britain's Great Man acting like a shoe salesman—and for our daughter, too. Once satisfied with the boot situation, Mr. Churchill grabbed up some umbrellas and off we marched into the rain. He went ahead with Ann, and Wayne and I followed. It was quite a sight to see this rugged but hunched old man, who so personifies the bulldog spirit of Britain, and the slim little American girl huddling together as they sloshed across that muddy garden, united by a common devotion to painting.

We stayed in the studio for a long time examining his pictures. Mr. Churchill and Ann talked and talked about artists and theories of art, and Wayne and I tagged along and listened. I was so happy. I felt as though my Ann had been singled out by the gods for a special favor, and had a sneaking idea she felt the same way.

Mr. Churchill gave us the grand tour. He took us around the garden of which he was so justly proud and then back to the main house. We all were wet, but that seemed to mean nothing to either Ann or Mr. Churchill, one of whom seemed as happy as the other after their little adventure in art.

Once back in the house, and relatively dry, Mr. Churchill continued the tour, taking us from room to room to see his letters and trophies and records, things which even during his lifetime had become of great historic moment and tradition. He took us into his bedroom where we had a glimpse of the more intimate side of this great man by seeing all the photographs of relatives and close friends who played such an important part in his private life.

After the tour we went to the old-fashioned, chintz-draped sitting room, where Mr. Churchill and Wayne began to talk about the political problem uppermost in their minds at that time—the problem of the peace treaties for Germany and Austria. Just as Wayne and I had felt a little outside while Mr. Churchill and Ann talked about art, now Ann and I felt a little apart as Wayne talked with him about diplomacy and the strategic problems of Europe. We were fascinated just listening to the two men. They went far afield from Austria, and soon we were listening to a full-blown discussion of all the major world problems.

The talk on Austria centered on the question of how a treaty could be written so that the country would not be turned over to the Communists. Wayne was hot on that issue then. He had seen how the Communists perverted the treaties with Hungary, Bulgaria, and Rumania in order to bring them within the Communist orbit, and he wanted no part of that for Austria.

The conversation finally was interrupted by the maid who entered, drew the chintz curtains, and wheeled in the tea cart. It was most pleasant in that sitting room, warmed by an open coal fire in the grate. In the absence of Mrs. Churchill I presided at the tea table and asked our host how he wanted his tea.

"Tea—no!" he roared. "It ruins my stomach. Never touch the stuff. I'll have whisky."

Mr. Churchill had a nickname for Wayne, calling him the "American Eagle," and on that rainy day he gave Wayne a photograph of himself, inscribing it: "To General Mark W. Clark—The American Eagle." Needless to say, it now is one of Wayne's most treasured mementos.

We had arrived at ten in the morning at the Churchill estate, and we stayed until well after dark. As far as the Clarks were concerned, we could have stayed for days listening to Mr. Churchill. We only hoped we hadn't overstayed our leave.

England was far from recovered from the war, and the British were still short of everything. The great coal strike was under way and that made things even more difficult. We moved into a hotel on arrival and were miserable there, with gas, lights, heat, and hot water rationed to a few hours a day. Fortunately, some kind English friends whose home was in the country rented us a flat they maintained for weekend use. It was on Park Lane, not far from our hotel, but it was in a different zone which had a larger ration of heat and light. And it was conveniently located.

Our fortune was short-lived, however. The very day after we moved into the new flat the area was rezoned and we had trouble again. We had no more light or heat or gas than we had before. All Britain seemed cold and dark and austere to us. But the people endured this hardship so bravely and well we could not bring ourselves to complain.

We did what we could to get along. The hot-water situation in our flat was so bad that Wayne had the habit of telephoning me just before he left his office so that I could start the bath running. There was real competition for hot water with our neighbors, and if we failed to start the bath running soon enough, others would get all the hot water.

There was no heat at all, and I wore all the warm clothing I could, including a fur coat, almost all the time I was in the apartment. A most welcome gift was a shipment sent to us by an American firm whose head was an Italian-campaign associate of Wayne's —a package containing a dozen beautiful wool sweaters. One was specially knit with a map of North Africa and Italy and red dots and black letters to show each place that Wayne used as headquarters for his Fifth Army and Fifteenth Army Group during the war. I, of course, didn't care what was on that sweater—it was warm and that was all I wanted. I was wearing it as usual one day while preparing Wayne's bath. Since we were going out to dinner that night, I also had on a suit and hat. Wayne arrived with his aide, who had been with him a long time. He walked into the tiny bathroom while I was still working on his bath, and as he crowded in, brushed me just enough to make me lose my balance. I tumbled into his tubful of water, hat, suit, sweater, and all.

Wayne reached for me as I fell, but missed. To add to the confusion, the doorbell rang. Wayne shouted for his aide to come help. "Renie fell in the tub," he called; "come give her a hand."

I don't know what the aide was thinking about, but he called back, "How far in did she fall?"

Wayne looked at me, looked at the map on my sweater, grinned a little, and shouted back, "All the way up to Naples."

None of which sounded funny to me then.

The food problem was difficult in London, too, in those times. Almost everything was rationed. Each person got one egg a week and two strips of bacon. I stood in queues day after day with bacon as my objective. I had ration coupons for six strips, two for each of us, but day after day my turn at the counter came too late and all I heard was, "Sorry, mum, no more bacon."

Then I always asked for cheese, plain yellow store cheese. Mr. Saunders, the greengrocer, was patient with me but he never had any cheese for me. Finally one day I said to him, "Don't you have any ordinary rat-trap cheese?"

He looked at me with a tired expression and said, "No, Mrs. Clark, we have only the rats today, and the traps, but no cheese."

Difficult as it was to get food from the grocer, it sometimes seemed almost more difficult to get a meal at a London restaurant in those rationed days. We were grateful, therefore, that our little flat had a kitchenette. That gave us a chance from time to time to get a meal for ourselves instead of going to a rationed restaurant.

In that situation, a gift actually forced on us by our Cockney maid was doubly welcomed. The girl, who worked in the apartment long before we moved in, brought us an orange one day. It was a tremendous orange, the size of an American softball, and since oranges were almost impossible to get on the London market that year, I was astounded that she offered me such a big one as a gift. So insistent was I that I didn't want to take it that we almost got into an argument. But then I realized she wanted very much to give us this gift, and I made a deal with her. I would accept it, I said, if she would agree to sit down with Wayne and me and share it with us. She agreed, and the next day we got together for our date with an orange. I divided it as nearly in thirds as I could, and the three of us sat at the table savoring this rare luxury.

The London Conference of Foreign Ministers was hardly over before we were preparing to go to Moscow for another meeting of the Council on the same issues of Germany and Austria. Wayne arrived in Moscow in March and stayed six weeks, and Ann and I joined him there after the talks were started. Spring came early to Moscow that year and physically we were quite comfortable.

Ann and I were especially enthusiastic about going to Russia because of our interest in the Soviet Union and Moscow and our desire to know what was happening there. Secretly I think we each lived in hope we would be able to pick up a sable or ermine or something equally magnificent at a real bargain price. But when we did shop around for sable in Moscow, we found it cost more there than in New York, and we both returned empty-handed.

We stayed at the Hotel Moscow and Wayne discovered very early that the Russians had wired his room and that our telephone was being tapped. There was another Dictaphone in the automobile the Russians provided for Wayne during his stay. Wayne and the other Americans in the delegation outfoxed the Russians, however, by making a game of it. The really serious conversations were held during walks along the sidewalk outside the Kremlin walls, and the Americans would be careful to keep out of earshot of the inevitable Russian agent following them. Then, for fun, they carried on weird and fantastic telephone conversations on the tapped phones, talking in pig Latin and double talk and saying things so mad and nonsensical that the Russian code experts must have almost gone out of their minds. And, of course, they always said terribly nice things about Russian officials in Vienna whom they didn't like. That was the surest way of getting those Soviets into trouble.

Ann and I apparently were not followed, and we did our best to see everything there was to see in Moscow, just as tourists do any-where. We saw the Russians' vaunted subway and had to admit it was a good one. There was a station around the corner from our hotel and often Ann and I would board the train for an exploration of Moscow and its suburbs. Mostly we went alone, occasionally with an interpreter Wayne sent with us.

In these explorations we hit upon what seemed to us a clever way of going about the city alone. We would board the subway station near the hotel and count the stations as we traveled out from the city into the suburbs—we always felt secure if we knew how many stations we were from home. Then we would climb to the street level for our daily surprise. We never knew what kind of neighborhood we were getting into until the final moment when we emerged from the subway and onto the street.

Each day we would walk around for a while in the vicinity of the subway station, taking care to keep our bearings so we wouldn't get lost from the subway entrance, our only landmark. Then, after looking into shops, walking past homes, and getting an idea of how poorly the people lived and what they bought, we would return to the subway and count the stations until we were back at the hotel.

Many things struck us. On the subways there were innumerable school children. But they were not children like ours. There was no gaiety in them, apparently no spirit, or at least no show of spirit. They sat silent and glum and expressionless. They seemed afraid, and didn't look at each other or exchange a word among themselves. I couldn't help remembering the unregimented verve and energy of our school children at home, children who laugh and play with a great hunger and zest for living, no matter where they are. These Russian children looked strong and husky enough, but each sat with hands in lap and head down. Never did one meet our eyes or show any curiosity about us.

Another impression was that Moscow lacked young men. All the time we were in Moscow we saw few if any young men on the streets. Indeed, women did the work, driving most of the automobiles, working on telephone poles, building buildings. Everywhere they did the street work, with picks and shovels, and they piloted the subway. We guessed that the young men were in the army, in mines and factories, but we never found out.

We learned about Russian prices, too, or at least the prices for things in our hotel. Our mouths watered for caviar by the time we got to Moscow and we began ordering double helpings regularly, twice daily. At the end of our stay when we got our bill we were staggered. We figured out that the price of one level tablespoon of caviar, with some black bread, was $1.80. We cut off the orders for double servings of caviar immediately and, in fact, had very few single portions sent up to our room after that.

As in any foreign country, there were language difficulties. When we visited the Lenin Library the Russian guide, in fair English, extolled the wonders of this famous library. Wayne listened as long as he could and then said, "We have lending libraries all over the United States."

The guide knew enough English to get along, but not enough, Wayne knew, to distinguish between the words "Lenin" and "lending." He was clearly dumfounded to think that in America there were "Lenin" libraries everywhere.

We were in Moscow but a short time. However, the picture those days painted in my mind was one of a city of resignation and discomfort and dirt and a city in which everyone seemed to be fearful of something. In our walks Ann and I never saw a house with curtains in the windows or flowers in the yard. The front yards were a mire of mud and waste and debris. Working people had to live where they were told to live and work where they were told to work. We learned that it was difficult for a man to change houses with another man even if it meant that each would be closer to his job. And it is the exceptional family that does not have to share its house or apartment with at least one other family.

There was some great beauty, but it seemed reserved for the select few in the Soviet setup, the big shots. The Moscow Ballet, for instance, is a thing of tremendous beauty. The ballet was born in Russia and the Soviets are proud of this art, as were the Russians of czarist days. But it is the rare "average Russian" who can get a ticket for the ballet. At least it was that way in 1947.

On the streets the people were poorly clothed, passive, subdued, and showed no interest in anything. Even foreigners like Ann and me, obvious foreigners, drew little attention.

The big crowds while we were there were at the Tomb of Lenin in Red Square. People were lined up for blocks, standing all day for their turn to pass slowly by the bier. I didn't see anyone in the crowd wearing shoes. They wore boots and the poorer among them wore cloth wrappings around their feet. The women all had old dark scarves tied over their heads.

During our days in Moscow I was able to talk with only a few Russian high-ranking officers, and that talk was little but chitchat at fairly formal social affairs to which Wayne took me. I would love to have gone with Wayne when he and others of the American delegation had dinner in the Kremlin with Josef Stalin, but that was an all-male as well as an all-night affair.

All Ann and I learned about the Russian people during our walks in Moscow we learned by looking, not listening. For one thing very few Russians speak English; for another, nobody seemed anxious to talk with us, or even willing. Not even the clerks in the shops in which we browsed approached us to try to sell us anything. Sometimes we had the uneasy feeling that we were invisible.

One thing Ann and I wanted so much to do in Moscow was to get inside the Kremlin. Its reputation intrigued us. So did its spires and minarets which we could see from outside the walls. Wayne tried to help us. He talked with Andrei Vishinsky, the Russian diplomat who was Wayne's opposite number at the conference, and Vishinsky said he would see what he could do. That was the end of it. Another Russian "pocket veto." There never was another reference to Wayne's request.

There was a strange quality about Moscow. Something was wrong. I sensed it right away but it took me a little time to realize what it was. Then it came upon me. I was looking at a sham city. The fronts of some buildings were newly painted and clean and bright; the sides and backs were dirty, run-down, cracked, and ugly. The Russians had done what they could to present a bold, clean front to the foreigners. They had slicked and polished what they thought the foreigners would see, neglected what they hoped the foreigners would not see.

The Foreign Ministers met in a building, for instance, with a beautiful façade in front. But when we sneaked a look at the sides and back, we found dirt and tawdriness. The back of the building was a mudhole, filled with refuse.

At the time of the conference the Moscow Hotel was opened to foreigners for the first time since the war. It was all painted and comfortable, but every window was nailed down fast. We guessed that the Russians wanted no falling or jumping incidents while the foreign dignitaries were in their capital.

One thing helped. There were old friends with us in Moscow. Gen. George Marshall was Secretary of State then, and head of the American Delegation. Wayne was his deputy for the talks on Austria. Gen. Lucius Clay was there from Germany, and Gen. Walter Bedell Smith was our Ambassador to Moscow. John Foster Dulles was with the delegation, as well as Wayne's close friend from North African adventures, Bob Murphy. It was good to see friendly and familiar faces in Moscow. We all felt that this kind of tonic, this kind of bridge to home, was important to us.

All the foreigners had been obliged to fly to Moscow over a route the Russians prescribed. That meant we were unable to fly directly from Vienna to Moscow but had to go by way of Berlin. On top of that, each plane carrying foreigners had to have a Russian navigator to make certain it did not wander off course and perhaps permit the foreigners to see something the Russians did not want them to see. The navigators didn't impress me or Wayne. He claimed they navigated by sight rather than instrument and said his navigator kept his nose glued to a window looking for familiar landmarks that would guide him to Moscow.

Wayne didn't want to fly back by way of Berlin. He wanted to go direct, by way of Warsaw. When he asked Vishinsky for permission, however, Vishinsky once again said he would see what he could do. Once again nothing happened. Days passed and there was no word. Wayne talked with Ambassador Bedell Smith and he went to work on the project.

Still there was no word until the very last day before we were to leave. Then the Russians said it would be all right for us to fly home by way of Warsaw. They went even further and said the Poles wanted to entertain us at lunch.

Our B-17 carrying Wayne, Ann, some of Wayne's staff officers, and me landed at Warsaw in the late morning. The Polish army was out in force, with all sorts of generals there to greet Wayne, along with a guard of honor. It was a big show.

After the greetings and the review were over, one of the generals asked Wayne if he would place a wreath on the tomb of the unknown soldier in Warsaw. Wayne said of course, and we got into a long motorcade to drive to the cemetery. The Poles had known Wayne would accept and had all kinds of soldiers out there at the monument. They even had the wreath all ready, and a loud-speaker system set up to carry the "few words" the Communists asked Wayne to speak. Wayne was ready with his "few words," but the Communists weren't.

What he said was: "This is a great privilege to be able to pay my respects to the deceased Polish soldiers. I know well how valiantly the Polish soldiers fought against the Germans when they served under me in Italy in the Polish Second Corps of Gen. Wladyslaw Anders."

There was consternation among the Communists. General Anders was a friend of freedom and no friend of theirs. I looked at them and had the feeling that they were horrified as though by a heresy. It probably was heresy to praise General Anders in Communist Poland. It was sad to realize that this man, who had fought so well and so hard as a Polish patriot against the Nazi aggressors, had become a figure the Poles were being taught to hate. Until Wayne spoke, there probably had not been one single word of public praise for Anders in Poland since the Germans were defeated.

Wayne's praise for Anders broke up the ceremony. The Communist generals couldn't end things fast enough, and inside of a few minutes we were on our way back to town for lunch.

After lunch we were driven back to the airport by a different, and appalling, route. The road took us right through the Warsaw ghetto, where tens of thousands of innocent people had been slaughtered. I had seen much of the devastation of the war, in several countries. But never was there anything to compare with this. The scars were unbelievable. There were no buildings. There were people living there again, but they were living in holes in the ground, like animals. Their pinched, hungry faces showed their misery. They grubbed in the dirt for anything they could find that might be useful. Most of them seemed to me to be in worse condition than those poor unfortunates who had made my heart ache in the refugee camps in Vienna.

As our plane took off from Warsaw for Vienna, the sight of those poor people stayed with me, hauntingly, frighteningly. For I realized now, more vividly than ever before, what misery and hatred the Communists had to feed on in Europe.

CHAPTER FOURTEEN

ᴏᴜʀ ʜᴏᴜsᴇʜᴏʟᴅ ɪɴ ᴠɪᴇɴɴᴀ ʜᴀᴅ ᴇxᴘᴀɴᴅᴇᴅ during our absence in Moscow, for Ann's white wire-haired terrier, Snootie, had had three puppies. That made it six dogs in the family.

From earliest childhood I had almost never been without a dog, but of all the dogs we ever had Snootie was the most like a person. Ann had trained her and she developed into a dog with a really remarkable personality. She had an endless string of tricks, including a piano-playing routine. Often we would have her show off at parties and always she was a hit.

But the most poignant memory of our dogs in Austria is of a little mongrel I named Puffy. Because Pal and Snootie went with us on every trip, we had become known in Europe as dog lovers, and, indeed, for anyone who visited us the fact was self-evident with four to six dogs running around the house. It was most natural, therefore, for friends in Vienna to ask us to help them find a pet. One friend asked us to look for a cocker spaniel for him during a trip we planned to Italy, and we began our hunt in Florence by inquiring among the hotel people there, who gave us an address to investigate.

I went there and was shocked. The "address" was a dungeon,

almost a cave. Dogs were very scarce in the war-torn European countries. Inside was a sickly, anemic dog with a litter of pups that looked only half alive and seemed almost certain not to live long. But one seemed a little more healthy than the others, and seemed to have a better chance of surviving.

It was a white puppy with long hair—breed unknown—and it looked so pathetic my heart went out to it. I decided I had to have it, not for my friend, because I could find no cocker, but for myself. The owner asked seventy dollars, fleas and all. I tried to wither him with my most disdainful look. He came down to thirty dollars. I still wouldn't buy. He said twenty-five, and the dog was mine. We put the dog aboard the train to return to Vienna. Every two hours I doctored him. His poor little body was covered with sores and he had never had enough to eat. He took a lot of care.

After about two weeks he began to look and act better. Soon he was as active, healthy, and happy as all our other dogs. And he became a fine pet.

Our maid, Augusta, loved Puffy. She lavished all her affection on that poor little waif dog, maybe because she too was a waif. She was a pretty little girl, very dark, serious, sweet, and faithful. She had no parents, no money, no relatives so far as we knew. She had no memory of any happy times in Vienna, only the memory of Hitler's armies, of war and defeat and occupation. Augusta was a terribly thin girl, and a terribly lonely one. There was something quite pathetic about the way she showered love and affection on that little dog, and gradually we came to accept the fact that the dog was hers.

When we finally were to leave Vienna, I gave Puffy a bath, dressed him up with a red ribbon, and had a tag made which said, "To Augusta from General and Mrs. Clark."

Augusta's eyes grew soft, and she burst into tears when she realized we wanted her to keep the dog. She hugged him, thanked us, and ran hurriedly from the room clutching her pet. It was the one thing in the world she had to love, the one living thing that was hers and hers alone. And I think it was the first gift she ever in her life received from anyone. Wayne and I watched her happiness and were all very grateful that something had made me insist on buying that pitifully sick little dog in Florence for what really was an outrageous price.

As our tour of duty in Vienna neared its close, I took stock of our experiences and remembered so many that had enriched our lives. There was the garden party in the summertime when Grace Moore was our guest. She was in Vienna to entertain American soldiers. After the performance we had her to a buffet supper for about 150 people. It was a perfect night, the moon low and lovely, spreading soft light through the garden as several violinists played Viennese waltzes.

Miss Moore had just finished a long performance for the soldiers but she still seemed fresh and full of energy. She was gracious and charming as she met all the people we had asked in her honor. Then, standing by the buffet table, she burst into song, picking up the music after it had started to play *Wein*.

It was a moment of enchantment as that wonderful voice floated across the garden, so gay and rich that it seemed to belong there among the trees and flowers. I thought what a shame it was that this voice could not always be heard in such a setting. There was something wrong with cooping up such beauty inside the four walls of a theater, and many of our guests that night, I am sure, thought the same thing.

One week later unbelievable news came from Germany. This vibrantly alive personality, this woman with such a zest for life, her great spark snuffed out in an airplane crash, had died. It was almost impossible for me to believe that only a week before she had stood in my garden so filled with life and caught up with the beauty of the night and the music that she had spontaneously broken into song.

Perhaps the most interesting meeting of all was the forty-five-minute audience Wayne arranged for me with the Pope in Rome. The Pope was grateful to the United States government and to Wayne because the Eternal City had been spared the fury of fighting during the war. Although Wayne and I are both Protestants, Wayne saw His Holiness many times during the fighting in Italy and they became quite good friends. Wayne arranged audiences with the Pope for soldiers in his Fifth Army, regardless of faith, during the war. It was after the war, during one of our visits to Rome together, that Wayne arranged an audience for me.

I was deeply impressed with everything about the Pope. His pictures were familiar to me, of course, and I had known that he was a man of great dignity and sensitivity in appearance. But never in pictures could I get the full impact of the deep sympathy, love, and understanding that are combined in the personality of His Holiness. He had the true and ideal characteristics of a father, which is what he is to Catholics the world over.

The hands of His Holiness were so fine they seemed almost transparent. I was fascinated with them, and with the enormous ring on his finger, as he toyed with the medal around his neck. But most of all I was impressed with his interest and knowledge about the world. He seemed aware of all things that were important, any place in the world. He asked detailed and intelligent questions about American life, getting down to happenings in various smaller cities in America, and his questions showed that he knew much about those cities.

Vienna was my home for exactly a year. Ann and I arrived on May 1, 1946, and we left in May of 1947 for that city of happy memory for us, San Francisco. It was to be Wayne's first stateside assignment in five years, the five years that began with such uncertainty and fear in 1942 when he went away to war. And Wayne decided we would go home in style, with a luxury vacation en route.

We went down to the Italian Riviera and then the French Riviera to play for a while before leaving for home.

We must have made quite a picture on that trip for we took along five dogs. The money we spent for their travel and care could have paid for a lot of things we needed, but both Wayne and I wanted our dogs along. There was Pal, of course, and Snootie and her three puppies, altogether quite a zoo to be carting around Europe. Our vacation over, we got to Le Havre in time to board the S.S. *America* for New York and home.

Home!

We hadn't had one, really, since the War College days five years before. But I was happy. The prospects for the future were all good. Not only were we going to be in the United States, but we were going to be at the Presidio, in San Francisco which we loved, among many old friends.

There were such happy memories of the Presidio. Ann was born there. Our first Army post, really, where Wayne and I had lived together as bride and groom. And it all seemed so permanent. Wayne was through with war, I knew. I was certain that if ever another war came along, younger men would step in to take their turn at the kind of soldiering Wayne had been through.

So our future was a straight line. Pleasant, interesting duty for Wayne for a few years at home, in the United States. I would be at his side always. No more loneliness, no more longing, and after a few years, retirement. Perhaps it would be at Camano, where the fishing was so fine. Wherever it was, it would be wonderful. I was joyous and at peace with the world.

The actual home-coming was a bit hectic, however. Dogs helped make it so. Only a few days after we arrived in San Francisco, where Wayne was to command the Sixth Army with headquarters at the beautiful Presidio overlooking the Golden Gate, we received an unexpected gift from a friend in New York. It was a great Dane!

We were a little appalled. Up to then the biggest thing we ever had in the way of a dog was our police dog, Mike, and he was a toy alongside this dog. The food problem alone was staggering. We had plenty of food for our five dogs, but the great Dane had to have almost as much as the other five together. He was such a beauty, though, that we took him into the fold and put him in an enclosure after having him checked by the vet. The vet said he was all right.

But the vet missed a virus that was incubating in the dog. Three days after we put him in the pen he died, and so did all the puppies. Only Pal and Snootie lived. They had been immunized well, the others only temporarily.

A year later Pal died, of old age more than anything else. He was thirteen. We had had him since Fort Lewis days and he had lived through countless experiences with us. He also was fairly well known around the country from the dozens and dozens of pictures that had been taken of him in Italy and published in American newspapers, and when he died we received hundreds of letters, wires, telephone calls, and messages of condolence. Many people were kind enough to offer us gifts of other dogs. We accepted, finally, a large French poodle named Paddy. He and Snootie became fast friends.

At the Presidio we were back in the peacetime Army again as we had not been since we left Fort Lewis, and I plunged into purely social problems, just as in the good old days. It was fun for me. I had enough experience behind me now that I was able to avoid many mistakes, and the work ran smoothly.

The thing that pleased me most was our post nursery, for which there was a real need. The problem was simple. Young officers with growing families frequently did not have enough money to hire baby sitters at the going price of $1.25 an hour plus carfare or taxi. The social obligations of Army life, however, still were heavy, and young officers and their wives had to accept many invitations and entertain. Remembering the problems Wayne and I had had when he was a captain, I felt the young officers and noncommissioned officers at the Presidio needed some help on the baby-sitting problem and went to work organizing the nursery. It was a fairly simple idea. And we had the funds to get started, what with four thousand dollars in the Women's Club fund, money earned through the Thrift Shop sale of secondhand things during World War II. The money was just sitting there with no place to be spent, and the Women's Club agreed to lend part of it to the nursery without interest to get the project going. The post itself found unused space which it let us have, and Letterman General Hospital came through with much of the necessary equipment, including sheets for the cribs and beds. Several members of the Women's Club painted the furniture and went shopping for toys.

When the physical requirements were finally met we hired one trained nurse and two practical nurses to run the nursery. We were so proud of it. Our nursery was big enough and well enough equipped to take care of two hundred children a day, and it usually carried the maximum. What the young parents on the post got was expert, trained care for their children at only twenty-five cents an hour with midmorning and afternoon milk and crackers at no extra charge—a fifth of what it would have cost to obtain an untrained high school girl for ordinary baby sitting.

The nursery was such a success that the women at Fort Lewis asked me to go up to Washington and help them organize the same kind of system. I did, and must admit I was delighted to see the idea catch on so well.

It was at the Presidio that Wayne and I celebrated our twenty-fifth wedding anniversary. We sent out invitations to old friends on the post and in the city. We had an orchestra and dancing. And the Officers' Club surprised us with a large and magnificent cake, surrounded by gardenias and inscribed with the words "Congratulations to General and Mrs. Clark."

Thanksgiving Day is always a big holiday on an Army post. The Army knows it is a day when men are more homesick than usual and tries to compensate in some way. Wayne and I went to one of the enlisted men's messes for Thanksgiving dinner. It was a fine mess, complete with all the latest gadgets, but basically it was a regular old-fashioned Army mess hall with long tables and stools. We rose from our seats when the Chaplain said grace.

When I sat down I went all the way to the floor, real hard.

They hadn't told me about one of their new gadgets. The stools were equipped with springs and swung back under the table as soon as they were released from the pressure of someone sitting on them. I was terribly flustered and felt every eye in the house was on me. And later in my confusion I bit into the red plastic top of a salt shaker which had gotten onto my salad somehow and which I mistook for a cherry.

Christmas Day added some more amusement to our life. Everything went wrong that day. For one thing it was raining hard, very hard. For another the electricity went off early in the morning. We

194

had house guests for the holiday. And to top everything, Ann's little Snootie ran away before breakfast and we all took off to hunt for her.

We all ran in different directions through that pouring rain, and finally Snootie was found, soaking wet and covered with mud. We were in much the same condition and completely out of sorts. We had eaten no breakfast and now it was too late even for a cup of coffee. Wayne and I barely had time to clean up and rush to Letterman General Hospital for our scheduled Christmas visit with the soldier patients.

Fortunately, our guests were our old and close friends the Griffiths from Seattle, and we could laugh with them about our troubles. We reminisced about the similar incident on Camano Island, when our dogs got into that terrible fight. Our other guest was Mike Mismanno, who, as a commander in the Naval Reserve had been on Wayne's staff through the Italian campaign. After the war he became a justice of the supreme court of the state of Pennsylvania, a position he still holds. But always he was a man of the rarest good humor, a man who could take in stride such things as a lost dog and an electricity failure.

The greatest thing the Presidio did for me was to give me back my family. It was only for a little while, but it was unexpected and therefore doubly appreciated. Ann was still with us, of course, and working harder than ever with her painting. She no longer was a student. In her own mind, at least, she was a professional and knew that painting was to be her lifework.

We lived in a beautiful house high on a hill in the Presidio, facing one of the most truly beautiful views in America. Before us was the Golden Gate and the fine, trim bridge that spans it. To the left was the Pacific Ocean. To the right was San Francisco Harbor, certainly one of the most picturesque in the world, and sometimes at night we would sit in our house and watch the ships go out to sea, toward Honolulu, Tokyo, Manila, Sydney. We could romanticize about the ships, some of which, we knew, were going to such storybook places as Samoa and the Fijis, the Coconut Islands, the balmy

South Seas. The lights on the ships were bright and big when they were going through the Golden Gate, and we watched them grow small and dim and then disappear as they went over the horizon toward the enticing islands of the Orient and the South Seas.

At this time Bill was stationed in Trieste, Italy, but his tour was completed and he flew out to California to see us. We kept then a long promise we had made to ourselves so many years before and gave him a present of an automobile. The old Buick with the flower holder that my parents had given us had been a real godsend, and we hoped we could give something as valuable to each of our children.

The day of Bill's return from Trieste seemed the ideal time for the presentation, and we planned the big surprise most carefully. We had Bill's brand-new automobile decorated beautifully in red ribbon and cellophane and parked it in front of our house with a spotlight shining on it. But of course it rained and the ribbon wilted. Red dye ran down the sides and over the hood of the automobile. It could have been splattered with mud, though, for all Bill cared about such nonessentials as red ribbon and cellophane. He was ready to jump for joy, and Wayne and I felt grateful that it was possible for us to make Bill so happy.

While at the Presidio Wayne got in some of his beloved fishing, both for trout in mountain streams some hours away and for salmon in the Pacific at our doorstep. He didn't fish from the shore, of course, but went out deep-sea fishing all the way to the Farallon Islands, well off the coast.

Occasionally I went with him and once I struck it lucky. I hooked and caught a 46-pound salmon and fought with him until I got him aboard. I was very proud of my catch and resented the fact that when they smoked that salmon and put it in cans, they labeled it, "Caught by Gen. Mark Clark."

Life was so good at the Presidio and in San Francisco, for Wayne and I always loved that city and had begun to feel it was our home. We talked about living there after retirement and enjoying its unbelievably fine weather and the warm hospitality for which it is so justly famed.

196

We let our love of San Francisco become known, so well known that a few years later, when Wayne was about to retire, somebody floated rumors that he planned to settle there and run for mayor. Nothing was further from his mind, of course. For to him, and to me, retirement meant an end to strife, military or political. It might mean work, hard work at a worthwhile job, but no politics.

Wayne and I had that very clear between us.

CHAPTER   FIFTEEN

IN 1950 WE HAD TO LEAVE OUR FIRST POSTWAR
home in the United States. It was quite a wrench to me to have to
say good-by to the Presidio, with all its happy memories. But once
again I learned that in the Army each new post carried with it a
special attraction and a special kind of happiness.

Our new post was Fort Monroe, Virginia, on Chesapeake Bay
overlooking famed Hampton Roads, where the Navy kept battle-
ships, carriers, cruisers, and other fighting ships. Wayne's new job
was Chief of the Army Field Forces, and as such he was in charge
of all training of our Army. As a professional soldier he was overjoyed with the command, which gave him the opportunity to put into
practice for the entire Army the many things he had learned in such
a long career of soldiering. It was a soldier's job and Wayne was
first and last a soldier.

But there was a big surprise for us almost as soon as we got to
Fort Monroe. A battleship was dumped right in our front yard. It
was not just an ordinary battleship, either. It was the proudest ship
of the fleet, the U.S.S. *Missouri.* On this ship was signed the Japanese surrender in Tokyo Bay on September 2, 1945. But proud as
she was, the *Missouri* got stuck in the mud right outside the window
of our new home.

198

Wayne took one look and sent greetings to the admiral. I don't think any admiral ever received such greetings before. Wayne's message read: "I see the battleship is here to stay."

The message was not, alas, appreciated, as the grounding of the *Missouri* came right in the midst of the Air Force–Navy controversy in Washington on the merits and vulnerability of our giant battlewagons.

Monroe was delightful to me. Our home there was old and big and gracious, made and planned for the quiet pleasures of an earlier day. I developed a beautiful rose garden with carefully tended paths which became a source of constant happiness to me, for I felt I was getting something of the flavor of the life the old Southerners had loved so well.

There was more than just the flowers and the spacious Southern home and the soft warmth of Virginia to remind us of the Old South. There was history all around us. The Casemate Club, completely surrounded by a moat with drawbridges, was an example. It was the club for the officers of Fort Monroe, but long before, it was the prison for Jefferson Davis—one of the oldest prisons, in fact, in America. Davis had been there almost two years, held in one small unheated room with only a bed and a Bible to comfort him, before his health failed and he was moved to another prison.

At the time we first saw it, the Casemate Club was old and so filled with history and tradition that the older officers and their wives seemed to think it should stay just as it was. I disagreed. I always had liked to try to improve and beautify posts, and if I ever saw a club that needed beautifying the Casemate was it. I did not want to wipe out the historical effect of that grand old building, but it was, after all, a club and the longer we were there, the stronger the urge became to repair it. It was simply too unattractive, drab, and dark—like a morgue.

Finally, I was asked to do something about it, and Ann and I went to work. We did it over completely, hanging blue drapes with Schiaparelli-pink walls, re-covering the dark furniture with gay chintz. New lighting was installed, and trailing vines in brackets which held electric candles lined the walls. We went all out and it was beautiful, nor had it lost its historic charm.

When the big opening night came I became suddenly afraid, almost afraid to go to the dinner. I feared the reaction of the elders, the retired officers and their wives who had liked the club the way it was. Ann and I thought we had done a good job and we liked the effect we had created, but as the time for the dinner grew shorter my confidence ebbed away. For a while I wanted to sneak home and hide. But my fears were groundless. Everyone seemed pleased and many were delighted with the changes. We had a gay and happy evening. And Ann and I were pleased as Punch to see the way the people flocked from one room to another to see the innovations—the television room, the game room, the ladies' luncheon room, and an adorable little nursery where families attending the parties could leave their children.

Fort Monroe was real Army. The honor guard marched frequently in the morning, with band. It was a grand sight to see those spick-and-span soldiers marching across the green of the parade grounds with magnificent Chesapeake Bay for a background. And always there was a little parade following the big one. A band of small boys and one little dog fell in behind the soldiers almost every time and marched so seriously, aping the soldiers so completely, that the effect was hilarious. Even the little dog seemed to catch something of the spirit and trotted on a straighter line than usual.

I was surrounded by friends whom we had grown to know and love on former posts. The Sullivans lived next door, the Howards were nearby, as were the Coburn Smiths, and many, many others who played such a large part in making our life a happy one.

We had many visitors at Fort Monroe as officers from a number of allied nations came to talk with Wayne about the training methods of the American Army. One visitor was a four-star British general. It was all very formal with a reception, dinner, a guard of honor—the works. But Wayne could tell me nothing about that when he came home. All he could remember was the shock he had had when the British general arrived. "It was the most fantastic experience," Wayne said. "I have an inferiority complex."

Then he explained: "That general started coming out of the plane and I thought he never would finish. More and more and more of him came out. Finally he made it. He was six foot eight!" Wayne, who usually towers over people, said he felt almost small in comparison.

Wayne and I flew to Canada from Fort Monroe to visit Field Marshal and Lady Alexander. Lord Alexander and Wayne had become fast friends while serving together in Italy, and Wayne had succeeded the Field Marshal in command of the Fifteenth Army Group. He was now governor-general of the Dominion.

We flew from Fort Monroe to Ottawa in February. It was an unseasonable 72 above zero at Fort Monroe, and a very seasonable 12 below zero in Ottawa when we landed four hours later.

At Ottawa we had to stand in the open for some time at the airport, greeting people and reviewing an honor guard, and I was chilled to the marrow before the ceremonies were over. Then from the airfield Wayne went to a men's luncheon and I went to the Country Club for lunch with the ladies. It was so nice and snug and warm in the Country Club living room that I was just beginning to thaw when the Canadians, accustomed to cold weather, said we would eat on the sun porch. By the time lunch was over I felt as though I were frozen solid.

That evening we went to a concert with Lord and Lady Alexander, sitting in their box. The gown I wore was decorative but not functional and I never did get warm. Toward the end of the performance I began to have the kind of ache that comes with the flu. And the theater was only the beginning of the evening. There was a reception and late supper afterward. Wayne and I stood beside Lord and Lady Alexander through the reception and there was no way for me to get away. No way voluntarily, that is, since I did get away involuntarily. I blacked out and kept from falling only by grabbing Wayne's arm. He stood on no protocol but took me upstairs and made excuses for me later.

I stayed in bed with my head on the royal pillow for the rest of our four-day stay in Ottawa. It was so warm there. And I believe that the kind bedside visits from Lord and Lady Alexander permitted me to get to know them better than if I had been up and taking part in all the social formalities they had planned. In any event, I didn't get out of that warm bed until it was time to leave for the airport and fly back to warm Virginia.

I loved life in Virginia at Fort Monroe. I felt utterly happy and carefree there and Wayne was extremely busy with his work, the kind of work he really loved. Occasionally he could break away and we would go fishing, but those opportunities were rare.

Ann was a joy. She had her studio at the fort and was moving ahead rapidly in her painting. Bill was an Infantry captain, stationed at Fort Benning, Georgia.

I knew in my heart that this happiness was stolen and only temporary. The Korean War was raging. It was like those last happy days at the War College almost ten years before, in 1941. Every happy and contented moment was something to be treasured. So I counted my blessings and lived each moment fully and joyously.

And then it came. Bill requested orders to Korea, and got them. It fulfilled his heart's desire. He reminded us how unhappy he had been not to get into World War II and how his dad had argued with him to get him to go to West Point instead of enlisting. Wayne then reminded Bill that he had told him at the time that he probably would have plenty of war to fight after he finished West Point.

So for the second time I sent a loved one off to war. How well I know what parents and wives go through while their dear ones are out on the front lines. How well I know the nagging fear and anxiety that becomes a constant and never-forgotten part of the consciousness of the ones who are left behind.

Eventually Bill was evacuated to the United States on a hospital airplane. He had three Purple Hearts, two Silver Stars, a Distinguished Service Cross and a battlefield promotion to major. He also had mortar-shell fragments in his lung, fragments which will be with him the rest of his life. It was a knee wound as well as the lung injury that finally led to Bill's medical retirement from the Army, in 1955. With those wounds he just couldn't keep up the pace of the Infantry.

202

We obtained a second son at Fort Monroe. Wayne's aide, Capt. Gordon Oosting, West Point class of 1946, and Ann announced to us one night that they planned to marry. We were delighted, for Wayne and I both loved Gordon and secretly I had hoped for a long time that Ann would marry him. But I guess you always get a special heart throb when your daughter announces she plans to leave you to set up her own home. I know I did.

Ann was radiantly happy and prankish. Nothing was important to her but her forthcoming marriage. The morning after they told us their plans Wayne was busy in his office and Gordon was on duty in the anteroom. Wayne needed Gordon quickly and pushed the buzzer. Nothing happened. Gordon was never like that before. He was a perfect aide who always snapped to when called. Wayne was puzzled and buzzed a second time. Never had he been obliged to do that for Gordon. Still nothing happened and Wayne, becoming irked, jammed his thumb on the buzzer button and kept it there until Gordon appeared.

His appearance was another surprise. He more or less slouched through the doorway, grinned, and asked, "You want me, Pops?"

Wayne exploded. "You 'pops' me, and I'll 'pop' you." he shouted.

Gordon was still in the Army and still Wayne's aide and he got scared. Hurriedly he explained, "Ann thought it would be funny, sir."

Gordon has been a wonderful son to us and husband to Ann. Wayne and I feel forever thankful for the superior man Ann married and the wonderful girl Bill took as his wife later. For my part, Gordon is one of the most admirable men I have ever had the privilege to know, and Audrey Caire, the beautiful girl from New Orleans who married Bill, and mother of our first grandchild, is an equal joy to us.

We didn't realize it fully until it happened, but there is no happiness quite like that of seeing one's children well married and set for long years of satisfying family life. When that happens a parent feels a great sense of accomplishment, something like a happy ending to a beautiful story.

Neither Bill nor Gordon remained in the Army. Bill was out by disability because of his Korean wounds, and Gordon, who like Ann is a deeply religious person, decided to go into civilian life where he could be more active in religious work.

The happy days at Fort Monroe ended in a terrible flurry of activity and a final burst of deep emotion for me. With Wayne gone off to Japan to take command of the United Nations forces fighting the Communists in Korea, I was left alone to make the preparations for Ann's wedding and face the job of breaking up our home once again and moving to a new one in Tokyo.

I had cried twice since my marriage to Wayne: once when Wayne left for war; the other time, when Bill left our happy home at the War College to go to West Point and, for the first time since my marriage, I was alone. Now, that night after Ann and Gordon were married and gone on their honeymoon, I returned to my bedroom and broke down and cried for the third time in my married life.

CHAPTER SIXTEEN

JAPAN WAS OUR LAST STOP IN THE ARMY. Wayne was sent there in May of 1952 as Commander in Chief, United Nations Command, to succeed his old friend Matt Ridgway, who went to Paris to head up the NATO forces. It was to be an eventful year and a half. It started for Wayne with the crisis over the prisoner riots at Koje Island in Korea and ended with the crisis over the armistice that stopped the shooting in the Korean War.

Wayne had gone on to Japan ahead of me and was at Haneda Airport to greet me when our airplane landed. The rain was pouring down. I didn't know it then, but we were having the *nubai,* or spring rain, which is difficult to live with but which does so much to keep Japan the lush, green, beautiful country that it is.

Rain or no rain, I was overjoyed to arrive in Japan. The main thing was that I would be with my husband again and that I would be able to help him at least a little bit to get through those trying days of the Korean War. It had been a long trip, too, with an all-day delay for engine repairs at Fort Lewis, Washington, and later delays for weather at Anchorage, and at Shemya in the Aleutians, and I was glad to be on civilized ground again. From Shemya we had taken the long hop to Tokyo, flying over water not far from the areas the Russians patrol off the Kurile Islands.

The drive home from the airport with Wayne gave me my first exciting view of the Orient. In the gray and misty rain, Tokyo looked like all the old Japanese prints I had ever seen. The little frame and paper houses were close together; the lanterns swung in the doorways of shops, more for advertising than illumination; and nearing the city we passed a huge, sprawling place that looked like a minor palace to me but proved to be an elaborate geisha house, one of the largest in the Tokyo area. Farther on we crossed a bridge and were faced with a high stone wall exactly like those in Japanese woodcuts. Behind it was a parklike area, the private grounds of a mansion once owned by a Prince of the Blood and later used by the American Army as a billet for visiting VIPs.

Everything I saw on that ride home was new and strange and entrancing. The Japanese really did carry those colorful and familiar paper umbrellas, slick and shiny with fish oil and rain water. They really did wear kimonos in the streets, but these were loose, comfortable-looking kimonos, not the stiff, binding kind which are worn on formal occasions. And the Japanese really did wear wooden clogs, called *geta,* which were held on by a thong that went between the big toe and the second toe. The *geta* had two wooden crosspieces under each foot which served as the soles of the footwear. On rainy days, such as this one, many Japanese wore *geta* with extra-high runners which raised their feet above most of the little puddles on the sidewalks and streets.

I divided my attention between the strange wonders outside the car and my husband inside. He was filled with questions about Bill, Ann, Gordon and the wedding and our friends and my trip. I answered as well as I could and gradually came to realize that although he looked much as he had six weeks earlier when he left Monroe, he had changed. The strain of Koje-Do and the prison riots and the burden of such a frustrating war in which victory was not the goal showed in his voice and his manner. He was tense and preoccupied and a little hardened. As he talked I came to realize what a terrible responsibility he had shouldered and what an awesome problem our country had to face in Korea. Men were dying at the front. A few men were listening to Communist lies day after day at the armistice talks in Panmunjom. And my husband even then was trying to find an answer to the fateful question of whether it would be worth the cost in lives to go all out to win the war. The question was whether the losses needed to win the war in Korea would save American lives in the future.

Wayne conferred at great length with his sea, air, and ground commanders. They all agreed the war could and should be won. Wayne was convinced that victory in Korea would save America another war in which the loss of American lives would be far greater than the cost of winning the Korean War. He recommended to Washington, therefore, that the decision be made to make the effort necessary to win the war. But the decision went the other way. History alone will determine, finally, whether it would have been better to have fought on to win the Korean War.

All these things were weighing on my husband as we drove to our new home in Tokyo, causing a tautness and strain I had not seen in him since the end of World War II. I had little time to be troubled that day, however. We reached our home, Maeda House, and I was enthralled. It was a mansion of thirty-two rooms with magnificent grounds. The furnishings were beautiful, for Penny Ridgway, Matt Ridgway's wife, had done an outstanding job in redecorating the house only a few weeks before when the occupation of Japan ended. Until then the United States Commander in Chief also had been the Supreme Commander for the Allied Powers in Japan—SCAP. General and Mrs. MacArthur and then General and Mrs. Ridgway had lived in the American Embassy close to downtown Tokyo while Japan was still occupied. But when the occupation ended, the week before Wayne arrived in Tokyo, the position of SCAP was abolished. Among other things, that meant that the Embassy went back to the State Department as the home of the new ambassador, our old friend, Bob Murphy.

The Ridgways had lived in Maeda House only a short time when word came from Washington that Matt was to move on to Paris to command NATO forces, succeeding General Eisenhower. But Penny earned my eternal gratitude for the great taste she had shown in choosing colors, draperies, and furnishings for Maeda House. The huge drawing room opened directly onto a long porch that overlooked grounds so large that they included a one-hole golf course. There also were tennis and croquet courts and a badminton net was in place. Wayne used to stretch his legs occasionally in the evening with a game of croquet or a walk through the well-tended, smooth dirt paths which seemed to wander on endlessly through the grounds.

When I arrived there were many servants, gardeners, and guards employed at the house. Some of them, I learned, had worked with the MacArthurs and the Ridgways at the American Embassy. When the war with Japan ended and the MacArthurs moved into Tokyo, they found the Embassy and residence in good condition, and a full staff of servants was on hand to greet them, men and women who had been working there on Pearl Harbor Day. Some had served Ambassador Joseph R. Grew years earlier, and during the war stayed on in the residence, maintaining both the house and grounds just as though the Ambassador still lived there. The neutral Swiss, who looked after American interests in Japan during the war, gave general supervision to the staff while the Americans were away. The old-time servants stayed on when Bob Murphy took over, too, but some of the younger people they trained during the postwar years went out to Maeda House to work for the Army.

Magnificent as Maeda House was, it never really was ours. We never felt it was our home. The chinaware, silver and table linen belonged to somebody else, was only borrowed.

The incident that made us think of ourselves more as guests than householders involved the icebox and a midnight snack. Like most people, Wayne and I liked to raid the icebox at midnight, and one night we raided the one at Maeda House. We found it padlocked and didn't even know where the key was hidden. We felt like strangers in our own home.

The cook, like most Japanese cooks, took his responsibilities most seriously. The food supply was one of them and if anything was stolen he would lose face. So he rigged a padlock to our icebox and kept the only key. We would have had to awaken him to get that icebox open. So—we went to bed hungry.

There was really little I could do to improve the gardens, but I could add to them. Almost immediately ideas came to me. I wanted fresh vegetables. I wanted home-grown strawberries. I longed to labor in the soil. Through an interpreter I told our gardeners what magnificent flowers they had created, how beautifully they had kept the grounds, and that I wanted them to show me some of the secrets of their success. I explained that I wished too to spend many happy hours gardening, not to improve on their way but so that I could absorb a little of their wonderful skill.

On that basis they welcomed me, and only once did I incur their disapproval. I cut all the dried flowers. The Japanese are frugal people, and the dead flowers had been left for seed for the following year. My basket was filled to overflowing when they discovered what I had done. With much arm waving, jabbering, and head shaking, they tried to explain. I hadn't the faintest notion what the commotion was about and sought out our interpreter. He at last explained to me and through him I told the gardeners I was sorry. I promised them, however, I would send for American seed and next year we would have even larger and more beautiful flowers. They all bowed low and seemed extremely pleased.

To me our house had a sad history. It was built by a great landowner and soldier, Baron Maeda, one of the wealthiest men in Japan. Because his first marriage was childless, the Maedas, as was the custom, adopted a boy child to carry on the family name. Some time after this the first baroness died. The Baron took a second wife, a beautiful girl of great dignity from a fine old Japanese family. She had been given the best of education and had command of several languages, but her family was not wealthy. This was not considered important, for the Baron was one of the rich men of Japan. Four children were born of this second marriage, one boy and three girls. The Maedas traveled together extensively and the children were educated in the best European schools.

209

It was at the time of the second marriage that the Baron built Maeda House. The main house was built in the Western manner, but connected to it was a delightful Japanese-style home. The Maedas used the palacelike Western home to entertain guests, but the Japanese house was the one in which they lived.

Life for the young Baroness and her four children was idyllic. There was more than enough for them and their world was one of security, luxury, and family happiness.

Then came Pearl Harbor and the Baron went to war. He was killed. But the Baroness lost more than her husband. Under Japanese law the adopted son of the first marriage was the legal heir to the estate, and there was little left for the Baroness except an older home much closer to downtown Tokyo.

Of course, I knew nothing of this story when I arrived in Japan. But after a few weeks at Maeda House I became conscious of the love, happiness, and infinite plans that had gone into the beautiful home and the magnificent grounds. I made inquiries and learned the story. I was told that Madame Maeda was helping to support herself and her children by writing daily articles for a Japanese newspaper and by giving language lessons.

All this I knew before I met Madame Maeda. Our meeting resulted from a chance conversation with the wife of a Japanese cabinet minister, who told me that Madame Maeda was her cousin. I asked if Madame Maeda had ever seen her home since she lost it and was told she had not. A little fearfully I suggested that perhaps she would like to visit her old home. I was fearful because I had no way of knowing how the Baroness would react to a return to the site of her lost happiness.

Very graciously Madame Maeda accepted my invitation to tea. I sent our car for her and she seemed happy to return to her old home. We walked all through the grounds and the house. She was most interested in the changes that had been made in the wallpaper and the general color scheme, and most complimentary.

That first visit started us on the path to a strong friendship, and it was not long before she asked me to have lunch with her. Her house was a fine old Western-style home on a hill. There was a tennis court down a terrace and a lovely garden in back. But the house itself no longer was hers. She rented it to a Tokyo newspaper whose owners and editors used the formal drawing rooms downstairs for conferences, round-table discussions, and for dinners and parties. Madame Maeda kept a small apartment upstairs for herself, and I could not help noticing that although her furnishings were of good quality, they were old and worn.

Madame Maeda served an excellent luncheon, however, and, as always, was most gracious and accomplished socially. There I met the Maeda children for the first time and asked them if they would like to come visit me at the house they had been raised in and see the grounds in which they had spent so many happy childhood hours. Their emotion was so strong none of them could answer and their mother had to accept for them.

They all came for tea in the afternoon. It was sad to watch them, for they seemed to be in a dream of bygone and happier times. They touched the trees they had climbed as children, and could hardly take their eyes off the courts on which they had learned to play tennis.

There was a poignant little scene at the chicken houses. The children remembered that when they lived in the great house they kept rabbits in the little houses which I had converted into chicken coops.

Madame Maeda was more meditative that day than during any of her earlier visits. She seemed to be thinking about the day when she was reigning queen at this grand home, and I felt strongly that her sorrow was not so much for herself but for her children.

There were many things of sadness in Japan, as in all countries. One day I went to Yokohama to present two thousand dollars' worth of gifts, which had been purchased by Americans for Japanese orphans, to representatives of twenty-eight orphanages in Kanagawa Prefecture, which includes Yokohama. It was quite a ceremony. The governor of Kanagawa and the mayor of Yokohama were there, and there was an orchestra of thirty blind children, all orphans.

I presented the gifts in the name of the American donors. There were blue washable uniforms for the girls, darker blue uniforms for the boys. There were new wool blankets, an assortment of sturdy toys, cans of powdered milk, diapers, wool underclothing, baseballs, bats, and gloves. There was a large operating lamp for the charity hospital, and there were even *tatami,* the thick, springy, rice-straw mats the Japanese use as flooring.

Ceremonies like this, for the unfortunate, always depress me, and I felt very bad that day. I could not help wondering what these children, these orphans, had in store for them in the future, how they could wring some pleasure and happiness from a world that had given them such a cruel beginning in life. The children, however, seemed happy that day, and the blind children most of all. I was glad that they were being taught something about music and that they appeared to love it. The orphanages could spend little on musical instruments, and the children had only the poorest kind. Most of them had mouth organs, but a few played a sort of imitation marimba. One seven-year-old boy was quite an artist with the instrument and the officials were very proud of him. They told me that at the orphanage they had an old battered piano and that this youngster, blind and with almost no help from a teacher, played with amazing talent.

And I was glad, too, that the children all were so clean. The clothing they wore was patched and mended, it is true, but it was also freshly laundered and pressed and the children apparently took pride in keeping themselves neat.

In Tokyo Wayne and I had some personal frustrations aside from such things as a padlocked icebox. Both of us, for instance, have always enjoyed browsing around a city, and Tokyo was packed with wonderful things to see along the Ginza and other shopping areas. But Wayne is six-feet two-inches tall; wherever we went among the short Japanese he stood out like a sore thumb. Just once we tried to walk through the streets and shops incognito. Wayne put on old civilian clothes and dark glasses, and we hoped that there would be so many Americans on the street that we would not be noticed. It was a vain hope. Wayne was spotted almost as soon as he stepped into the throng moving slowly along the side-walk. And once he was spotted, the crowd closed in. It was a friendly, curious crowd, but nonetheless a crowd. Our dream of a quiet prowl through Japanese shops went glimmering.

I knew how much Wayne missed because of this constant attention. Alone I attracted no attention at all but was just another American "dependent" wife looking for bargains and souvenirs. Nobody could see me over the heads of the crowd, and my picture wasn't often in the papers. The result was anonymity and freedom —well, almost freedom. By regulation a guard and interpreter had to go with me everywhere. The overwhelming majority of Japanese in Tokyo were friendly to Americans and almost all American women felt completely safe in going into the business districts or almost anywhere else alone. But my husband was commanding the United Nations forces fighting the Communists in Korea, and among the seven and one-half million people in Tokyo there were some rabidly anti-American Communists who might conceivably have attacked the commanding general of the United Nations Command or his wife.

I was fortunate in having Mrs. Kazuko Aso as a friend in Tokyo. She is the daughter of Shigeru Yoshida, the Prime Minister of Japan for so many years, and also, because his wife was not living, his official hostess, helping him with English and, I believe, sometimes advising him. Father and daughter were very close.

Mrs. Aso took me to back-alley shops, quaint other-worldish places which specialized in fine artisanship. The people worked in everything from paper to silver and my home in Charleston now has many of the beautiful things the Japanese craftsmen make.

My particular joy was the *obi,* the formal sash a woman winds around her waist outside her kimono. Spread out, the *obi* is about a foot wide and ten to twelve feet long, and Japanese women wear it wrapped so tightly that it is like a board. It is made of heavy tapestry silk, and the colors and designs are magnificent. One I was particularly fond of had a white background enlivened by gold and silver threads. The design was a great splash of pastel colors woven into a picture of a ricksha filled with flowers.

213

I even made place mats for my dinner table from *obi*. I did this by removing all stitching so the silk could be spread to its greatest width. Then the *obi* was cut down the middle, lengthwise, giving two rather wide strips. From each of these, I cut nineteen-inch sections, to form the place mats for the head and foot of the table. The remaining strips I used to form an unbroken place mat down either side of the table. I like to think the idea was original with me. At least I am certain I never saw any others like it in Tokyo.

It was fun to shop for *obi*. They were found in little old shops tucked away in back alleys as well as in the big modern department stores on the Ginza, but it was always far more fun to poke around in the little stores than in the big ones. These resembled living rooms more than shops, and customers went through sliding glass doors into a little open vestibule. The shop floor was raised about eighteen inches from the entranceway, and the floor was of rice-straw *tatami,* which meant that if I wanted to step up into the shop itself I would have to take off my shoes.

Like many Americans, I preferred to keep my shoes on and therefore just sat on the open edge of the shop floor. The proprietor, who invariably seemed to be a little old man in a black kimono, then would spread out his wares before me. I found this far more pleasant than standing at a counter in the Western-style department stores. It was more like visiting a friend than shopping.

Another joy in Tokyo was that of the flowers and the blossoms. The cherry blossoms in April are all that the tourist books say they are, solid masses of white and pink that make the world seem wonderful, and tulips, jonquils, lilies, and pansies were everywhere. I was so delighted by the beauty that I wrote a friend that I imagined heaven to be just like this.

Tokyo usually is called a man's town, but there were some wonderful things for women there, too. The shopping, of course, was wonderful, with silver shops, jewelry shops, pearl shops, silk shops, curio shops, and art shops among the finest in the world. Then the Army itself provided us with fine services. At the post-

214

exchange beauty shop, where I went, they had Japanese girls who were expert operators. And the prices were astounding. It cost only sixty cents for a fine shampoo or a wonderful manicure or even a pedicure.

One Japanese service that Americans learned to love was the massage at which the Japanese are expert. Men and women, many of them blind, are trained to give a massage as good as any I have had anywhere in the world. They work on nerves and nerve ends, using some of the same principles that Japanese jujitsu wrestlers use in their matches. The study of the nerves of the body, applied with equal effectiveness to jujitsu and massage, is an ancient art in Japan, and surprisingly enough, an hour-long massage in our own homes cost only a dollar.

Wayne refused to get bogged down in social activities in Tokyo as he had been in Austria. He had the great volume of the Korean War work as his excuse, and begged off social functions as much as possible, but even so, our life was a very busy one. Whenever we had a rare free evening we would have a quiet chat upstairs before dinner and then dine in complete relaxation. Those evenings made Wayne happy and helped to refresh him for his labors in both Japan and Korea.

One of those evenings I will never forget. Wayne came home a little late and decided not to change to fresh clothing. "I'm going down there and eat just as I am," he said, "without a tie."

When the dinner call came we walked out into the upstairs hall. Wayne was full of life and energy, happy to be able to live for a few hours just as though he did not have the cares of a war on his shoulders. We walked down the hall and Wayne looked longingly at the wide winding banister that lined the formal staircase to the great reception hall.

"I will," he mumbled. I didn't know what he was talking about until I saw him straddle the banister and slide down it like a small boy.

Japanese servants are wonderfully well trained. Three of them were at the foot of the stairs. They bowed low when the general reached the end of his slide, just as they bowed low every evening when we descended the stairs for dinner. Maybe they hid smiles with their bows that night, but if they smiled, it didn't show.

Wayne, in a playful mood, asked, "Didn't General MacArthur ever do that?"

At last the servants were shocked. One gasped, "Oh no, sir."

CHAPTER SEVENTEEN

THE JAPANESE THINK OF THEIR HOMELAND as a link to heaven. They call their emperor *Tenno Heiko,* "Son of Heaven." During our stay in Japan we met the Emperor and Empress a number of times and found them far more folksy and human than their titles or the pomp and ceremony that surrounded them would seem to imply.

Wayne and I saw plenty of this pomp. The Crown Prince Akihito reached his eighteenth birthday while we were in Japan, and there were ancient ceremonies of investiture which officially designated him heir apparent to the throne of Japan. The ceremonies of the Imperial Family of Japan are perhaps the oldest still followed anywhere in the world. The Japanese claim that the first emperor, Jimmu, ascended the throne in 660 B.C. and that the present emperor, Hirohito, is 124th in an unbroken line of descendants. The ceremonies handed down through the ages certainly carried an atmosphere of great antiquity.

Invitations to the investiture ceremony were most detailed. The women invited were told they were to wear long dresses with long sleeves, and that they were not to wear black or purple, black being too depressing and purple only for royalty. The guest list included the leading foreign diplomats in Tokyo at the time. Wayne was the only military man invited. There were a large number of Japanese officials who had earned the honor by their service to Japan and a large number of Japanese noblemen whose families, down through the ages, had been close to the throne.

The Imperial Chamberlain met Wayne and me when we arrived at one o'clock at the palace, which is hidden in a vast parklike area that lies behind moats and great stone walls in the center of Tokyo. The Chamberlain escorted us to an elevator which took us to a huge drawing room where the Japanese officials and titled nobles were gathered. We chatted with them for a little while and then the Emperor, Empress, and the Crown Prince were announced.

The Crown Prince looked such a little boy. He was still in his teens, slightly built, rather handsome but so very young-looking. The Imperial Family greeted the guests formally and then left to meet other guests who were in other rooms. Soon word came that we were to move on to the banquet hall. As we walked we passed Japanese musicians kneeling on the floor and playing the music of the ancients on bamboo flutes pitched so high they almost hurt our eardrums. Inside we were shown to our places, which were lower than the dais on which the Imperial Family was to be seated. When the Emperor, Empress, and Crown Prince entered, everyone rose.

The banquet itself was most strange to me. The Japanese had anticipated that the foreign guests might be confused, so they provided little printed diagrams with English-language notations that told us what the food was, its meaning, and where it would be placed before us. Each dish was symbolic. There was one dish for longevity, another for health, a third for good luck. It all looked pretty enough, but my palate was not trained to relish the strange foods put before me. There was carp, which we were told was symbolic of male power and strength. The carp is a symbol of masculinity in another way in Japan. Every May 5, on what once was called Boys' Day, every Japanese family flies a great paper or silk carp from its housetop for each son in the family. A paper or silk eel is flown for the girls, the symbol signifying grace, slenderness and femininity.

The carp was all right to eat, for me, but other dishes were difficult. We were served thin slices of raw fish, chilled. With it we got some soy sauce, mustard, and horseradish which we mixed together ourselves in a shallow china sauce dish. Then we were served octopus soup. All this we ate with chopsticks.

The food was served in grand style. It was carried into the banquet hall by silent, beautifully trained servants. Each serving was on an individual square lacquer tray.

Beside each place at the table was a gift, a fine, round lacquer bowl decorated in gold with the Imperial Crest, the sixteen-petal chrysanthemum. In addition each guest was given a beautiful white box, also carrying the Imperial Crest. During the luncheon I peeked into the box at my place and saw that it was empty, but after we left the table somebody, probably one of the chamberlains, returned and packed the remaining food on each plate into one of the white boxes. We found two of the food-filled boxes in our car when we started for home.

Many months later we had a much more enjoyable and less ceremonious luncheon at the palace with the Emperor and Empress. Wayne and I were the guests of honor. Bob Murphy, our Ambassador, was the only other foreigner there, and the five other guests were Imperial Household Chamberlains and Ladies-in-Waiting of the Empress. I was secretly relieved when the luncheon turned out to be Western style. We sat on chairs and ate Western food with knives and forks. The table was set beautifully, with orchids of all sizes and varieties filling the center with a great mass of soft, delicate color.

The food this time was delicious, worthy of the finest of American or French cuisine. The service was gold, right down to the knives and forks. Although neither the Emperor nor Empress drink intoxicants, there was red and white wine and champagne for the guests. And at the end of the luncheon we were served coffee rather than the usual tea. Many Japanese prefer coffee but can't afford it, and in downtown Tokyo there are many fashionable places which serve only Brazilian coffee and little cakes, but only the more well-to-do can afford the prices.

At this small palace luncheon for ten we talked with the Emperor and Empress through the official court interpreter, since neither the Emperor nor the Empress tried to speak English with us. They did seem well informed about the world, however, for all the cloistered life they lived behind the moats and walls of the palace. As parents, too, they were keenly interested in what their son, Crown Prince Akihito, would find during the trip he planned to make to the United States.

The Emperor was most interested in the Korean War and plied Wayne with questions about the military prospects, the chances for armistice, the economic and political issues involved, and the probable over-all effect on Japan. Wayne was impressed with the caliber of the questions the Emperor asked and came away convinced that the man on the throne of Japan was one fully capable of grasping the meaning of the historic events taking place around him.

The Emperor and Empress arranged one of our gayest little outings in Japan. We were their guests at the Imperial Duck Reserve for a duck hunt, although actually they were hosts in absentia, for the custom is for them to extend invitations only, but never to accompany the guests in hunting the ducks. And a Japanese duck hunt is different from any other in the world.

The reserve is about an hour's drive out of Tokyo. There is a pleasant hunting lodge where we rested and chatted after the drive and where we received instructions on how to hunt ducks, Japanese fashion. Prince Takamatsu, brother of the Emperor, and his beautiful princess acted as hosts and explained the business to us.

From the lodge it was but a short walk to the hunting grounds. The ducks, thousands of them, were swimming on a big lake surrounded by a dike or levee. There were a number of concrete shelters around the lake looking like pillboxes cut in half with one side open.

Each shelter was connected to the lake by a very deep and narrow canal, some twenty or thirty feet long. At the head of each canal was an iron grating which literally served as a doorway to the lake. The grating could be raised to permit the ducks to swim from the lake to get the food spread as bait in the narrow canals. In the face of the shelter there was a speakeasy-type peephole from which the grate and canal could be seen without alarming the ducks.

Helpers were all over the place. Two hid at the head of the canal to raise the grating and hurry the ducks toward the shelter, after the food. Another stood at the peephole to give us the signal to begin the hunt.

This was a hunt without guns. Our weapons were oversized butterfly nets on long poles. We huddled behind the shelter as quiet as church mice, waiting for the signal that would send us running on tiptoe to our assigned places over the canal. We were divided into two groups, one to run to either side of the water.

Finally the keeper at the peephole raised his hand—the signal that the grating was up and the ducks were coming in. We got ready to run. At the proper moment the keeper threw down his hand.

I was mighty clumsy at this point of the operation, but I noticed that nobody was being particularly graceful. For one thing the ground was wet and slippery, and for another, the pole and big net were terribly awkward to handle, particularly when you had to run with them over slippery, wet ground, without making a sound.

I did the best I could to remember how we used to run silently as Indians when we were little girls, but I'm afraid the memory didn't do me much good. I felt I was making as much noise as a herd of elephants as I struggled out with the net and the pole.

There were two phases of the run. First we ran to our assigned positions at the foot of the sharp, head-high rise that led to the edge of the canal. Once in position there, we were given the second signal which started us clambering up the skiddy, muddy ground. Everything was supposed to be silent until we were in our places looking down on the ducks.

Then, again on signal, everybody started shouting and keepers waved their arms, all in an effort to frighten the ducks. And it did. They went wild trying to get out of that bedlam. The only place for them to go was up, straight up from that narrow canal, whose walls rose four or five feet above the water.

The ducks were frantic and flew wildly from the water. That was when we were supposed to catch them in our nets. We all waved the long poles and hoped a duck would fly into our nets or that we could bag one with a clever stroke. There may be more science to it than that, but that was all I could figure to do.

Most of the ducks got through the row of nets but a few were caught each time, helplessly entangled in the webbing. We made a number of forays at the ducks, moving from one shelter to another, and I even caught one myself, although I always have suspected that the orders were out to the keepers to continue the hunt until every guest had caught at least one. I know there was no skill in my catch. All I did was run out there, stick the net over the water, and hope something would fly into it.

The unscheduled feature of the afternoon came when an admiral waved his net so frantically that he knocked off the hat of the British Ambassador.

Throughout our stay in Japan our association with the Japanese people on all levels was most pleasant. I never once detected any rancor left over from the war. Certainly there was none on our side among the Americans serving in Japan, and none in my heart.

The friendliness of Japanese toward Americans was particularly evident in the country and smaller towns, where the people saw less of Americans than did the people of the big cities. In the country, away from our military establishments, an American still was something unusual. In the cities, however, people were so accustomed to seeing Americans that they took little notice of us, and we moved among them, quietly and at peace.

CHAPTER EIGHTEEN

LIFE IN JAPAN WAS VERY BUSY FOR US MOST of the time and the tourist holidays we took were few and far between. Wayne bounced back and forth between Tokyo and Korea constantly to work on both the war and the truce talks. The armistice problem was a ticklish one for many reasons. For one thing, President Syngman Rhee of the Republic of Korea did not want a truce, and Wayne's job with him was made even more difficult because Wayne never was quite certain but that Rhee might be right and the armistice nothing but a snare and a delusion.

In Tokyo I was kept busy with all manner of activities. I once jotted down my activities for one day. I will admit it was one of the busier days, but there were many just about like it.

At 9 A.M., I met at my house with a group of American women to work out a program to organize the American Girl Scouts in every prefecture in Japan.

Two hours later, at 11, there was a meeting of the executive council of the Women's Club.

At 12:30 P.M., Wayne and I went to the palace for luncheon with the Emperor and Empress.

At 3 P.M., I had a tea at the house for some people just in from

223

the States. I hadn't met them, but we had mutual friends who asked me to extend courtesies to the visitors.

At 5:30 P.M., we had cocktails for sixty people in honor of Gen. J. Lawton Collins, the Army Chief of Staff who was visiting from Washington, and Gen. Maxwell D. Taylor, who had just arrived to take over the Eighth Army in Korea from Gen. James A. Van Fleet, who was retiring.

At 7:30, we sat down to a dinner in honor of the two generals. The emphasis that day was on high-level, formal business. When you lunch with the Emperor and Empress of Japan and dine with the Chief of Staff of the United States Army on a single day, you have had quite a dose of formality.

Sometimes these formal functions were more fun than others, such as the Air Force party Wayne and I were to attend together one night. At the last minute Wayne had to fly to Korea, and I wanted to refuse, but the officer who arranged the party insisted that I come anyway. Shortly after I arrived I was introduced to a young officer, along with many others. At first I paid little attention to him, but gradually I became aware that every time I walked to a new group of people, this young officer walked with me.

I had been with the Army long enough to know what had happened. The poor fellow had been assigned to watch over me, and I knew what a thankless assignment that was, particularly when he probably had to leave his wife or sweetheart standing off in a corner somewhere.

But he was a very nice young man, the kind of young man you like on sight, and it became something of a game. Every time I went from one group to another I would call him with me. That little gesture was fun for me and I meant it to be fun for him. At least it let him know that I knew he was under orders and that I sympathized with him.

Dinner was served at a large number of small tables, and my place was at a table with Gen. O. P. Weyland, commanding general of the Far East Air Forces, and a few other very high ranking officers. But there was no place for my young man.

224

It was difficult to keep a straight face, but I did my best as I told General Weyland that I wanted his young officer to sit at our table. There was great scurrying among the waiters, and the place settings had to be crowded together a little bit, but my young man got to dine with his big boss that night.

After dinner I again began moving about from one group to another, with my young officer right at my footsteps. I couldn't escape him. But I had to stop him this time. I turned, and as quietly and privately as possible, I said, "Young man, I don't know where you are going, but I am going to the ladies' room."

He turned beet-red with embarrassment, but he had such a fine sense of humor that when I smiled a little to show him I thought the whole thing was very amusing, he broke into a broad grin.

As I settled into a routine, I found that there were many demands on the time of the wife of the commanding general, more, perhaps, in Japan than anywhere else we had been. Social luncheons, just for fun, were all but eliminated from my life, and never was I able to take time to sit down for an afternoon of bridge or to read a book. It got so that I never accepted a luncheon invitation unless it was for official reasons or a charity of one kind or another. My entire time was spent trying to help Wayne by visiting hospitals and orphanages and attending various public functions. He simply did not have the time to attend himself, and I became something of an unofficial representative for him. In this capacity, I visited not only hospitals and orphanages, but art shows, museums, dairies, and the hydroponic farm which provided so much of the fresh vegetable supply for our men in Japan and Korea.

The hydroponic farm was of great interest to me. It was about an hour's ride by automobile from Tokyo, on the highway toward the big air base at Tachikawa. The ride itself always fascinated me, for the highway passed through several small towns whose little shops crowded the road on either side. We had to drive so slowly through those towns that I always got a good view of what the shops had to offer. There were umbrella shops, china shops, brass shops, stores that sold nothing but kimono cloth, souvenir and curio shops, and shops specializing in the entrancing objects of the religions of the East. These included miniature wooden shrines, fine candlesticks, gay paper streamers, and all manner of things that make religious observance a thing of beauty for the Japanese.

The streets always were crowded and street vendors chanted the special calls they had for their wares. The flutes played to call people to the noodle wagon, and the candy man clapped two blocks of wood together and chanted that he had "sweet things" to sell. There were even men who carried two large bowls of goldfish suspended from a bamboo pole balanced over their shoulders.

The hydroponic farm was in open country, back from the road. There vegetables were grown in chemically treated beds of sand or gravel. The farm was developed very early after World War II when American Army doctors said that, because of the use of human fertilizer, Japanese vegetables were a possible source of dysentery. The Japanese protect against it with most careful handling of vegetables in the kitchen, but the risk remains. Besides that, the American housewives who began moving to Japan in the summer of 1946 were not accustomed to washing all their vegetables in what the Japanese called "medicine water," and the doctors just didn't want to take any chances.

The fertilizer is collected daily in Japan by men who drive oxcarts. Rather, they lead the oxcarts, for the Japanese rarely ride on horse- or ox-drawn wagons because of the heavy tax they have to pay for the privilege of riding. That means they move through the streets of the communities, including Tokyo, at a snail's pace, with their loads of aromatic "night soil" fertilizer stacked in their wagons in what Americans called "honey buckets." It was always a hazard on Japanese roads to be caught behind one of those wagons. The roads for the most part are narrow, and if any traffic was coming the other way cars would get stacked up behind the slow-moving honey-bucket wagon. When that happened, even on the hottest summer day, Americans rolled up their car windows tight. I always felt great sympathy for those American families who rode in open jeeps and had no windows to roll up.

Perhaps the most pleasant and personally rewarding of my "duties" were the many parties I gave at Maeda House for children from the orphanages and the neighborhood. On designated afternoons about fifty children ranging in age from six to twelve would come to the house for a few hours and I would serve lemonade, ice-cream cones, cake and cookies, and usually have balloons as favors. The Japanese make wonderful balloons in all shapes and sizes and the kids loved them. I always showed an hour of movies, usually Mickey Mouse, a great favorite with the Japanese children.

Women of the WAC helped me at the parties and seemed to enjoy watching the children play every bit as much as I did. I was both sad and happy to see the children. I was happy to see their joy and to see how hard they tried to make the best of what they had. But I was sad that they had so little. They were always so clean, even though soap was an almost priceless luxury. Their clothing was patched and their socks darned, but always their clothes were clean when they came to my house. But more than that, these children were remarkably well behaved, always careful not to do anything that would annoy or bother us.

I always noticed that the Japanese children never reached for a cookie or piece of cake or anything else. Nor would they ask for anything. They restrained themselves and were content to eat only what was passed to them. That meant harder work for the WACs and me, for we knew those children wanted to stuff themselves and had to keep a constant watch to see that each one had enough to eat.

These parties really were not a duty. There was nothing official about them, and Wayne made a formal ruling that they had to be paid for with personal funds, not with official entertainment money. But I am convinced they paid dividends in Japanese-American relations. Those little Japanese children, I feel confident, always will have a little more understanding of Americans and a little more sympathy and warmth for the people who took the trouble to give them ice cream and cake and Mickey Mouse movies.

I will admit there was a selfish side to those parties. It always made me feel warm all over to see these Japanese orphans, who had so little, have some fun and some goodies for a little while, anyway.

There was work to be done, too, with our own soldiers. The Korean War was still going on. Back home it must have seemed that it had settled into a stalemate, but people were still getting hurt. Our American casualties were running about five hundred a week during all those months of the armistice talks at Panmunjom. The wounded were divided into several categories. Those who could return to duty after short treatment were held in hospitals in Korea. More seriously wounded were flown to Japan, and some were then flown to the United States.

Once a week I visited hospitals. It was a two-way morale mission. The men seemed to like to have a woman stop by and talk with them, and Army public relations people would follow me around to take pictures to send to the families back home. This was the kind of Army public relations few know about, for very few of those pictures ever went to the newspapers. Each picture was meant for the families of the wounded men so that mothers, wives, and sweethearts could see the kind of treatment the men were getting.

In addition, I wrote a little personal note to go with each picture. I knew from bitter experience how much I appreciated letters from people who had seen my Bill when he was in the hospital in Korea or Japan, and I hoped that my letters meant something to the families of these other men wounded in the same war. The letters of gratitude I received from the parents I will treasure all my life.

On a typical day that I remember I talked with fifty-one wounded soldiers. Pictures were taken with forty-five. The other six were wounded so badly, blinded, or their faces so terribly scarred that pictures could not be taken. The men were lonely and homesick. Those who were not too sick physically always seemed to enjoy talking with a woman and seemed thankful that someone thought they were important enough to be visited. I always tried to dress up a bit and wear rich, gay colors on these visits. The men seemed to be partial to soft, fuzzy hats with glittering beads.

With the Korean War and the armistice talks continuing and a new relation with a free Japan developing, there was a constant stream of official guests to Tokyo. It seemed we had an official luncheon about every few days for people from Washington, and in nearly all cases the guests were men. Much as I liked to listen to the talk of these people who were making and implementing United States policy, I found after a while that these luncheons made it difficult for me to do anything else and told Wayne I would prefer to have a cottage cheese and tomato luncheon by myself. He looked at me disapprovingly. "I prefer you to be there," he said. And that was it. Just as in Austria, he wanted me at the table when he had an official luncheon or dinner. Many of the men were old friends of ours, particularly those in the military. And, as Wayne pointed out, at many luncheons we had people from Korea, and they appreciated the chance to talk with a woman after so many months in the battle zone.

The list of luncheon guests in Tokyo would be just about as long as the number of days we lived there. Field Marshal Alexander came while he was Minister of Defense of Great Britain. Marshal Juin of France came up from Indochina. Senators came quite regularly. We entertained the dignitaries from Italy and then New Zealand. The Chief of Staff of the Ethiopian Army came to lunch. So did a Greek general.

One of our most interesting guests was Mrs. Franklin D. Roosevelt. I was doubly pleased, first because we had so few women guests and secondly because I was fond of Mrs. Roosevelt. We had a long talk about places and people we both knew, and I recalled to her how gracious she had been the time I visited her at the White House for a large luncheon, and how I had appreciated the fact of her moving from group to group to be able to speak with each individual guest.

Mrs. Roosevelt said that she so loved and enjoyed people that she never saw her old friends often enough or met as many new friends as she would like. She said she was particularly interested in meeting the men who were making history and their families.

I remarked on her vitality. She seemed even more energetic than she had been ten years earlier when I knew her in the White House. In Tokyo she continued to write her newspaper column, even though it meant she had to stay up a good part of each night to do it. She said that she required little sleep and that, in fact, she had found she seemed to get along better without too much sleep.

Mrs. Roosevelt asked all manner of questions about the work I was doing with orphans and in the Army hospitals. Graciously she assured me nothing I could do would have been more gratifying to the parents of wounded soldiers than to continue sending the letters and pictures to them after my hospital visits.

The guests came from all parts of the world, particularly from countries having troops in Korea, and as the armistice talks moved closer toward their conclusion, the guests came in increasing numbers. Without exception, they were delightful, interesting people and people well worth knowing and talking with. But the luncheons were a strain and consumed a great deal of time. Wayne had to think of his job and of getting enough rest to do it properly. As a result we entertained as much as possible at luncheons and as little as possible at night.

When I arrived in Tokyo I found that Wayne had let his calendar get jammed full for night and day for weeks ahead. My first project was to determine which evening functions were duty and which were not. Wayne works at such a terrific pace, and with such concentration, from early morning to late at night that I was determined to keep as many evenings free for him as possible. That was essential, I felt, to keep him fit to continue the high-pressure work he was doing, running a war on one hand and conducting armistice talks on the other.

Even the clock was against him in Tokyo. Midnight in Tokyo is 10 A.M. in Washington. I never fully realized until I arrived how many times the Pentagon gets an absolutely urgent idea between the hours of 11 A.M. and 3 P.M., Washington time. That time spread is 1 A.M. to 5 A.M. in Tokyo. Time after time Wayne

230

was called out of bed between those hours, often with messages requiring immediate action.

Gradually I sifted the invitations to find which ones could be declined, and after a while we were able to eliminate everything except absolutely official functions which we were duty-bound to accept. In addition, we kept every weekend free, from Saturday noon through Sunday night, when the situation in Korea would permit. Wayne used many of those weekends to make inspection trips through Japan and Korea, but at least he was away from his desk, out in the open air and enjoying a change of scene. I went with him on all those trips and particularly enjoyed seeing the various places in Japan.

We got a real thrill in the fall of 1952 when word came through that our old friend Ike was elected President of the United States. Wayne had known and worked for both President Roosevelt and President Truman, and admired them, as did I. But this was something entirely different. This was a lifelong friend winning the highest office in the world. I was happy because I knew that Ike would take to the White House a deep and understanding patriotism and unquestioned honesty and integrity.

After the elections Ike flew out to Korea, and Wayne, of course, saw him there. Unfortunately, the President-elect did not come to Japan, and I did not get to see him.

Our first and only Christmas season in Japan was gladdened by a visit from Ann and Gordon, who flew in from San Francisco with our old and dear friends, Mae and Ben Swig, of San Francisco. We made such wonderful plans for them to visit everything we liked so much in Japan—and then had to scrap all of them. There was an avalanche of official visits, and the pressure of the work kept mounting until Wayne had to ask to be excused from traveling. Ann and Gordon, however, refused to go anywhere outside Tokyo without him. Ann brought that wonderful soft look to Wayne's eyes when she told him, "I flew over here to see you, Daddy, not Japan."

Ann was tremendously impressed with Japanese art. She spent

231

a good deal of her time in Japan visiting museums and art galleries and exploring little shops. What impressed her more than anything else was the way the Japanese people use their art treasures. She found that in rich homes and poor, there is a strict limit on the number of artistic displays shown in a single room. Classically, the Japanese put only one vase or picture in a room so that all attention is centered on one thing. In that way, the Japanese reason, they can feel the full impact of the beauty without being distracted by other things. When one particular piece has been on display a length of time, it is carefully put away and another object of art is brought out.

Ann also was entranced with Japanese landscape gardening and with the stunted dwarf trees, the *bonsai*. These trees, fully matured and perfectly proportioned, are so stunted that a full-grown oak may be no more than two or three feet high.

Wayne was able to take one trip with Ann, Gordon, the Swigs, and me. We went to Osaka, the industrial and financial center of Japan; to Kyoto, the grand ancient capital of the emperors; and to Nara, which was the capital of even more ancient emperors. Nara is known particularly for the spotted deer that roam the magnificent old parks. The Japanese say they try to keep those parks as much as possible as they were a thousand years ago. Temples and shrines ring the big parks, and beautiful old stone lanterns stand side by side like soldiers along the pleasant walks that lead to the shrines and temples.

On New Year's Eve we went to the Fujiya Hotel, nestled in the lush and beautiful Hakone Mountain pass which provides ever-changing views of majestic Fujiyama. In that magnificent hotel with our children and friends, it was a quiet and absolutely perfect holiday eve.

Next day we drove the two hours back to Tokyo for the official New Year reception. Wayne and I stood in the reception line for what seemed like hours, shaking hands with slightly less than two thousand people. Everyone was there—Japanese, American, and United Nations officials, diplomats, soldiers, sailors, Marines, and airmen. Two days later, on January 3, we bid a tearful farewell to Ann and Gordon, sorry we could not be returning with them to the States. It seemed almost cruel to return to Maeda House, empty now without the children, who had made it so gay and happy with their young laughter.

Wayne and I went down to dinner alone in our huge dining room. It never had seemed so vast and so completely inappropriate for a dinner for two. Our hearts were heavy and filled with loneliness.

And then the servants did something I shall always remember as a prime example of the exquisite sensitivity of the Japanese. They sensed our mood and our loneliness and did their best to counteract it. And their best was very good.

One surprised us by bringing our canary bird downstairs from our bedroom. He put the cage on the great table and the bird immediately burst into song. Another servant led in our two frisky puppies, who scampered about the table begging for tidbits.

The canary and the puppies changed our mood completely. We were busy and laughing and talking again, and I put some records on the phonograph and Wayne and I brightened considerably. Instead of giving vent to the emotions which were so close when we began that meal, we wound up telling each other how grateful we were to have not only each other but all the other countless things and friends that had blessed our lives.

CHAPTER NINETEEN

During the new year period it was natural for us to take stock of ourselves and the things around us. We had been in Japan and the Far East for eight months. The paramount thing, peace in Korea with or without victory, still was unattained. Because of that, our enthusiasm for everything else was tempered.

Wayne was doing everything in his power to negotiate the kind of truce his government had decided it wanted. He did not necessarily agree with the policy; he would have preferred to go on to victory, being convinced that victory would be worth the price because of the greater number of lives and treasure that would be saved in the long run. But as a soldier it was not his job to set policy. He let his views be known through channels, and that was as far as he could go. When the orders came to him, he complied and worked for the national policy objectives as hard as he could. It was frustrating and sometimes heartbreaking work.

Against that background, we still found things to be thankful for. We liked the Japanese people. They seemed to like us and to appreciate that we were interested in their welfare. They also seemed to appreciate the work I was doing for their orphanages, schools, churches, and other charitable efforts. In this work I had the opportunity to mingle freely with the Japanese, and I came to feel strongly that the Japanese people had a true friendship for Americans.

It was exciting and interesting to live in Japan. But during that New Year period, with our beloved Ann and Gordon so recently departed, Wayne and I realized sharply that nothing can fill the void and longing which people have for their own country and children. We were homesick. And we realized that only by living in a far-off land could we understand to the fullest the blessings of being an American.

There were compensations, of course. There was Yoshiye Ikuoka, for instance, our little neighbor. She was four years old when we arrived in Japan, and lived in a little house not far from ours and on the road Wayne took to work every day. After we had been in Tokyo awhile, Wayne mentioned to me one night that he noticed an old man with a little girl in his arms who waved to him from the same street corner every morning when he was on his way to work and every evening when he returned. He said he was going to stop and say hello.

He did. The little girl was all embarrassed and giggly at such attention, and the proud old man who was her grandfather bowed low, Japanese-fashion, with great tears of emotion welling up in his soft eyes.

That was the beginning of a strange and wonderful friendship. Wayne looked forward to seeing the little girl and her grandfather every morning and evening. "It helps put things in perspective for me," he said one evening. "When I see that little girl smile and wave to me each day, it's a constant reminder that what I'm dealing with out here is not just maps and Army units and strategic targets, but real people, living, laughing, loving people whose lives depend on what we are doing."

Wayne began stopping at that street corner quite frequently to say hello to Yoshiye and her dignified old grandfather. Many times I was with him. Sometimes they exchanged little gifts. We gave her a doll and other little trinkets. She gave us such traditional Japanese gifts as lacquer boxes, and as a farewell gift at the end of our tour of duty she and her grandfather gave us a fine photograph album, which is becoming a traditional Japanese gift item.

After the friendship between Wayne and me and Yoshiye had blossomed, I began inviting her to the children's parties at Maeda House. She was so pretty and always so clean. Even though she was less than five, her mother touched up her face for these parties with a little lipstick and rouge, a common adornment of little Japanese girls. Yoshiye always wore Western-style dresses, as did most of the little girls in Tokyo and other Japanese cities. Japanese are most adaptable and they learned early that Western clothing is more convenient for outdoor wear than the traditional kimono.

After I got to know Yoshiye, I began buying American dresses, sweaters, and dolls for her from the PX, to say nothing of candy and cakes, and I would stop by her corner and give her the little presents. Often Yoshiye and I talked through an interpreter. I enjoyed these talks, and I remember one in particular. It was toward the end of our stay in Japan and I had just told Yoshiye that we were going home to the United States. She said she would miss our dogs, Pal and Spottie. "Won't you miss me, too?" I asked.

"Oh, yes," she said, with the complete honesty of childhood, "but I'll miss the dogs more."

Yoshiye was something less than a complete dog lover, however. When she came to our house she treated Pal and Spottie with the utmost respect, as though she didn't quite know whether or not to be afraid of them.

The grandfather, Rokunosuke Ikuoka, was as interesting to me as the little girl. He was a wonderfully educated man, most dignified and formal. Whenever I invited Yoshiye to a children's party, he brought her, and during the parties he and I would have a chance to talk, each time through an interpreter. Always he talked about how glad he was that the Americans had come to his country and how much the United States had done for Japan and was teaching Japan. He said that democracy, as the Americans lived it, was something the Japanese had to learn.

Often we talked about little Yoshiye. I told him she was growing so big that he would not be able much longer to hold her up to see the general ride by. Mr. Ikuoka looked sad. Through the interpreter he said, "My granddaugther is a joy to me. She is obedient always. But I am troubled because she is growing up so rapidly. I realize there will not be many more years when I will be able to hold her in my arms so she can wave to the general. The high spot of each day is when we see the general. On Sundays I am sad. Sundays seem like a long day. I do not know when the general is going to his office, so most Sundays I do not have the chance to see him."

Mr. Ikuoka was too old to work himself, but lived with little Yoshiye and her parents, who supported the family with the earnings of a little shop.

There was a touching scene when Wayne and I left Maeda House for the last time, on our way to America. Yoshiye, her grandfather, her mother, and all her other relatives were standing on the same old corner. They waved Japanese and American flags. Wayne had the car stopped and got out and picked up little Yoshiye in his arms. The friendship between the general and the little girl was well known in Japan by that time and there were photographers there shooting pictures frantically. Next day the Japanese newspapers, which were mailed to us in San Francisco, published the pictures and said that as our automobile drove away, Yoshiye waved and called, "Dear Uncle Clark, *sayonara* [farewell]."

Animals were part of our life in Japan, too, as they had been part of my life since I was a little girl. The Society for the Prevention of Cruelty to Animals had established a branch in Japan, with both foreigners and Japanese taking an active part. Lady Lorna Gascoigne, wife of a former British Ambassador, and Mrs. Lindesay Parrott, wife of the *New York Times* correspondent, had been instrumental in getting it under way after the war, and it was a going concern by the time I arrived.

The highlight of the Society's work while I was in Tokyo was a Mardi Gras celebration in which we raised eight thousand dollars to help run the animal hospital which the Society had established. The Mardi Gras was one of the highlights of the Tokyo social season, and the Emperor's brother, Prince Takematsu, who was interested in the Society, sometimes lent his palatial home to the Society for the celebration. During the occupation, the Mardi Gras night was one of the few more or less formal functions at which all Japanese and foreigners could meet on an equal footing socially.

We also had our personal pets. We not only had the dogs and canaries we always keep around the house, but we had lots of others.

Strangest of all, perhaps, was the cricket, which is thought to be good luck. Japanese love crickets as pets and keep them in little bamboo cages that can be held in the palm of the hand. The crickets live on various kinds of greens, and we fed ours cucumbers and mulberry leaves. We came to like our little cricket and his song, and I kept him on my desk in my home office.

I always thought of my cricket as a grasshopper and even called him "Hopper." The Japanese consider their crickets good-luck omens, and certainly my cricket brought me good luck in the form of enjoyment. As I spent many hours at my desk, I came to look upon my cricket as a companion, and his song frequently kept me from being lonely at my work.

There was a distressing aspect to this pet, however. I was told that the life expectancy of a cricket was three months, so I knew my enjoyment of him would be short-lived. Quite consciously I began to count the months, then the weeks, and finally the days he would be with me.

Each morning when I uncovered his cage he would chirp merrily and in time I became certain that he also waved one of his long legs at me in greeting. Then one day he lost a leg. How it happened nobody ever knew. And the strange thing was that Hopper didn't seem to mind, but was just as merry and loud as ever. And certainly his health didn't suffer. For Hopper lived an entire month longer than he was supposed to. And when he died

238

the gardener and I buried him with appropriate ceremony under a beautiful blooming camellia tree.

Most bothersome of our pets were our cats. When I first arrived I found three cats living near the greenhouse. They were so very sick and pathetic that I took them in, cared for them, and fed them daily. That was a mistake, because somehow the word got around among the cat population of Tokyo. How the other cats got into our grounds, surrounded by a great stone wall, I never learned. But they did, in companies and battalions.

I took a cat census one day and found we had twenty-eight grown cats, ten kittens and more on the way. Our dogs chased the cats all over the place, trampling flowers and vegetables and spreading confusion and noise generally. Vainly I tried to give the kittens away. Nobody really wanted them, and all I got was excuses. I never could bring myself to stop feeding those cats, and I just would not permit our people to drown the kittens. So we were stuck with them. And every night they yowled.

The cats, the dogs, and the crickets were for fun. The children in Japan and Korea were not. There were thousands, particularly in Korea, who had to be fed and kept warm and helped and educated, war orphans and waifs who somehow had to be kept alive and strong until they were old enough to take care of themselves.

The American people answered the need magnificently. CARE packages flowed into both countries. Soldiers of the Twenty-fifth Infantry Division founded and supported an orphanage near Osaka, Japan, and American soldiers of all outfits bought CARE packages at counters in the post exchange in Seoul and other cities, packages they contributed to the needy.

After I had been in Japan for a while and realized the needs of the orphanages, I thought that even more had to be done. I wrote to a number of friends in the United States, to newspapers, to philanthropic organizations, and to the Save the Children Federation of New York. I asked them to support a new effort, "Operation Blanket," to get clothing and blankets from the States to the orphanages of both Japan and Korea.

The response was overwhelming. Not only did I get blankets and clothing, but checks began coming by mail, big checks, some for two or three thousand dollars. "Operation Blanket" fast outgrew me. I could not handle it alone and arranged for five Army chaplains to help. By this time the flood of blankets and clothing from the United States was so great that we had to get a warehouse in Tokyo to receive them.

There in the warehouse the chaplains and their helpers and I sorted the supplies and arranged distribution. The chaplains were familiar with the various orphanages and kept themselves acquainted with the needs of each one so as to meet the requirements. Eventually the program became so big that a nationwide radio broadcast was arranged. I spoke from Tokyo. Clare Boothe Luce spoke and urged people to join the campaign. They did. School children throughout the States collected things for the Korean and Japanese orphans.

I was overjoyed with the results of my brain child. "Operation Blanket" gave me more pleasure and a greater feeling of accomplishment than any other single such undertaking of my life. And I got an unexpected experience from "Operation Blanket." I got to go to Korea. Wayne never would have let me go just for a visit—there had to be a reason. When I told him I wanted to fly to Pusan with a load of blankets for orphans, he decided that was reason enough and permitted me to go.

Wayne had a strict rule against junkets to Korea by women. He just wouldn't let them go unless they were going to do something useful in connection with the war. This ruling made him somewhat unpopular socially in Tokyo, for many women, ambassadors' wives and Army wives, were eager to go take a look around Korea. They wanted to see as much as they could, get as close to the war as they could. Wayne's reasoning was simple. When a woman goes into a war zone there are complications. There have to be special quarters, with special guards; transportation has to be provided. It means soldiers are taken away from other duties directly connected with the war, in order to make certain the woman visitor is safe. While Wayne was in command, therefore, no woman got to Korea without a good reason, and only the fact that the orphans were part of the United Nations' responsibility enabled me to take the blankets and clothing to them in Pusan and Seoul.

I was appalled by the misery I saw at Pusan, the refugee center. It was the tip end of the Korean peninsula, as far as those poor people could run from the war, and there they were crowded into vast refugee camps, shantytowns, and tent cities. There weren't even enough shanties and tents to go around, and many had to live in open lean-to shelters.

The refugee problem as such was far too big for me. That had to be handled by governments and by the United States Eighth Army and the United Nations Command. Estimates said there were anywhere from two to four million refugees in South Korea. I concentrated on the orphans. We never could get enough of the things we needed for these poor children, but every bit helped and we did receive aid supplies by the ton.

In Pusan I talked to a little Korean boy who had picked up a smattering of English. I asked him his name. His answer always epitomized the tragedy of Korea for me. He said simply, "I'm nobody from nothing."

It did my heart good, though, to see the warmhearted generosity of the Americans for these people. Many, or perhaps most, American infantry and air units "adopted" Korean boys as mascots. Soldiers and airmen adopted Korean children, sometimes legally, most times informally for the duration. The soldiers taught their mascots to speak English and tutored them in reading, writing, and arithmetic. They sent home for cowboy outfits and toy guns and sombreros and jeans to dress up the little Korean children like American children.

But there just weren't enough units in Korea to take care of all the orphans, so more had to be done. The soldiers themselves took care of some of this work. Units "adopted" whole orphanages and did what they could to help the children. Beyond that, there was need for the more formal system of aid offered by Korean and American welfare organizations which collected and distributed the supplies needed by the orphanages. My trip to Pusan was made to get firsthand knowledge of how much was needed and how much could be handled through the welfare distribution facilities.

But my big impression on leaving Korea was of the volunteer work done by the American servicemen themselves. This was more personal. The Korean children were able to see their benefactors, to play with them, to know them. And I am certain that hundreds and hundreds of those children now have a lifetime sympathy for America and Americans because of the help, attention, and love shown to them by our American soldiers in uniform.

During the visit to Pusan I met Madame Syngman Rhee for the first time. She is a Viennese, much younger than President Rhee. She was unusually active in helping her husband in his task of ruling his war-torn country, and every paper on which he worked went through her hands. Despite this responsibility and the great load of work she assumed, I found Madame Rhee charming, pretty, and relaxed. She has a sweet smile and was most affable. The one thing I found a bit difficult was that she wore nothing but the Korean costume, which I must admit I do not admire. I could understand why she did it. She was a foreigner married to the president of the Republic of Korea and wanted her husband's people to know that she had cut her ties with Europe and had cast her lot with them. The Korean dress was the outward manifestation of this decision.

But to me the Korean costume was unbecoming. It is made of lovely fabrics, but fashioned so strangely that the woman's dress looks roughly like a tent with arms and a head stuck out from the top. There is a short, bolerolike jacket with long, flowing sleeves. The skirt starts high, almost at the armpits, and billows out to the ground. It looked like a maternity dress to me, but every Korean woman, rich or poor, wears the same-style dress, almost without variation.

Wayne and I had dinner with the Rhees. Their home was terribly cold. The Koreans developed what we call "radiant heat" some four thousand years ago, building fires in little ovens in the brick foundation of their homes from which heat flows under the

242

floor through a system of flues. In some houses the kitchen stove supplies the heat for the ducts under the floors. But the Rhees kept their house cold.

The President was affable and interesting. He speaks quite good English, having run a school in Honolulu for many years and having lobbied in Washington for Korean independence for even more years during the Japanese occupation of his country. Officially Wayne had to oppose many of Rhee's ideas and policies, and Rhee was a stubborn, determined leader who battled right down the line against American ideas he did not like. Wayne had one political trouble after another with President Rhee, real basic political arguments. That's why I always have to laugh when I hear the Communists call Syngman Rhee an American "puppet." He's nobody's puppet, and never could be.

Wayne realized that too, and respected him for his independence. And as things developed, Wayne always retained his personal admiration, respect, and fondness for Rhee, no matter how hard they were fighting over matters of policy.

Madame Rhee was and is of utmost importance to the President. She even mothers him a little to make certain that he conserves his strength and maintains his health. She personally arranged his diet and supervised the preparation of his food so that his health would be safeguarded.

Of course, that cold room at the Rhee home did not jibe with my idea of safeguarding the President's health. I like rooms warm, good and warm, and that room seemed awfully chilly to me. But it didn't to Madame Rhee, possibly because she wore woolen clothing and a little bolero jacket lined with rabbit fur. Before the dinner was over Madame Rhee was perspiring, and I was almost shivering.

Finally Madame Rhee said, "I am so hot I can hardly stand it." She was the President's lady. And the servants did hear her. They opened the doors to the outside and let in the wintry winds.

Then I really did shiver.

After that first visit Madame Rhee insisted that I return and see Seoul. Wayne was more than a little irked. It seems Madame Rhee was always inviting women to come over from Japan to visit her and Wayne believed she wanted me to come to Seoul to break the ice so that she could have other visitors despite his ban on such visits. His theory was that Madame Rhee was lonely for the companionship of women, and I think perhaps she was. I know that when I visited Pusan and later when I visited the Rhees in Seoul, she could not spend enough time with me. Personally I found her charming and liked her very much. We had much in common, particularly a fondness for dogs, and we talked long about her little dog, its habits and eccentricities, and my Pal and Spottie in Tokyo.

As a native Viennese, she plied me with all sorts of questions about the people of her family home, the buildings, the food situation, whether there was enough fuel and clothing to keep the people warm in winter. Madame Rhee was accustomed to tragedy and misery, having seen enough of it in her adopted country for some years. But she still had a warm and active sympathy for the plight of the Austrians.

Later the Rhees returned our visit and stayed at Maeda House. It was a busy time. The President brought a large staff to help him try to work out an agreement with the Japanese. We went so far as to hold a dinner for the Rhees and Japanese—a trying event, for Rhee was breaking bread with his old enemies for the first time in years.

Finally I was able to go to Seoul for Korean relief. While there I arranged to fly by helicopter to several hospitals nearby to visit with the wounded soldiers. Seoul was less than sixty miles from the front lines then, and from some of the hospitals I could hear the explosions of the big guns and even see some of the pillars of smoke that billowed up from the shell bursts.

I was perfectly safe back in the hospital areas, far from the active front, but it gave me a strange feeling to see and hear war. I always considered that I had been "in the Army" ever since I had married Wayne more than a quarter century before. But there in the hospitals in Korea I was seeing and hearing the violence of war for the first time, even at such long range.

CHAPTER TWENTY

HONGKONG, SAIGON, MANILA, AND FORMOSA are names of romance and adventure to most Americans, and they were to me. So I was overjoyed when I got an unexpected chance to visit what seemed to me the most glamorous of them all, Hongkong.

Marshal Juin visited us from Indochina in early 1953. Wayne arranged for him and his staff to fly back as far as Hongkong, and asked me if I would like to go along. "Why don't you go for a joy ride and the shopping?" he asked. "The airplane has to go down there and back, anyway."

Wayne couldn't get away himself, but there was no reason why I shouldn't go. Hongkong is an island and a peninsula, separated by a harbor that is considered one of the three most beautiful in the world, along with those of Rio de Janeiro and Sydney, Australia. I had seen Rio, and to me Hongkong Harbor was more beautiful and certainly was more exciting, full as it was of everything from ocean liners to little Chinese sampans.

The governor, Sir Alexander Grantham, and his lady heard I was coming on to Hongkong alone and graciously asked me to be their house guest. We never had met and I was most pleased with the invitation. But I was not prepared for the welcome I got. When I

245

arrived Lady Grantham met me and said, "Welcome to Government House, Maurine."

I was familiar enough with British people, their habits and customs, to know that something was strange. It was unheard of to address anyone by first name at first meeting, and rare to call anybody by first name any time. It just didn't seem British to me at all.

Lady Grantham saw my perplexity and smiled with a little mischievous glint in her eye. Then she laughed. She said she would have to ask my forgiveness, but she just wasn't able to resist the temptation, for her first name was Maurine, too. Neither of us had met many people with that name, and we compared notes. We found it all went back to Ella Wheeler Wilcox, who wrote such popular books and magazine stories so long ago. It seemed that Lady Grantham's mother and my mother each had been impressed with a Wilcox novel entitled *Maurine,* so each had given that name to her daughter.

All this started us off on a good footing toward firm friendship. We became very close in a short time, much closer, I think, than we would have been if our first names hadn't been the same.

Lady Grantham showed me Hongkong. There was the shopping, the best perhaps in the Orient. There were tax-free British woolens, the best in the world at what seemed ridiculously low prices to me. There were Chinese silks, lingerie, and linens which I was assured had come from China before the Reds took over. As wife of the commanding general of the United Nations forces fighting the Chinese Reds in Korea, I did not want to get caught trading with the enemy.

There were French perfumes, tax-free or almost so. There were fine shops for hats and dresses. In fact, there were all sorts of things I had not seen since I had been in Tokyo, which still did not go in too heavily for luxury shops.

Sir Alexander and Lady Maurine took me on a tour of orphanages and hospitals, in which each had a deep interest. I was impressed both by the needs of the colony and the amount of construction work under way to meet them. Civil war in China and the victory of the Communists there had made Hongkong a refugee center. Poor Chinese who had fled their homes on the mainland to escape the Reds

246

were crowded into shantytowns that spread up incredibly steep hills. Sometimes the shantytowns were more like cliff dwellings. I was told that, exclusive of the British military stationed in the colony in such great numbers while I was there, there were estimated to be more than two million Chinese residents. The terrible problem of how to house and feed all those people and find work for them faced Sir Alexander daily.

I was fascinated by Hongkong. To me, Hongkong was the Orient of the storybook, and I loved it and was genuinely sorry to leave.

But what a pleasant surprise was in store for me in Tokyo! I no sooner got back than Wayne told me I was going to return to Hongkong almost immediately, and with him. Armistice talks in Korea were at a stalemate. The fighting was little different, although men were getting killed and wounded every day. But nothing big was under way or anticipated from either side. Down south, trouble was brewing in Indochina, where the French were having a difficult time with the Communist forces of Ho Chi-minh, and Wayne's French friend Marshal Juin wanted him to come to see what could be done by America to help France in her difficult situation. Washington had approved.

Wayne decided that since he was going to Indochina, he would make a stop in the Philippines. As commanding general of the Far East Command, he had over-all responsibility of the American ground, sea, and air forces there, and this would be his first opportunity to inspect them. He also scheduled a stop on Formosa to confer with Generalissimo Chiang Kai-shek and with the American officers assigned to the island to help Chiang build up his anti-Communist ground, sea, and air forces.

Wayne was deeply concerned with the war in Indochina and wanted to try to sell Marshal Juin on the idea of training the Vietnamese troops in the same way the United States Army had trained the Republic of Korea troops and made them into a reasonably good army. Wayne feared the Communists would shift the weight of their attack in Asia from Korea to Indochina and said he knew from experience that any defense in that area would have to depend in large part upon the people and their own army.

Wayne had prepared the way earlier by conducting Marshal Juin on a tour of ROK training camps in Korea. The French Marshal was impressed. Now, in Indochina, Wayne was going to try further to impress the French that the Far East Command could help them train the Vietnamese.

The invitation to Saigon was extended by the French High Commissioner, M. Jean LeTourneau, who was host at a formal dinner at the official residence, a magnificent building constructed along the lines of a European palace. The French, of course, are magnificent hosts, and everything was just right.

The dinner guests gathered in a large drawing room for cocktails before dinner. There was real elegance about the group, an air of Old World grandeur. I wore my most formal gown, with a long train, and felt almost queenly as the High Commissioner gave me his arm and we started together down the long, grand stairway that led from the drawing room to the dining room below.

Then, in this most elegant of all settings, the humor came back into our lives. Either somebody stepped on that train or it got tangled in my feet. But whatever the cause, I tripped and then fell down the last few steps. Mack Sennett used to get laughs with scenes like that in his old two-reel silent comedies.

Men came from everywhere. They were dashing men, in resplendent uniforms, epaulets, and ribbons, and I couldn't help noticing as they helped me up that their trousers were so tightly fitted that they had a little difficulty bending over to help me to my feet. But, as I said, the French are magnificent hosts. The High Commissioner and his people were so charming that they quickly put me at ease and the evening resumed its pleasant pace.

We traveled much within Indochina. We flew from Vietnam to the tiny kingdom of Cambodia and spent a day at the astounding Khmer temple, Angkor Wat, the vast and beautiful architectural wonder which was lost in the spreading jungle for so long.

In Vietnam we went from Saigon, in the south, to Hanoi in the Red River Delta rice area of the north. There we stayed with the French commanding general. Wayne flew with him to the front, which was so close, while the women in the party were taken by automobile to the port of Haiphong. It was a short ride but a memorable one. The area was infested with Communist guerrillas, and the French feared an ambush and sent a heavy guard along with us. I always said they sent tanks, but Wayne said they were light armored cars. That has been a family argument ever since. But I was there and Wayne wasn't, and I believe I have been "in the Army" long enough to know the difference between a tank and an armored car. These were tanks.

The countryside through which we traveled was tragically deserted. The rice was lush in the fields, but there was nobody there to harvest it. The fighting had swirled into the paddy fields, and all the farmers had been forced to flee with their families. It was particularly pathetic to me because I had seen the desperate need for rice in Korea and, to a much lesser extent, in Japan.

We lunched at a French outpost in the hills behind Haiphong, then boarded a French boat which took us back up the Red River to Hanoi.

In the Philippines we went to beautiful Baguio, the summer capital high in the mountains, as guests of the American Ambassador, Admiral Raymond Spruance. In Manila we toured the bustling, busy city, and I was amazed at the amount of activity here in this city of the tropics. I guess I had expected to find that the heat made everyone sleepy and lazy, but there was more noise and traffic and confusion in Manila than in almost any city I had ever seen.

Much of Manila had been repaired and rebuilt, but there still was ample evidence of the ravages of war. Manila was a battleground in 1945. Artillery and mortars had broken great buildings. The Japanese army set fire to the old walled city which the Spaniards had built. The walled city still was unrepaired and was being kept more or less as the Japanese had left it, a war-built memorial to the war.

In Manila there was a very strange remnant of the war, the "jeepney." In the past tiny ponies had pulled little carts through the city as buses, and some of these pony carts, gaily painted and flying tassels from the canopy on top, still operated. But the "jeepney" was taking over. This, as its name implies, is a converted jeep, with the rear seat cut away and an open bus compartment built on to seat about four people on each side. The jeepneys would speed through the crowded streets at a mad pace, and I never did learn whether they ran regular routes or just wandered where the passengers wanted to go.

We stayed at Clark Field, north of Manila, in the Philippines. On one flight from Clark field into the Manila airport Wayne asked the pilot to fly over historic Bataan and Corregidor, where so many Americans fought and died in the heroic rear-guard action at the beginning of the Pacific war. It was thrilling to see those famous battlegrounds from the air, even though the jungle growth had covered all sign of combat.

We circled over Corregidor several times, seeing "Topside," the flat-topped mountain where the American paratroopers dropped in 1945 to begin the battle to recapture the island. Then the airplane circled some more so we could see "Bottomside," where the Infantry landed in small boats on a sandy beach that was turned into a frightful slaughterhouse by withering Japanese machine-gun fire.

It was hard to realize that this lush, green tropical island once was the scene of such life-and-death conflict. Nothing could have seemed more peaceful than the little island with waves lapping gently on its shores.

Our tour also took us to Taihoku, capital of Generalissimo Chiang Kai-shek on Formosa. The Japanese built Taihoku and it had the look of a Japanese city in some ways, although the realities of the tropics had obliged the Japanese to alter their traditional ideas of architecture and city planning. Balconies shaded the sidewalks before the shops, much as the Spanish shelter walks from the hot sun. This type of architecture, in fact, was common in the Orient, even in the British-built city of Victoria on Hongkong.

Wayne and I arrived at Taihoku the day Madame Chiang Kai-shek returned there from the United States, where she had undergone extensive medical treatment. Despite her long illness, I was impressed with both the vitality and beauty of this woman. We drove to the Chiangs' country house not far outside the city for dinner. Our route was along a highway lined with tiny houses and rice

250

paddies, and suddenly we were in another world of lotus ponds, spreading shade trees, unbelievable flowers.

The house itself was big but not particularly luxurious. Everything was pleasant and comfortable, but not overly elaborate. Chiang Kai-shek is not the old-style, luxury-loving Oriental potentate. In fact, he makes a fetish of being a Spartan. The simple uniform he wears, without decoration or insignia of any kind, is a kind of symbol of his attitude toward pomp and luxury.

Madame Chiang speaks fluent English with an exceptionally good choice of words and phrases. The Generalissimo said not a word of English, and I had the feeling he did not understand it, either. The Missimo, as the Chinese call Madame Chiang, served as his interpreter part of the time, although an English-language secretary, Sampson Shen, was at the Generalissimo's elbow all the time and took over when the Missimo wanted to talk with someone on her own.

She talked with me at length about her role on Formosa. She had familiarized herself with my interest in orphanages, hospitals, women's work, and the Scouts, and talked a good deal about the things being done in those fields on Formosa. Madame Chiang was active herself in all these things, and linked them to the Formosa defense system which dominates the life and thought of the island.

She founded the Women's Alliance, which seemed to be, in effect, a huge volunteer factory to make uniforms for the Nationalist troops. The Alliance took over an enormous building and stocked it with hundreds of American sewing machines. It operated buses which picked up women and children from all parts of the island and took them to Taihoku. Each group would stay in the capital for one week, and the children would be sent to schools and nurseries while the women spent their week sewing for the soldiers. The Women's Alliance provided food and shelter for all during their stay in the capital.

Madame Chiang approached her task with great energy and imagination. One of her most successful projects was started in the spring of 1950 when the Nationalists still were dazed by their loss of the mainland and when people on the mainland hardly knew what

251

had happened. Morale was the big problem. Madame Chiang went to work on the rice-drop project. Every night Nationalist transport airplanes would fly deep into China from Formosa and drop hundreds of small bags of rice. In each bag was a letter from a Chinese on Formosa. Each letter was worded differently, and signed differently, but each carried the same central message, that the people on Formosa had not forgotten their brothers under Communist rule on the mainland. The rice was a token of that remembrance and a promise of greater help in the future.

Madame Chiang ran the campaign to get the letters. She broadcast appeals for each Chinese on Formosa to write the letters for the rice bags. Her appeal met with such unexpected success and response that in ten days she had to go on the air again and ask the people not to send the letters any longer. A huge room at Taihoku airport was filled with them and no more could be handled.

The Missimo also was active in working with the Chinese Women's Army Corps, with orphanages and hospitals, in army, navy, and air force relief, and many other things that contributed to the general strength and morale of the Nationalist forces.

Our meal at the Chiang home that night was a delicious Chinese dinner of almond soup, shark's fin soup, a dish of chicken and walnuts, and a dish of beef and green peppers. During dinner I had a chance to listen to the Generalissimo. What struck me most forcibly was that he considered himself a revolutionary. That was not the picture we had in the United States, and I asked questions. The answers I got through an interpreter put Chiang Kai-shek in a new perspective for me.

Briefly, Chiang pictures himself as the revolutionary fighting all Chinese oppression. He rose to power in revolt against the old war lords. He became a world figure in the struggle against Japanese aggression. And he suffered his most terrible defeat in the war with the Chinese Communists. But to Chiang each of these forces was tyrannical, each stood in the way of the achievement of the Nationalist Revolution which Chiang is convinced is still under way. In his view the oppressors have changed, but the rebels have not, and he is a rebel. To him the war lords, the Japanese, and the Communists were more than anything else enemies of his revolution.

After dinner I forgot my manners and gasped in wonder at a mass of orchids growing on a matting nailed to a wall. They were astounding plants. One trailed down four or five feet in absolute splendor. I admired them out loud, which is something that never should be done in the Orient. For Madame Chiang, like the well-trained Oriental hostess that she is, insisted that I take it with me. She drew the largest from the matting and called a servant to take it to our airplane.

The Chiangs already had put enough things into that airplane. They had loaded it with watermelon, cantaloupe, pineapple, and other fruits. The watermelon interested me most. It did not look as good as our rich, red melons. It was a sort of orangish yellow inside, but the flavor, somehow, was better and sharper. It reminded me that many things in the Orient cannot be judged by our American standards. I set up the orchids in our home in Tokyo and they grew luxuriantly. Later, when we moved back to the United States, I gave them to Ann for her new home in San Mateo, California.

After the return from our brief trip to the southern areas, I plunged back into my regular routine. Every morning, in my office at my home from nine to twelve, I dictated letters to the families of wounded soldiers I had visited in the hospitals. It took every morning because I had talked with fifty to sixty wounded men each week, and that meant a lot of letters to be written. One afternoon a week was spent in the hospitals, two or three afternoons were devoted to orphanages, and I entertained orphans at my home whenever I could find time.

The schedule was more difficult than I realized. One noontime, after I had finished dictating my letters and was sitting alone at my desk, my throat tightened up and I had difficulty breathing. I was extremely uncomfortable and the attack persisted. I telephoned our Army doctor and he asked me how far I was from my bed and then said, "Mrs. Clark, you move very slowly to your bed and lie down right away, just as you are. I'll be right over."

He didn't waste any time. He made a quick examination and said I had suffered a mild heart attack. Then he called the ambulance and got it on its way before telephoning Wayne. The call caught Wayne just as he was about to sit down to lunch with a group of important visitors from the United States. Wayne heard out the doctor and then took off for home without even excusing himself from his guests, and sent an aide back to the luncheon table to explain.

I was in the hospital for over a week and had to stay quietly at home for another month. Wayne tailored his schedule to permit him to spend every possible minute with me. He did have to make one flight to Korea while I was in the hospital, but he made it very fast.

The gratifying thing to me was the unexpected result of my visits to wounded soldiers and my letters to their parents. After I had been in the hospital a few days and the doctors said I could receive visitors, the soldiers began to come to see me. They were men I had visited earlier, in the same Army hospital, before I became ill. And behind them came letters from their parents, the people to whom I had written. They were all most solicitous and kind. My recovery was relatively swift and complete, and there has never been a recurrence. Indeed, there is a good deal of doubt that there was a heart attack in the first place, for later tests showed no evidence that I had ever suffered one.

I have always believed that one of the big factors in my quick and complete recovery was my happiness over the visits from those wounded soldiers and the letters from their parents. These made me feel I had been able to do some good and that my efforts had been appreciated.

CHAPTER TWENTY-ONE

I HAVE SEEN MARK WAYNE CLARK WEEP ONCE, and once only.

It was the night he came home from Korea exhausted after signing the armistice that ended that unhappy war. It was the one time in my life that I saw him really uncertain, really torn between duty and conviction. His duty was to sign the armistice, but his conviction was that victory was possible and would have been preferable in the long run. But he also was convinced that if there was no determination to win the war, then it was better to sign the armistice and stop the killing. We were taking almost ten thousand United Nations casualties a month even during the lull that came with the armistice talks.

He did not like the part he had to play as the only United States Army general in history who signed an armistice without victory. More than anything else, though, that night, he feared the United States of America had made an historic mistake, that it would pay an awesome price in years to come for the respite from war it got through the Korean armistice.

I sat by helpless. This was one problem with which I could not cope. There was nothing I could say or do that would ease him at that moment.

255

The Korean War had dominated our life in the Orient. It was the big job for Wayne, the reason for his assignment. He worked with the Japanese problems, too, of course, but Japan was a free country and Wayne did not have the occupation command duties that General MacArthur and General Ridgway had before him. There was plenty for him to do in Japan. He had to work with the Japanese government to plan defense of the Empire. He had to negotiate on the problem of American bases. He had to liquidate the occupation, which meant moving headquarters and other units from the big buildings the occupation forces had used in downtown Tokyo and other cities for almost seven years. New camps and headquarters had to be built outside the cities, and whole new communications systems had to be set up. And Wayne had general responsibility for the procurement system in which Japanese industry earned about a million dollars a day turning out equipment for use of United Nations forces in Korea.

There were so many things on which Wayne had to take action that he had to work with a very tight schedule. Each morning staff officers came to him individually with problems on which he had to make decisions. There were so many that Wayne had to budget each man to a time limit, some men getting as little as three minutes to explain their problem, others with more weighty problems getting ten or fifteen minutes or even more. Wayne found he simply could not afford to work any other way because there were not enough hours in the day to hear out each staff officer more fully. The staff officers cooperated wonderfully and Wayne said they became expert in condensing their presentations.

The armistice came in Korea after high drama. In October of 1952 Wayne suspended the talks because they were getting nowhere. He had his senior delegate, Maj. Gen. William K. Harrison, tell the Communists that the talks would remain recessed until they agreed to four alternative U.N. proposals or came up with something new of their own.

The recess lasted until April, when the Communists finally indicated they might be willing to talk. From a personal viewpoint, that ended my tours of Japan and the Orient. Wayne was just too busy. He flew to Korea so often I once told him he seemed like a commuter. Some of his trips actually were on a commuting basis as he would leave home early in the morning, complete the three-hour flight to Seoul, talk with Gen. James A. Van Fleet or President Syngman Rhee for a few hours and then fly back home for work and a late dinner. Most times he would stay over in Korea.

It was a seven-day-a-week job for Wayne from April on, and he worked most nights. It seemed to me that he and his staff officers were working beyond human endurance, but he used to tell me that the excitement and importance of the work pumped adrenalin or something through the blood stream and made it possible for men to work harder than they ever had before.

The break in the peace talks came gradually. The first step was the agreement of the Communists to exchange sick and wounded prisoners. The United Nations Command had urged that exchange long before Wayne ever got to Tokyo, and had repeatedly requested it since. The Communists never accepted the suggestion, however. When they advanced it themselves, they tried to make it appear that this was a brand-new idea which they had come upon through a spirit of humanitarianism.

Wayne flew over to Korea with Secretary of the Army Bob Stevens to see the first prisoners to come out of the Communist camps. Some seemed in pretty good condition, but others were broken in spirit and body, and many said that they had left buddies behind who were far more sick than they.

Wayne always believed that there was a deep motive behind the Communist agreement to exchange the sick and wounded. He believed the Communists were trying to exert mass psychological pressure on the peoples of the United Nations to make them force their governments to back down on the one issue that then blocked an armistice.

That issue was forced repatriation. In UN prison camps were 68,000 Koreans and 15,000 Chinese who vowed they would fight to the death against anyone who tried to force them back to their

Communist homelands. The Communists wanted every one of these men. The United States declared it would force nobody back to communism.

Wayne always believed that the Communists agreed to exchange the sick and wounded to make the people of the free world even more anxious to get their prisoners back. He said he believed the Communists released the sick and wounded as a sort of appetizer to whet the desires of the free people to get back their prisoners at any price. Wayne was very proud of the way the free peoples understood the principle, accepted it, and resisted the Communist lure.

The exchange of sick and wounded made us dare hope for armistice, however. And with that hope came a small personal hope for Wayne and me. Actually it was a big family hope, small only because of the comparison with the far greater issues that were involved in the war and armistice in Korea.

In October of 1952 our Bill had telephoned me from the States on my birthday. He was recuperating from his Korean wounds and in New Orleans to see his girl. After the usual birthday greetings and family small talk, Bill broke the news to me. He had met his girl. She was beautiful. She was wonderful. She was the girl for him, and they were going to marry. It would be in the summer. Her name was Audrey Caire. She was of a fine old New Orleans family. Her father was a leading New Orleans physician, an obstetrician. I would love her. Bill did. All this poured over the trans-Pacific radiotelephone circuit in a torrent.

Wayne was both happy and glum. He had missed Ann's wedding because of this Korean War, and now he might miss Bill's. There was nothing in sight in October that gave him reason to believe the war would be over by summer. And I told Wayne I just wouldn't go back without him. It looked as though we both might miss Bill's wedding.

Perhaps it was selfish of me, but from the time of that telephone call, I was unable to separate in my mind the time of the armistice and the time of Bill's wedding. I must confess that often my prayers were that the armistice would come in time for Wayne and me to fly back for the wedding. Sometimes I felt a little guilty about this. I told myself over and over that in the big scale of things it was quite unimportant whether or not I saw my son married. In the big scale there were the lives of hundreds and thousands of Americans and others, and beyond even that might be the fate of our nation. But I was a mother, and I did so want to be with my son on the great day of his life, to share even a little bit in his happiness. And I eased my sense of guilt by telling myself that the armistice I wanted was the same armistice everyone else seemed to want and it really didn't hurt anyone just because I had a special selfish reason for wanting it to come quickly. I thought it was a harmless selfishness.

To me it always has seemed important that parents share in the greatest of the joys of their children. It creates a bond for later years, a common memory, and I wanted that bond between Wayne and me and Bill and Audrey.

The armistice talks were resumed in late April. There was great optimism, then pessimism. Things looked good at the beginning but soon bogged down into the same old arguments. Wayne was busier than I had ever known him to be. There were the talks at Panmunjom, the offers, the counteroffers, the angry charges. There were the talks with Syngman Rhee, who threatened time and again to break up all consideration of a truce by taking off on his own. And there was the war which flared into big fighting from time to time in that last summer.

Finally, as though out of the blue, the Communists agreed to the armistice. Wayne flew to Korea to sign it. The date was July 27, 1953. At two o'clock in the afternoon Wayne broadcast a short message to the world. Then he telephoned me and I told him it was one of the most magnificent I had ever heard. To me it was. I thrilled to his words when he said, "I cannot find it in me to exult in this hour. Rather, it is a time for prayer, that we may succeed in our difficult endeavor to turn this armistice to the advantage of mankind. If we extract hope from this occasion, it must be diluted with recognition that our salvation requires unrelaxing vigilance and effort."

The words were all Wayne's. No speech writer had penned them for him. They were his words, his feelings, his fears. I knew. I had

259

seen him fall asleep from sheer exhaustion the night before while he wrote them.

The armistice was signed in the morning and Wayne broadcast in early afternoon. But hours later it still was difficult for me to believe that the war was over, that at ten o'clock that night the guns would be stilled in Korea for the first time in three years and one month. I sat at home waiting for Wayne to fly back to Tokyo. I thought of my son and the permanent injuries he bore from the Korean fighting, and of the thousands of mothers whose sons were killed or wounded in the costly but inconclusive fighting.

I wrote letters to my closest friends. I told one that I still felt weak and trembly and that I felt as though I should whisper when I talked about the war and the armistice. I asked myself what it was going to mean, whether the armistice was an act of wisdom or a grave mistake that would lead to something far more terrible and costly than the Korean War had been. And I felt a little empty because, for the first time in history, the United States had failed to fight a war through to victory.

Late in the evening I got a telephone call from Haneda Airport. Wayne had landed and was leaving for home. I knew it took just a half hour for the drive and I began to prepare to receive him.

I heard the car roll up on the gravel driveway and the servants hurry to open the front door. I followed them and stood there to greet him.

His appearance shocked me. He was a different Wayne. The stimulation was gone, and so was the adrenalin that had kept him on his toes through all those long, terrible months of strain and work. The job was done and he no longer had to call on all his reserve energy.

Wayne threw his arms around me and kissed me.

"I've got news for you, Ma," he said.

"I know all about it, dear," I replied. "I heard on the radio."

"No," he said, "you haven't heard this. I've made my decision. I've had forty years in the Army. I'm turning in my soldier's suit. We're going home, Ma, so pack up your marbles.

"I've thought it all out. We fly home for Bill's wedding. After that I'll go up to Washington and tell the President. I feel that is the proper way to do it."

He took a deep breath and then continued.

"I almost did it another way," he said. "Yesterday flying over to Korea I thought it all out. I wanted to make the announcement of my retirement right away, right after I signed the armistice. I thought I would leave the building after I had signed and talk to the newspapermen there, the fellows I have come to know. I thought I would tell them first.

"But on the airplane flying over, I decided against it. I'll go to Washington and tell Ike. That's the better way."

Wayne was a tired man. The toll of all those fifteen months finally showed on his face and in his body. He was able to relax for the first time.

"We'll go home and go fishing, Ma," he said with a little smile.

Then the piled-up exhaustion took over. He just sort of sagged into a chair.

And that was when I saw him weep.

CHAPTER TWENTY-TWO

ALL THROUGH THAT SUMMER OF 1953 WAYNE wondered whether the Korean armistice would be signed in time for us to fly to New Orleans for Bill's wedding. He had missed Ann's marriage. It just couldn't be that both his children would marry without their dad being present. The wedding was scheduled for August 3, and Wayne had his air officers figure out the latest time he could leave Tokyo and get to New Orleans for the wedding day. They reckoned that with the fourteen-hour time differential we could leave Tokyo on August 2, Japanese date, and arrive in New Orleans in time for the wedding. Wayne even had them work out an emergency flight plan on that basis.

Bill's wedding received much publicity because of the uncertainty about whether Wayne could be there. Once when Wayne returned from Korea a newspaperman at Haneda Airport in Tokyo asked him whether the armistice would be signed in time for him to reach New Orleans for the ceremony. Wayne said things were touch and go in Korea and that he just did not know.

The newsman then asked, "Which would you rather do, go to your son's wedding or sign the armistice?"

Wayne replied, "Go to my son's wedding. I know the results of that affair are going to be successful."

The uncertainty of going or not going was almost more than we could stand. Bill had asked his dad to be his best man. He and all the Caire family could make only tentative plans until we knew ours.

As it developed, the emergency flight plan did not have to be used. The armistice was signed on July 27, which gave us ample time to fly to New Orleans together.

On the flight over, Wayne relaxed more than he had in many months. The cares and strain of the Korean War were through for him. He had done his job and was retiring. It was the future, therefore, we talked about that day. Wayne talked and talked about fishing and building a home on Camano Island on Puget Sound. Fishing was a symbol of freedom to him and to me, and when we spoke of going "fishing," we meant we were going to live our own lives, free to go and do as we pleased. We had not been able to do that for many years.

The future offered many roads. In the beginning the most alluring to us was the road to Camano Island and complete freedom. Then the new roads began to open before us. Big business was after Wayne, and many job offers were received. Some of the offers were for more money than we ever had dreamed of, fabulous salaries plus a home and everything that went with it.

We had to consider these offers most carefully. We were going to have four children now, and it would be wonderful to be able to make enough money to leave them comfortably situated. We talked about it incessantly, wondering whether we had the right to refuse these offers which would mean so much to the lives of our children.

There were other offers with less money but with more basic appeal to us. We had to decide whether our main duty was to spend the rest of our lives building an inheritance for our children or to spend the remaining years making each other happy. The temptation to accept one of the big money offers was great.

We came to no decision on the airplane, and after we landed in the United States we had little time for further consideration. Our first stop was San Francisco. Mayor Elmer Robinson declared a "Mark Clark Day," with a thrilling ticker-tape parade down Market Street to the Palace Hotel, where, at a luncheon for more than a thousand people, Wayne made a speech. It was a most cautious speech. He told me before he went on that he did not want to swing from the hip in this first speech at the things he thought had been done wrong in Korea.

I was happy that he took that attitude. We were getting out. We were going to live our own life in our own way. I did not want him mixed up in a controversy, and I did not think the time was right for any complaint about the armistice. The ovation Wayne received in San Francisco impressed us both with the deep desire the American people had to end the Korean War. Wayne repeated to me over and over that he, too, thought the war should have been ended, that as long as the United States was not determined to win the war, it was senseless to continue to spill American blood and that of our Allies.

From San Francisco we flew to New Orleans and arrived the day before the wedding. It was a bad spot for Audrey, who had never met us. She and Bill were at the airport when we landed, and the poor girl was shaking like a leaf, worried sick about whether her prospective in-laws would accept her and like her. She needn't have been, of course. She is the kind of girl anyone would warm to at first sight. In the first place she was a striking beauty and had modeled professionally and done some television work. But even more appealing than her beauty was her personality. The very fact that she was nervous and worried about meeting us was symbolic of the humility which helps to make her such a lovable woman.

I had already come to like Audrey through her letters. But I was bowled over, sold lock, stock, and barrel, when I saw her. She was every bit as beautiful and charming and friendly as Bill had said, and I was proud of him for having made such a wonderful choice.

The wedding was at noon the next day. It was a formal ceremony in a huge, impressive church. Audrey was so beautiful I thought of her as a storybook bride.

So they were married and I gained a daughter.

Audrey and Bill left on their honeymoon to the Broadmoor Hotel at Colorado Springs. It was not difficult for Wayne and me to say good-by to them because after we completed a quick trip East we were to join them in Colorado and they were to fly with us to Tokyo, where they would spend the last part of their honeymoon. I was overjoyed by this plan for it would provide me an opportunity to learn to know our new daughter-in-law.

From New Orleans Wayne and I flew north to Washington. We stopped en route at Charlotte, North Carolina, to visit our dear friends Dr. and Mrs. Paul Sanger. Paul had been a surgeon with Wayne in Italy. There, a newspaperman at the airfield flabbergasted Wayne with a simple question. He asked whether it was true Wayne was going to become president of the Citadel, the military college of South Carolina. That was supposed to have been a close secret, and Wayne had to dodge the question. He was considering the Citadel post seriously, but had made no decision.

Consideration began under auspicious circumstances while we were still in Tokyo and shortly before the Korean armistice was signed. Things were going badly in Korea. It looked as though agreement with the Communists was just about out of the question, and Wayne called a desperation conference of his top air and sea commanders, Gen. O. P. Weyland and Adm. Robert Briscoe. He told them that things had reached a low point. Syngman Rhee was being tough, threatening to break up any armistice that was signed. As Wayne put it, the Communists at Panmunjom were "spitting in our faces." Wayne asked Weyland and Briscoe to let their imaginations run rampant and try to come up with some plan by which the Communists could be put under such military pressure they would have to sign an armistice. The question he asked was: "What can we do to influence the situation within the limitations imposed upon us?"

In the midst of this conference Wayne was handed a radiogram. It said: "If you intend to retire should truce be signed would you be interested in the presidency of The Citadel. General Summerall has retired but an acting President could continue until next June."

It was signed: "James F. Byrnes, Governor of South Carolina."

Wayne's immediate reaction was that he wanted any job but the one he had. But after letting off steam with that wisecrack, he wrote a more thoughtful reply. He radioed back to his old friend Jimmy Byrnes: "Grateful for message. Am definitely interested in Citadel presidency having long looked forward to retirement at appropriate time which should not be too far away. Nothing would please me more than being associated with that great institution. Depending upon situation here expect to be in Washington within month for conference. Could then see you and discuss this situation. Warm regards."

The Citadel was very much in our minds during all our consideration of job offers. It did not carry with it the fabulous money that some of the other offers did, but it did hold promise of the kind of life we both wanted. We were thinking of the Citadel when we arrived in Washington. Wayne went to the White House to give Ike the official signed copy of the Korean armistice. After the presentation Wayne talked privately with Ike and told him, "I'm going to turn in my soldier suit."

The President was surprised. Wayne still had seven years to go before compulsory retirement age, and Ike apparently had never considered that Wayne might want to retire earlier. Finally he agreed that after forty years' service, Wayne was entitled to retire if he so desired, and he accepted with regrets, but asked Wayne to return to the Far East for a few months.

Later that afternoon Mamie Eisenhower telephoned me to say she had just learned from Ike that I was in town and to chide me for not getting in touch with her. I explained that I had thought about it but decided she was far too busy and I hadn't wanted to trouble her. Mamie chided me again and said she always wanted to see me. She suggested lunch for the next day. I was pleased with the invitation, of course, but had to decline because, as I explained to her, we were staying in Washington that night only to take Mother Clark to dinner and were leaving early the next morning.

Governor Byrnes was unable to get up to Washington to see Wayne, and Wayne was not ready to decide without visiting the Citadel, so that decision had to be deferred. In the meantime we had to get back to Tokyo to clean things up and wait for Wayne's successor. En route, in San Francisco, newsmen crowded around

Wayne again. There were reports he planned to run for mayor of San Francisco. This was a much easier question than the one about the Citadel. Wayne didn't have to dodge it because it was just not true. So he told them the only thing he was going to run for was "cover."

En route to Tokyo, Audrey, Bill, Wayne, and I stopped at Ed Pauley's luxurious Coconut Island in Hawaii where life is of unbelievable splendor and ease. Pauley has two rules for guests. They must wear shoes for dinner and go barefoot the rest of the day. It was a happy and wonderful stop on our return trip to Tokyo to wind up our life in the Army.

In Tokyo I got to know and fully appreciate Audrey. During her three weeks there she became my daughter and no longer was merely the girl my son married. And when Audrey and Bill left, I felt much the same kind of unhappiness and desolation that I had earlier in the year when Ann and Gordon had completed their holiday with us. There was a difference this time, though. This time we knew we too were going home.

By the time Audrey and Bill left, we were caught up in a whirl of farewell parties and receptions. The Army, Navy, and Air Force had farewell parties for us, as did the diplomatic representatives of the United Nations in Tokyo. We took a final fishing trip, despite weather so bad that even some of the crewmen got seasick. Japanese government officials gave us farewell dinners, and since Wayne no longer had the excuse of Korean War duties, we had to accept most of the invitations. Each party was fine and wonderful and enjoyable in itself, but there were so many we began to wear out.

Finally Gen. Ed Hull arrived to take over from Wayne. He was a welcome sight to us, for we wanted badly to go somewhere and rest and then resume our planning for the future. The job offers still were coming in, and Wayne used a simple yardstick to measure each one. The questions were: "Will I be happy in what I am doing, and will I have a little time for fishing?"

The Citadel offer looked best of all from many points of view, but Camano Island looked good, too. Wayne and I both thought

267

it probably would be Camano or San Francisco near our children, but we also wanted to look into the Citadel proposition very thoroughly.

I had a special uneasiness, too. I had learned in thirty years with Wayne that if he was happy, I was happy, but if he was unhappy so was I. I was not at all certain how happy he would be if he suddenly shed all responsibility and work, and I was not certain at all that Camano was the answer for us. In fact, in the back of my mind, I was a little worried about his decision to retire from the Army ahead of time. I feared he might have regrets. He had always worked at such a terrific pace, had always loved the Army so much, I feared that he might be making a mistake in retiring so many years before he had to.

Wayne tried to still my fears and told me he wanted retirement more than anything in the world. He said he wanted to be free so we could live as we wanted to live, do what we wanted to do. We talked about our future as we could, holding family conferences in hotel rooms and in airplanes, weighing one factor against another, planning, hoping, worrying. But still we were undecided. There was no doubt that the Citadel was eager for Wayne to take over, and Governor Byrnes flew up to New York to see us on the "Mark Clark Day" there in October of 1953.

There was a repetition in New York of San Francisco's Mark Clark Day parade in the summer. Wayne sat high in an open convertible and waved to the people who crowded the sidewalks and leaned out open office-building windows throwing ticker tape to the street. Audrey and I rode in a second convertible behind him. The wind was high that day, and the motorcade rolled swiftly through the streets, and by the time we reached our destination, the Waldorf, we were hanging on to our hats and our hair was blown every which way.

After the celebration quieted down a bit, Governor Byrnes took Wayne aside and began talking about the Citadel presidency. The big thing Byrnes wanted Wayne to do was to fly down and take a look at the Citadel. Wayne knew if he did, he would probably accept. We flew down to Charleston with Governor and Mrs. Byrnes and arrived on a Friday. We were met at the airport by many dignitaries and taken to the Citadel, where Wayne took a review of the Corps of Cadets. I watched Wayne closely. His eyes got a bit misty as he watched those fine young men parading by so smartly, spick-and-span in their uniforms, and he sneaked a look at me as though to say, "Renie, I'm throwing in the towel, this is it."

Byrnes knew the way Wayne felt, too. Wayne was reminded of how much the Citadel cadets looked like "The Long Gray Line" at West Point.

There was the business about the house. Byrnes had written to us before we ever saw the Citadel that the President's House was run down and would need repairs. Wayne had replied how important a house was to us, how each of us took great pride in our home, and asked the governor to send us photographs of the President's House and blueprints of the floor plan. Governor Byrnes came back with a letter that the state would build us a new house, as the Citadel needed a new President's House anyway.

When we visited the Citadel we realized how true that was. The old house was too far gone to repair adequately. Termites were in the foundations and the timbers. The house itself was so old-fashioned that it did not have the facilities we felt we needed.

The governor went over the plans for the new house, plans he said would be put into effect whether Wayne took the post or not. Later it was decided the old house would be torn down. The road that ran behind it would be closed to make room for a garden that would run all the way down to the Ashley River marsh.

The entire picture he outlined for us sounded wonderful. And, after Wayne took the job, the governor and the state made good on every promise. They even let Wayne and me work out the plans with an architect and supervise the construction, in a loose sort of way. The result was a dream house of which Wayne and I are most proud, and of which we believe the state of South Carolina can be equally proud.

But the big factor that swung Wayne over to take the job and give up his dream of fishing at Camano was that of the cadets themselves.

269

"I saw in those bright young faces," he told me, "a love of country, love of God and love of everything good. I saw that there was plenty that could be done at the Citadel to help them, to build up the student body so that more young men could get the fine training the college had to offer.

"Renie," he continued, "this job is a challenge and it obviously carries the opportunity to do a satisfying job. Besides, I have worked with young men all of my forty years in the Army, and I knew when I saw those cadets parading by me that I wanted to keep on working with them."

Wayne didn't tell Byrnes right away. We flew to Charlotte for a couple of days to visit with the Sangers. There we took time to think the problem through. After two days, Wayne phoned Governor Byrnes to tell him he would accept the post.

We never have had reason for a single regret. All my fear that Wayne might be sorry for his decision to retire from the Army seven years before he had to proved groundless. As Wayne put it himself, the switch from the Army to the Citadel was a "gentle transition."

Of course, he is still Army in spirit, devoted to it and its ideals. Wayne is proud that three generations of Clarks were graduated from West Point—Dad Clark, class of '90; Wayne, class of '17; and Bill, class of '45.

I realized this pride so sharply the day Bill's first child, our first grandchild, was born. Audrey and Bill were at Fort Benning in Georgia and Wayne and I were on our way to Washington when Bill got a telephone call through to us.

"It's a girl, Dad," he announced proudly.

Wayne's rejoinder was happy and lighthearted, a quick joke such as he so often has on the tip of his tongue. But lighthearted and joking as they were, the first words he said to Bill showed how close the Army was to his heart and mind. For Wayne said, "My goodness, Bill, they'll have to make West Point coed."

From Charlotte we flew to Washington, where there was something that had to be done first, before we took up our new life at the Citadel, something I had long dreaded.

Wayne had to go to Washington for the retirement ceremonies.

I was afraid they would be too emotional, that the strain of leaving the Army after forty years of service would be too much. If there had been a graceful or logical way for me to have escaped, I think I would have taken it. But my fears were groundless, and there were no tears for us on retirement day. Wayne was not at all sad, but looked forward happily to a life of our own choosing, a life he felt we had earned through those long years so often marred by anxieties and, most of all, by separations forced by duty.

The ceremonies of retirement were strictly Army. There was a big reception at Fort McNair, where we had lived so happily in 1940 and 1941 and where I had cried in a clothes closet when my family was broken up by the war. At the reception Wayne saw friends, close friends, whom he hadn't seen for years. There was nothing sad about the ceremony or the reception. It was more like a graduation, with Wayne leaving something he had loved, the Army, for something he also would love—a quieter, more free and perhaps happier life.

It was a day of reminiscence for me. I had been "in the Army" with Wayne for almost thirty years, and here we were at Fort Mc-Nair, with all its many memories. Many of the friends we had made in three decades in the Army were there, each one's face reminding us of one experience or another.

I felt a deep sense of gratitude for the privileges and happiness and experiences I had enjoyed during my Army years, and above all the friends I had met, the people who were of lifelong importance to me. Consciously, on that day of high emotion, I thought to myself: "If I had to do it all over again I would choose the Army life above any other."

But I realized the time had come to leave the service. I had served my time, just as my husband had served his. I had contributed a little, my husband a great deal. I was terribly proud of his record and his contributions, but now it was time for something different, something a little more quiet and restful. High Army rank had brought us many privileges, but it also had put heavy demands on us. We had lived in a goldfish bowl in a sense, and our time never was our own.

Until Pearl Harbor we had much freedom, but after the war, with Wayne holding high command in Vienna, in San Francisco, at Fort Monroe, and in Japan, we no longer were able to live the average life of the Army post with other people. Virtually all our time was "official" time, and the luncheons and dinners we gave were for official guests, not our own intimate friends. The official guests almost invariably were splendid and interesting people to know, but we could not relax and play with them as we could with intimates. Entertaining usually was work instead of play.

Many times in Vienna and Tokyo, I had anticipated with mixed emotions that day of retirement. I had so longed to be an average Army wife, free to come and go as I pleased, free to play bridge or go to a picnic or play family cards or go to the post movie. I missed running my own kitchen. In Tokyo, for instance, our kitchen was such a busy place I was in the way when I entered it. We ran three messes from our kitchen there. One was for Wayne and me and our guests. Another was for the American Army officers and men who were assigned to our compound. The third was for the Japanese servants and gardeners. There was far too much going on in that kitchen to permit me to go puttering around as I liked to do. I didn't even plan our meals. The Japanese cook would just send up the menu, all printed, for me to approve.

Now it would be different. Out of the Army, we would live as we desired. We would entertain our intimates, our close friends, at parties that were play, not work. The kitchen would be mine. Wayne and I could fix our own Sunday breakfast, as we liked to do. I would prepare the menus. I would do the shopping. I would control my own home.

No, that day of retirement was not sad. I was grateful for what we had through our years in the Army, and I was happy that Wayne and I together had decided that now we wanted something different.

CHAPTER TWENTY·THREE

L IVING AT THE CITADEL HAS BROUGHT US JOY.
We have time to be together, to plan future improvements for this
college, to fish, hike, watch television, to be with the many charming
friends we have made here and welcome the old acquaintances that
are constantly passing through Charleston.

It was a novel experience and tremendous thrill to plan our new
house and watch its construction. Now we are living in our "dream
house"—a gracious, beautiful home in every detail. I revel in the
grounds that extend to the river marsh and are enclosed by a typi-
cally Southern, white pierced brick wall. Usually, evenings around
sundown Wayne and I walk among the myriad of flowers I have
planted or play a game of croquet.

Next door to us live our dear friends, the Sullivans. Maj. Gen.
Joseph Sullivan is administrative dean of the Citadel, and Marge is
my closest companion, just as she was in Vienna, the Presidio, Fort
Monroe, and Tokyo. I believe Marge and I have a rare relationship,
for in nine years of almost daily association we never once have
had a disagreement of even the most trifling kind. At the Citadel
we play gin rummy together, and when our husbands are busy with
Citadel work in the evening, we spend our evenings together, some-

times eating at her house or mine, sometimes at a hotel restaurant in town.

The relationship between Sully and Wayne has been unique, too, I believe. Classmates and friends at West Point, they have been together for an usually large part of their Army careers. It was Sully who drove Wayne home over a short cut through the redwood groves from Monterey to San Francisco the day Ann was born. Sully was with Wayne all through Italy and stayed with him in Vienna and then in Korea and Japan. It was no accident that he came on to the Citadel with us. Wayne appointed him dean so they could continue to be together.

For the first year at the Citadel we were further blessed by the presence of Audrey and Bill. Bill was due for ROTC work, and the Army assigned him to the Citadel as an instructor. They lived near us and we had the joy of seeing them almost every day. Bill's Korea wounds finally deprived us of this happiness, and he was retired from the Army with a disability discharge. He has accepted a splendid position with a bright future in Los Angeles, but the only trouble, from our selfish parental point of view, is that his headquarters are on the other side of the country. That means all four of our children are on the West Coast, just as far as they could be from Charleston without leaving the United States. We fly there when we can to see them and they visit us, but it couldn't possibly be often enough for Wayne or me.

The first year at the Citadel was exciting for us. One of the highlights was the visit from President Eisenhower, on whom Wayne bestowed an honorary degree. It was a great day for the Citadel. Governor Byrnes was there, along with many other notables of the state, and we had a garden-party reception for the President. There were about 150 guests in all.

Wayne got an unexpected little thrill from the day. Some of the Secret Service men who came on ahead of Ike were agents who had flown to Casablanca in early 1943 to safeguard President Roosevelt. They had worked closely with Wayne at Casablanca and now worked closely with him again in Charleston. As they made preparations for Ike's security, the Secret Service agents and Wayne traded reminiscences of Casablanca and the safeguards taken to protect President Roosevelt while he was in North Africa for his wartime meeting with Prime Minister Churchill.

The security arrangements were simple. After taking a review of the Corps of Cadets, Ike was to go into the bedroom wing of our house, and an agent was to stand guard before the door in the house and the doors leading from our bedrooms to the little patio just off the lawn. The plan was to keep Ike in the bedrooms until all the guests were gathered on the lawn, and then he was to go out through the patio to greet them.

Ike wouldn't have it that way, though. He walked into the living room, told me he and Mamie were building a new home at Gettysburg and he wanted to see ours. The Secret Service men were thunderstruck.

The only other time I saw Ike since we returned from Tokyo was in the White House, the day Wayne gave him an award for the American Heart Association. I went to the White House with Wayne but did not go into the room with him to see Ike. Ike greeted Wayne and then asked, "Where's Renie?" Wayne said, "She's outside," and Ike demanded that I be brought in to see him. He gave me a big kiss and we chatted for a little while. I was happy to see that he had not changed, essentially, from the cheerful, happy man we had known before he became President.

We were privileged to have visits from other old and dear friends at the Citadel. The visits had one important difference from most of those we had from friends during the years Wayne held high Army commands. In the old days our friends could visit us only for official reasons. And an official reason meant work and formal social functions and precious little time for relaxation and the kind of talk old friends always want to have when they meet. But at the Citadel, people could visit us just for pleasure, for a reunion, for a long talk.

Francis Cardinal Spellman spent a night with us in Charleston. We always consider ourselves most fortunate to have a few hours to talk with the Cardinal, and the evening he spent with us was no exception. It might have been, though. On the Isle of Capri, long before, we had been given an ash tray of Italian porcelain. The ash tray is beautifully colored and has a delicately lettered inscription in Italian. At our new home at the Citadel, I put it in the guest room because it harmonized with the coloring of the fittings in the room.

When we showed Cardinal Spellman into his bedroom I saw Wayne grab that ash tray quickly and hide it in his pocket. A little shudder ran down my spine for I knew what a terrible social error Wayne had averted so narrowly. I suddenly realized that the Cardinal spoke and read Italian fluently and also what was inscribed in Italian on that ash tray. It reads: "A guest is like a fish. After three days it stinks."

The Cardinal has a keen sense of humor and I am certain he would have passed off that inscription with a smile. But even he might have paused a moment to wonder just what kind of hosts Wayne and I were.

One of the rewards that comes from educational work is the mutual inspiration educators and students give one another. Sometimes I think the educator really gets the best of the bargain. This much I know: Wayne has learned much from his work with the young men at the Citadel. He has come to understand and sympathize with the problems of young Americans in a new setting, a setting different from the Army life in which he was accustomed to watching young men.

To me life here is somewhat similar to that of an Army post. I thrill to the marching music of the band as it plays for parades, and I love to hear the bugle sound taps in the evening. Being closely associated with the young cadets makes one feel youthful. The sight of their eager faces, their quick firm step, inspires me to throw my shoulders back and not feel my age.

For nearly a whole year these cadets and veterans had seen our new home being built. I knew how curious they must be to see how it looked on the inside after we were living in it and asked Wayne if it would be in order to invite the entire Corps of Cadets and Veterans, fifteen hundred strong, to tour our home at specified times. He said he thought it a fine idea provided it was not too hard on me. They came, at stated days and hours. Wayne and I shook hands with each one at the door, and they were given a complete tour of every room in the house with all objects of interest explained.

Our home is somewhat like a museum because some of our things do have historic value. I am always amused when people ask me, "What period is your home?" and I have to say that it is of no particular period, or all periods—just a hodgepodge gathered from having lived practically all over the world. To us these things have cherished memories of glorious, happily spent years. I gaze at the crystal chandelier which once hung in the palace of Franz Joseph, and I'm reminded of Austria—or at the Japanese screen from Tokyo, or a lamp from South America. In our dining room is a set of gold-rimmed dinner plates with a different division insignia in the center of each plate. The set of twenty-four was made for Wayne in Italy. On either side of the fireplace in the library stands a pair of cannons which were presented to my husband in England. These reputedly were used in the defense of Longford Castle against Oliver Cromwell.

We do not live in the past. I never have. I always have lived for the now and the tomorrow, but it is good to realize how you got to the "now," and all those mementos help us.

And there is one memento of my life with Wayne that I shall always cherish above all else. There is nothing tangible to this memento. It is a thing of memory, glorious, undying memory.

It came on New Year's Eve, December 31, 1953. We were at the Fairmont Hotel in San Francisco, where Wayne was working night and day on his book *From the Danube to the Yalu*. We had returned from the Far East, and Wayne had just retired from the Army after forty years of service, a fact which in itself made this New Year's Eve a special one.

He was so tired from working on his book, which he was hurrying to complete so that we could move to our new Charleston home, that he did not feel like celebrating that night with a lot of people. I felt that this first New Year's Eve after retirement was a special one that we should share with no one, and I was happy. We had a